VICTORIA AND DISRAELI

Victoria and Disraeli

THE MAKING OF A ROMANTIC PARTNERSHIP

THEO ARONSON

MACMILLAN PUBLISHING CO., INC.
New York

Macmillan Publishing Co., Inc.
866 Third Avenue, New York, N.Y. 10022

Library of Congress Cataloging in Publication Data
Aronson, Theo.
Victoria and Disraeli.
Bibliography: p.
Includes Index.
1. Victoria, Queen of Great Britain, 1819-1901.
2. Beaconsfield, Benjamin Disraeli, 1st Earl of, 1804-
1881. 3. Great Britain—Kings and rulers—Biography.
4. Prime ministers—Great Britain—Biography. I. Title.
DA554.A726 1978   941.081'092'2   78-8181
ISBN 0-02-503490-1

First American Edition 1978

Printed in the United States of America

For
William Tallon

Contents

Illustrations

Author's Note

The title of this book indicates its scope. It is a study of the personal relationship between Queen Victoria and Benjamin Disraeli. Yet, in order to present this relationship fully, I have felt it necessary to trace the individual emotional and political development of both Victoria and Disraeli during the years that preceded their romantic partnership. Only by doing this can one come to a complete understanding of their mutual attraction. But here again, I have dealt only with this development in so far as it affected their future partnership. With Queen Victoria in her various other roles as monarch and matriarch, I have not concerned myself. Nor have I dealt with every aspect of Disraeli's life. He is not discussed as a novelist, and his public career has been confined to those areas that are relevant to his subsequent relationship with the Queen. He has been treated as a personality first, a politician second. This book is, quite simply, a study of the growth and flowering of a remarkable relationship between two remarkable people.

I should like to express my gratitude to Her Majesty Queen Elizabeth II for her permission to republish passages from various printed sources of which the copyright in the original text belongs to Her Majesty. For arranging this, I must thank the Librarian at Windsor Castle, Sir Robert Mackworth-Young.

I am deeply indebted to the National Trust, Hughenden Manor, for permission to study and quote from the Disraeli Papers. Among the mass of Disraeli's superbly catalogued papers there are almost three thousand items under the heading 'Royal Correspondence'; I am most grateful to Mrs Barbara North whose efficiency and courtesy during the time I spent working on these and other papers at Hughenden Manor was unfailing. I must also thank the National Trust for permission to reproduce several pictures at Hughenden Manor.

My thanks go, too, to Sir Francis Sykes for permission to reproduce the portrait of Henrietta, Lady Sykes; and to the Radio Times Hulton Picture Library and the National Portrait Gallery for permission to reproduce several pictures of which they hold the copyright.

To Mrs Evelyn Hawley, O.B.E., Secretary of the Primrose League, I am also very grateful for help and interest.

Several published works have proved invaluable. Chief among these are the exhaustive six-volume *Life of Benjamin Disraeli* by W. F. Monypenny and G. E. Buckle and Robert Blake's superb biography, *Disraeli*. Extremely helpful, too, have been *Victoria R.I.* by Elizabeth Longford and *Queen Victoria* by Cecil Woodham Smith. All other books consulted and to which I am indebted, are listed in the Bibliography.

For other information, material, advice and help, I must thank the British Museum, London, the Library of Congress, Washington, and the South African Library, Cape Town.

My final thanks are to Mr Brian Roberts whose expert advice and unfailing interest have, as always, proved invaluable.

Prologue

It was, on the face of it, a most extraordinary relationship. What could Queen Victoria possibly have in common with Benjamin Disraeli? Why should the Queen of popular imagination—the dowdy, unsmiling, unapproachable, matter-of-fact Widow of Windsor—be attracted to this flamboyant, honey-tongued and ageing exotic? She was so four-square, he so *outré*. With her dumpy shape and her dour expression, the Queen looked like nothing so much as a disgruntled German *hausfrau*; with his dyed ringlets, his parchment skin and his hunched shoulders, Disraeli had the air of a decaying *roué*.

And their personalities were so different. Where he was said to be wily, Oriental and sphinx-like, she was known to be as honest as the day was long. Victoria sat on the most important, most firmly-established throne in the world. Dizzy was looked upon as an adventurer, a parvenu, a man whom the Queen herself somewhat inaccurately described as having 'risen from the people'. The adored Prince Albert had once said that Disraeli 'had not one single element of the gentleman in his composition' while Victoria had described him as 'unprincipled, reckless and not respectable'.

His very name—for he was born D'Israeli—was synonymous with Jewry, and the Queen had once refused a peerage for Lionel de Rothschild on the grounds of his being a Jew. A '*Jew* baronet' she would not object to, but she drew the line, she announced, at 'a *Jew* being made a Peer'.

But there it was. By the mid-1870s this seemingly incompatible couple were hand in glove. That Queen Victoria was enamoured of her bizarre Prime Minister there was no shadow of doubt. Indeed, their relationship was one of the most romantic of her life. The years in which they were closely associated became an idyll for her; the happiest period of her long widowhood. During them, she was transformed, in Dizzy's extravagant phrase, into 'The Faery Queen'.

And he was hardly less enamoured of her. Not only did her status fire his always colourful imagination but, as a female sovereign, she brought out all his brilliance, all his romanticism. He could never, he admitted, have been as happy in the service of a king. Politically, the two of them were in almost complete accord. Victoria was only too ready to give her blessing to her Prime Minister's high-flown schemes. On a more personal level too, Victoria stirred the emotions of this extraordinary man. His wooing of her was not all political. Emotionally he responded to her hardly less than she did to him. 'I love the Queen,' he once wrote, 'perhaps the only person in the world left to me that I do love. . . .'

But there was even more to their association than a successful personal and political relationship. The effects of this unlikely partnership far outlasted not only Disraeli's term of office, but his life. For, in a way, Benjamin Disraeli re-fashioned Queen Victoria. She emerged, from their years together, greatly changed. And she remained, for the rest of her life, very much what he had made of her.

For the first half, and more, of her reign, Victoria was a Coburg queen. She had been raised by her Coburg mother, the Duchess of Kent; she had been advised by her Coburg uncle, King Leopold of the Belgians; and she had been fashioned by her Coburg husband, Prince Albert. Even after Albert's death, the Queen remained Albert's pupil, Albert's creation. Alive or dead, the sober and high-minded Prince Consort guided Victoria's thinking. Her one wish, the inconsolable widow had cried out, was to remain faithful to her late husband's ideals; to continue along the path that he had so conscientiously mapped out for her.

And this, for a dozen or so years after his death, is what she did. But during Benjamin Disraeli's first, and short-lived, term of office in 1868, the Queen's resolve began to melt in the seductive warmth of his manner. And in the half-dozen or so years of his second premiership—from 1874 to 1880—she set out along a very different and infinitely more glorious highway. For the last twenty-five years of her reign, Victoria was the revered, the awe-inspiring, the almost mythical Queen Empress; a fittingly venerable and imperious monarch of the greatest empire that the world had ever known.

And the transformation had been brought about, to a very great extent, by Disraeli. This is not to say that Queen Victoria had not always been a strong-minded and highly individual personality; throughout her life she remained shrewd, conscientious and eminently practical. But it had needed this astute and imaginative statesman to open her eyes to the possibilities of her position, to recognize the underlying romanticism and emotionalism of her nature, to encourage and bring into full flower her latent sense of majesty. The old Queen who drove through the clamorous streets of imperial London on the occasion of her Diamond Jubilee in 1897 was very much Disraeli's masterpiece.

The story of how the paths of these two complex and dissimilar personalities came to converge—both politically and emotionally—is one of the most fascinating of the nineteenth century.

PART ONE

The Coburg Queen

Chapter One

Throughout her long life, there was one thing on which Queen Victoria always depended. This was, if not exactly the love, then at least the support of a man. Masculine guidance, attention and protection were all but indispensable to her.

The need seems to have had its roots in her childhood. Her father, the Duke of Kent—fourth son of King George III—had died when she was only eight months old, in January 1820. It may well have been this lack of a sympathetic and reassuring male presence in the household at Kensington Palace that started Victoria on her life-long search.

There was not, unfortunately, much chance of finding a strong male arm among the members of her late father's family. Princess Victoria's pack of 'wicked uncles'—King George IV and his brothers—were hardly of the stuff of which mentors are made. One could not possibly hope to benefit by their advice; still less by their example. And in any case, Victoria's mother, the widowed Duchess of Kent, was on such bad terms with her royal brothers-in-law that she kept her precious daughter well away from them. The coming reign, she had long ago decided, must in no way resemble the ones preceding it. Victoria must look elsewhere for masculine direction.

There was, in fact, one person in the household at Kensington Palace who was only too anxious to fill the gap left by the untimely death of the Duke of Kent. This was Sir John Conroy, the Duchess's comptroller. Handsome, ambitious, overbearing and unscrupulous, Sir John Conroy was the dominant figure at Kensington Palace. The Duchess had complete faith in him. Indeed, so thick was the still young and attractive Duchess of Kent with her comptroller that it was assumed they were lovers. Conroy certainly behaved as though he were master of the household.

Determined to secure a powerful position for himself in the years ahead, Conroy kept a tight grip on the future Queen. He saw to it that the young Victoria was kept isolated from the Court (in 1830 the florid King George IV was succeeded by his more simple-minded brother, King William IV); he packed her off on a series of semi-royal progresses through the country; he schemed to get himself appointed as her future private secretary. If the young Princess Victoria did indeed feel a lack of masculine support at Kensington Palace, it was not through any want of trying on the part of Sir John Conroy.

But his efforts counted for nothing. Victoria hated Conroy. He was the last person in the world in whom she would ever confide; to whom she would ever turn for advice or guidance. Some imagined that her abhorrence sprang from the fact that she had once caught him in the act of making love to her mother, but Victoria herself was always to deny this. She certainly resented his familiarity towards the Duchess of Kent but she resented, far more, his arrogant attitude towards herself. And the more Conroy tried to force his will, the more she resisted him. The result was that relations between Victoria, on the one hand, and her mother and Conroy on the other, became increasingly strained.

By nature lively, warm-hearted and frank, the young Victoria was forced to cultivate a cool, somewhat withdrawn manner. To the Duchess, Conroy and their circle, she appeared stubborn, wilful and far too independent for her own good. To the general public, she seemed unusually self-possessed. Only to her devoted governess, Baroness Lehzen, could the unhappy Victoria reveal her true, and very engaging, self.

Loathing the one man who could have been a father-figure, Victoria came to rely, ever more heavily, on another. This was her mother's brother—King Leopold of the Belgians. Indeed, Uncle Leopold became the first in the line of men who were to play so important a role in Queen Victoria's career.

2

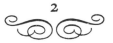

During the first twelve years of Princess Victoria's life, her Uncle Leopold lived in England. He had arrived there, in 1816, as the young and handsome Prince Leopold of Saxe-Coburg, to marry Princess Charlotte, only child of the future King George IV and thus heiress apparent to the British throne. The marriage had been short-lived. Within eighteen months Princess Charlotte had died in childbirth.

Robbed of his chance of being the husband of a queen, Prince Leopold was none the less able to console himself with the thought that he would one day be the uncle of one: for, in the year after Princess Charlotte's death, Leopold's sister married the Duke of Kent. Less than a year after that, Victoria was born.

At one stage during Victoria's girlhood, Leopold had fondly imagined that he might become regent for his niece. Surely the now childless King George IV and his equally childless heir—his brother who afterwards became King William IV—would both be dead long before Victoria turned eighteen? And surely the British government would rather have the young, popular, respectable and hardworking Prince Leopold as regent than yet another of Victoria's profligate, extravagant and idle paternal uncles?

But Leopold dared not push his claims too hard. King George IV liked him no better than he liked Leopold's sister, Victoria's mother; and when William IV succeeded his brother, the new King made it quite obvious that he liked Leopold even less. So Uncle Leopold had to content himself with weekly visits to Kensington Palace and to waiting for the day when his niece would ascend the throne.

But for someone of Prince Leopold's ambitions and abilities, the position of uncle to a queen was not going to be nearly good enough. He still hankered after something more spectacular. Not until 1830, however, when he was already almost forty years old, did an opportunity present itself. Prince Leopold was offered the throne of newly independent Greece. After a period of agonizing heart-searching, he refused it. The whole project was too fraught with uncertainties. Within a year he was made another offer. This time it was the newly independent Belgium that was hawking its throne. After yet another period of indecision (not for nothing was Leopold referred to as *Marquis Peu-à-Peu*) he accepted it. In July 1831, not long after his niece Victoria's twelfth birthday, Prince Leopold set out for Brussels. He was never to live in England again.

Out of sight did not, as far as both Princess Victoria and Uncle Leopold were concerned, mean out of mind. On the contrary, from Belgium King Leopold exerted more influence on his niece's mind than he had ever done at home. For there now began that stream of letters between *My dearest Love* and *My dearest Uncle* that were to be such a feature of Victoria's early years. Denied sympathy, affection and encouragement in her own home, Victoria sought it from her Uncle Leopold. He now became, as she put it, like a father to her.

What was he like, the first of the men in whom the ardent young Victoria put her trust? By his forties, King Leopold of the Belgians had lost pretty well all his dashing good looks. He had also lost most of his youthful charm. He was now a thin-lipped, paper-faced, pedantic and circumspect creature, old beyond his years. 'His pomposity fatigues,' wrote that acidulous diarist Charles Greville, 'and his avarice disgusts.' But King Leopold was no fool. Astute and far-sighted, he was developing into one of Europe's most successful monarchs. As such, he was of inestimable value to the young Victoria. Not only did Uncle Leopold have a thorough understanding of the relatively new concept of constitutional monarchy but he was only too ready to impart this knowledge.

Impart it he certainly did. For year after year his letters, heavily larded with advice, encouragement and protestations of affection crossed the Channel to Kensington Palace. To his palace of Laeken in Brussels went Victoria's answers—appreciative, questioning, and no less affectionate. With her distant uncle, Victoria could be far more frank, confiding and natural than was possible with most of the people surrounding her at home. No letter from dear Uncle Leopold, no matter how heavily pedantic or tediously instructive, was received with anything other than unfeigned gratitude; no teacher could have hoped for a more willing pupil.

'I am much obliged to you, dear Uncle, for the extract about Queen Anne,' she wrote in the winter of 1834, 'but must beg you, as you have sent me to show what a Queen *ought not* to be, that you will send me what a Queen *ought* to be.'

Dearest Uncle needed no second bidding. This task, he answered joyously, 'I will very conscientiously take upon myself on the first occasion which may offer itself. . . .' And take it upon himself he did. As the young princess matured, so did the stream of Uncle Leopold's maxims, aphorisms and exhortations gather force.

Uncle and niece met again, for the first time in over four years, when King Leopold visited England in the autumn of 1835. Victoria was then sixteen years old. Uncle Leopold in the flesh turned out to be even dearer than Uncle Leopold on paper. 'What happiness was it for me,' noted the ecstatic Victoria, 'to throw myself in the arms of that *dearest* of Uncles, who has always been to me like a father. ...'

Nor did the fact that King Leopold had a new wife lessen his niece's appreciation. Leopold's Queen, who had been born Princess Louise d'Orleans, eldest daughter of Louis Philippe, King of the French, was a kind-hearted, mild-mannered young woman, nearer in age to Victoria than to her husband. Flushed with excitement at her Uncle Leopold's visit, Victoria was no less ready to fall in love with her Aunt Louise.

The return of the royal couple to Belgium left Victoria desolate. Months later she was still writing to tell her uncle how *hard* it was for her that he should be so far away 'when I recollect the happy time when I could see, and be with you, *every* day.'

Uncle Leopold was far too astute and prescient a man to let such adoration on the part of the future Queen of England run to waste. It must be gainfully channelled. He must use it to improve, not only his own position, but the position of his house—the Coburgs.

3

King Leopold did not need to look far for the means by which to retain his hold on the future Queen. In fact, he did not need to look at all. Of one thing the Coburg family was never short: young males. Not without reason would Bismarck one day refer to Coburg as the stud farm of Europe.

King Leopold's eldest brother, the Duke of Saxe-Coburg-Gotha, had two sons. The elder was named Ernest and the younger Albert. And it was Albert—devastatingly handsome and about the same age as Victoria—whom King Leopold had in mind as Victoria's future husband. In the spring of 1836, in the teeth of violent opposition on the part of Victoria's much less agreeable uncle, King William IV (who had his own, quite different ideas on the important question of Victoria's future husband) her cousins Ernest and Albert arrived on a visit.

One look at the tall, well-built, blue-eyed and brown-haired Prince Albert and the passionate young Victoria melted. She could not praise him highly enough. His nose was beautiful, his mouth was sweet, his teeth were fine, his expression was delightful: 'full of goodness and sweetness, and very clever and intelligent'. And not only was he 'extremely handsome' but he was accomplished, clever, reflective.

'I must thank you, my beloved Uncle, for the prospect of *great* happiness you have contributed to give me, in the person of dear Albert,' she wrote. 'Allow me then, my dearest Uncle, to tell you how delighted I am with him, and how much I like him in every way. He possesses every quality that would be desired to render me perfectly happy.'

King Leopold could hardly have expected better than that.

The worldly King might have been put out, however, had he been able to read his niece's journal for the following spring. For in it, the seventeen-year-old girl dwelt, at considerable length, on the attractions of an altogether different sort of young man. This was her second cousin, Charles, Duke of Brunswick. With his long dark hair and moustachios, Duke Charles was a Byronic-looking figure—swash-buckling, romantic, wicked. Adding to his air of bravado was the fact that he had been expelled from his country and its regency entrusted to his more conventional brother, William. The young Victoria, who saw Duke Charles on several occasions that spring, was clearly fascinated. She could hardly take her eyes off him as he lounged in his box at the opera, his great fur coat slung over the back of his chair and his long hair parted in the middle and 'hanging wildly' to well below his ears; the style might not suit ugly people, she decided, but it certainly suited 'these handsome ones'.

In the Park, she would see him at even closer quarters. He was so handsome, so elegantly dressed, so 'ferocious-looking', so 'very wild and odd'. In short, there was something about this desperado, with his bold stare and his shady reputation, that set Victoria's pulses pounding. She had noticed him looking at her; what if he were to speak to her?

Fortunately, she was never put to the test. But that her imagination was set aflame by this unconventional, rakish and sensual-looking gallant there is no doubt. It is the first indication of Victoria's taste for theatrical and mysterious-seeming men that was to run side by side with her appreciation of the sturdier masculine virtues.

4

Within a few weeks, she had more important things on her mind. Just after two o'clock on the morning of 20 June 1837, her uncle, King William IV, died at Windsor Castle. The dawn of that momentous day was just breaking as the carriage bringing the Archbishop of Canterbury and the Lord Chamberlain came clattering pell-mell up the driveway to Kensington Palace. With a cotton dressing-gown over her nightdress and her long fair hair falling about her shoulders, Victoria came downstairs to receive the two men. She would not allow her mother (with whom, by now, she was barely on speaking terms) to accompany her beyond the door of her sitting room. She entered it, she says, *alone*. The men fell to their knees and as the Lord Chamberlain began to speak of her uncle's death, Victoria knew that she was Queen.

Her first letter, written some two hours later, was 'two words only' to her Uncle Leopold. She ended it, 'Ever, my beloved Uncle, your devoted and attached Niece' and signed it 'Victoria R.'

At half past eleven that morning she held her first Council in the Red Saloon at Kensington Palace. 'A hum of half-suppressed conversation . . . fills that brilliant assemblage; that sea of plumes, and glittering stars, and gorgeous dresses,' runs one description of this historic meeting of the Queen with her Privy Counsellors. 'Victoria ascends her throne; a girl, alone, and for the first time, amid an assemblage of men.

'In a sweet and thrilling voice, and with a composed mien which indicates rather the absorbing sense of august duty than an absence of emotion, the Queen announces her succession to the throne of her ancestors, and her humble hope that divine Providence will guard over the fulfilment of her lofty trust.

'The prelates and captains and chief men of her realm then advance to the throne and, kneeling before her, pledge their troth, and take the sacred oaths of allegiance and supremacy.'

Thus, with characteristic flourish, was the scene later described by a dandified young author and aspiring politician named Benjamin Disraeli.

Chapter Two

Just as Queen Victoria always needed the support of a man, so did Benjamin Disraeli depend on the love, encouragement and sympathy of women. 'A female friend,' he once wrote, 'amiable, clever, and devoted, is a possession more valuable than parks and palaces; and without such a muse, few men can succeed in life, none be content.'

Disraeli was at his best in female company, particularly in the company of older women. For whether it be as a wife, a mistress or a friend, Disraeli invariably sought out women older than himself. They alone seemed capable of giving him the uncritical affection and admiration his egotistical nature so ardently craved. In fact, they were more like mothers than lovers. If Queen Victoria spent much of her life in search of a father-figure, Disraeli spent his in search of a substitute for his mother.

Benjamin Disraeli, who had so much to say about everything else, had surprisingly little to say about his mother. Quite clearly, there was very little affection, very little rapport between them. Of his father, on the other hand, he was very fond. Both parents were of Italian-Jewish stock. His father, Isaac D'Israeli, was the son of a Benjamin D'Israeli who had emigrated to England from Italy in the mid-eighteenth century. His mother, Maria Basevi, was the daughter of a Naphtali Basevi who had likewise left Italy to settle in London. In later years, Benjamin Disraeli was to glamorize his origins with much flowery talk of descent from a family of 'aristocratic' Spanish Jews who had settled in Venice; while others (and Queen Victoria among them) liked to think of him as a poor Jewish boy who, by virtue of his own brilliance, had overcome all obstacles to rise to the top.

The truth was more prosaic. Disraeli's origins were neither as romantic as he pretended nor as obscure as was sometimes maintained. Both Isaac D'Israeli and Maria Basevi, when they married in 1802, were members of wealthy, talented and relatively distinguished families; and their second child, Benjamin, was born, on 21 December 1804, into a prosperous middle-class home. He grew up in a comfortable, red-brick, white porticoed house near Gray's Inn, in London. Isaac D'Israeli was a sceptical, mild-mannered, bookish man; Maria was a prototype Jewish mother—happy to devote herself to her home, her husband and her four children.

But, from the start almost, the relationship between the mother and her eldest son was unsatisfactory. Perhaps she felt closer to her only daughter, Sarah; perhaps she lavished more affection on her two younger, more dependable sons; perhaps she did not give Benjamin the admiration he felt he deserved.

For that he deserved admiration, Benjamin had no doubt whatsoever. Nor was his conceit entirely unfounded. In the first place, there were his good looks. Even in boyhood, Benjamin Disraeli's appearance was striking. He might have been born British but his ancestry was obvious: he looked like an Italian Jew. His hair was black, glossy, curly; his skin was sallow, his eyes were dark, his nose was hooked. Among his flaxen-haired, pink-cheeked and blue-eyed schoolmates, he was very much the odd-man-out. There was something un-English too, about his manner. Here he seemed rather more Italian than Jewish: Disraeli was proud, vain, flashy, quick-tempered, extravagant, emotional, warm-hearted. He was also a good deal brighter than his contemporaries: quick-witted, inquisitive, eager to learn and anxious to shine. The boy was determined, not only to dazzle in company but to make his mark in the world.

How he would do this, he was not yet certain. All roads lay open to him, bar one. This was a career in Parliament. The parliamentary oath could be taken only by Christians. It did not matter if one were of the Jewish race; one could not be of the Jewish faith. Not until 1858 would this bar be removed.

But before Benjamin turned thirteen (and before even he could have had any ambitions to enter Parliament) the barrier disappeared. In March 1817 his father—the skull-capped, scholarly, retiring Isaac D'Israeli—quarrelled and broke with the local congregation, and with active Judaism. Although he did not convert to Christianity, he was talked into having his children baptized into the Church of England. From now on Benjamin Disraeli would be a practising, if not very convinced, Christian.

If Benjamin's mother remained resolutely unimpressed by her precocious son, one cannot altogether blame her. His early career was hardly spectacular. His deeds were not nearly as dazzling as his words. On leaving school (he attended a somewhat obscure establishment named Higham Hall) he was articled to a firm of solicitors. With this proving too tame an occupation for someone of his overweening ambitions, the youngster (by now the surname had been transformed, in three generations, from Israeli, via D'Israeli to Disraeli) plunged into a series of disastrous financial and literary adventures.

Speculation in South American mining shares landed him in a debt that would take decades to clear (by his late thirties he would still owe over £20,000); a foray into newspaper publishing proved a complete failure and landed him in still more debt; his first novel, *Vivian Grey*, written anonymously and satirizing his former associates on the newspaper venture, earned him more virulent criticism than hard cash. It was no wonder that Maria Disraeli should sigh that although her Ben was a 'clever boy' he was no 'prodigy'.

But if Mrs Disraeli was not prepared to concede her son's genius, there were other women who were. One of these was Sara Austen, the childless wife of a solicitor by the name of Benjamin Austen, through whom Isaac D'Israeli had once hired a house. 'There is no fascination so irresistible to a boy,' wrote Disraeli in *Vivian Grey*, 'as the smile of a married woman.' And if Disraeli, at twenty-one, was no longer a boy, Sara Austen was certainly a married woman. She was, in fact, to be the first of that parade of older, maternal women with whom Disraeli was to become enmeshed.

2

In the year 1825, when Disraeli turned twenty-one, Sara Austen was almost thirty. She was an attractive woman, cultivated, clever, talkative, anxious to make some sort of mark on the world of the arts. Saddled with a worthy but boring husband, Sara was immediately taken with the young Disraeli. The features which others might find affected or ridiculous—his sensitivity, his arrogance, his foppishness—she took as signs of his brilliance. There was a great deal more, she apparently decided, behind those Byronic looks, those flamboyant airs and those dandified clothes, than many imagined. Although she might well have fallen in love with him (some of her letters reveal a considerable depth of feeling) Sara also had great faith in his abilities.

And Disraeli was hardly less taken with her. For someone with his egocentric nature, admiration was essential; from few younger women could he hope to get the enthusiastic, yet uninformed, admiration that Sara Austen lavished on him. Whether or not she became his mistress one does not know. Nor is it particularly important. What was important, for the young Disraeli, was that he felt able to confide in her; to reveal to her his dreams and ambitions. With Sara Austen he felt cherished and appreciated.

When he admitted that he was writing a book, Sara was delighted. She would be his Egeria. Together, they would make a perfect partnership. She would help set his feet on the road to greatness.

The book was *Vivian Grey*. Throughout its length (five volumes ultimately) Sara Austen was at his elbow. She read, she listened, she suggested, she corrected and, above all, she enthused. 'I have now gone through it twice,' she gushed, 'and the more I read the better I am pleased. . . .' Lest even the publisher guess at the author's identity, Sara copied out the entire manuscript herself. It was she who negotiated the contract and when—on the discovery of the author's identity—the world seemed to be falling about Disraeli's ears, it was Sara Austen who hurried him away on a continental holiday.

With the couple went the long-suffering Mr Austen. At this stage of his wife's infatuation with Disraeli, Austen was not yet pestered to advance the young man money; although, at the end of the holiday, he was obliged to remind Disraeli that he still owed £26 of his share of the expenses.

The three of them set out for Paris in the August of 1826. From there they travelled, via Geneva (where Disraeli was thrilled to be rowed on the lake by the boatman of that *beau idéal* of all romantically-minded young men of the time—the late Lord Byron) to Italy. This was Disraeli's first experience of a southern land. He responded to it immediately: to the blazing sunshine, the glowing landscapes, the melancholy ruins, the flamboyant palaces, the opulent churches; indeed, to the whole colourful Mediterranean atmosphere into which he always seemed to fit so much more happily than he did into the temperate pattern of Victorian England. His letters home were ecstatic.

Through it all Sara Austen continued to adore and mother him.

'Really he is an excellent travelling companion,' she reported to his sister Sarah, 'so satisfied—so easily pleased—so accommodating—so amusing—and so *actively* kind. . . .' She fussed over his health ('once or twice I have heard him complain of a little faintness from the excessive heat'); she kept an eye on what he ate; she saw to it that he was comfortably lodged.

Back in England, where Disraeli at once plunged into a sequel to *Vivian Grey*, Sara again did everything she could to ease his path. Nothing was too much trouble for her: she criticized, she copied out, she acted as his agent. He had only to demand that she undertake research on this or that subject for her to fall to it at once. When he needed money, she saw to it that her husband paid up.

But already Disraeli was tiring of her. It would have needed a more exceptional woman than Sara Austen to hold, for any length of time, the attention of this mercurial and conceited young man. He was finding her too pressing, too voluble ('Mrs Austen speaks French with even greater rapidity than she does English' was his laconic complaint to his sister) and, as a lawyer's wife, she was not nearly smart enough for the socially ambitious Disraeli. In addition, he was going through a difficult stage. The excitements and disappointments of his feverish search for either fame or fortune had left him feeling despondent and frustrated.

'I am one of those to whom moderate reputation can give no pleasure,' he once sighed. As things stood, his reputation was hardly even moderate. His father warned him not to be in a hurry. One could not become a great man in a day. But to someone of Disraeli's temperament, such advice fell on deaf ears.

3

In his dejection, Disraeli turned to another woman. This time it was his elder sister, Sarah.

In 1828 Isaac D'Israeli left London and bought a graceful, red-brick Queen Anne house called Bradenham, in Buckinghamshire. In this more leisurely country atmosphere, brother and sister came to know each other, and to appreciate each other's qualities, much better than they had in London.

In the year that their father bought Bradenham, Sarah turned twenty-six, Benjamin twenty-four. In some ways, she was a tamer version of her brother. Equally dark and attractive, Sarah was less striking to look at, bright, sharp and amusing, she could not match his glitter, his intellect nor his wit. She was steadier, quieter, less impetuous than he. But then Disraeli was not looking for an equal; still less for a rival. He was looking for a confidante. And his sister Sarah was certainly that.

Together they explored the beautiful countryside about Bradenham: the woods, fields and villages of a rural, manorial England that was gradually beginning to strike a chord in the heart of this romantic young man. Together they discussed his position: his debts, his ambitions, his writing. Like Sara Austen before her, she encouraged him, she admired him, she ultimately devoted herself to him.

At this stage of her life, Sarah Disraeli was engaged to a young man named William Meredith; after his sudden death in 1831, she seems to have given up all thought of marriage. From then on she lived only for her brother. Her feelings for Benjamin, wrote a friend of the family, were 'a passion bordering on romance'.

And his were hardly less for her. 'I have no wife, I have no betrothed; nor since I have been better acquainted with my own mind and temper have I sought them,' he wrote to her on one occasion. 'Live then, my heart's treasure, for one who has ever loved you with a surpassing love. . . . Yes, my beloved, be my genius, my solace, my companion, my joy . . . we will feel that life can never be blank while gilded by the perfect love of a sister and a brother.'

It was, on the face of it, an odd letter for a brother to write to a sister but one must always make allowance for the fact that Disraeli's pen often ran away with him. Yet he loved Sarah and although he could never abide by his resolve to 'live only' for her, he greatly appreciated all that she did for him.

Thanks, in some measure, to the aura of understanding and tranquillity created by his sister Sarah, Disraeli gradually emerged from his period of mental and physical lassitude. He began writing again. By the spring of 1830 he had finished a new novel, a picture of high life entitled *The Young Duke* ('What,' asked his father with a fine Jewish shrug, 'does Ben know of dukes?'). He began to be invited out. That equally dandified young novelist, Edward Lytton Bulwer, asked him to a dinner party. Disraeli arrived wearing green velvet trousers, a canary-coloured waistcoat, silver-buckled shoes, lace cuffs and his hair in glossy ringlets. The sparkle of his talk astonished them all. To the women he made a particular appeal; and they appealed no less to him.

'In society nothing must be discussed. . . . In society never think,' he wrote in a style foreshadowing Oscar Wilde. 'Talk to women, talk to women as much as you can. This is the best school. This is the way to gain fluency, because you need not care what you say, and had better not be sensible. They too, will rally you on many points, and as they are women you will not be offended. Nothing is of so much importance and of so much use to a young man entering life as to be well criticized by women.'

But what perhaps revived him most of all was his resolve to tour the Mediterranean and the Near East. For some time now Disraeli had become increasingly interested in his Jewish origins. He had even begun a novel about a twelfth-century Jewish hero, named David Alroy. Perhaps by travelling to the land from which his race had sprung he could finally restore himself, both mentally and bodily. He decided that he must pay a pilgrimage to Jerusalem.

4

Disraeli's celebrated, sixteen-month-long tour of the Near East was part ecstasy, part education, part debauch. Together with his sister Sarah's fiancé, William Meredith (who was to die of smallpox in Cairo on the return journey), he travelled to Spain, Malta, Corfu, Albania, Greece, Turkey, Cyprus, the Holy Land and Egypt.

It was difficult to decide which was the more exotic: the sights he saw, or the clothes he sported. He certainly spared no effort to impress and amaze. In Malta, ignoring grumblings in the Officer's Mess about 'that damned bumptious Jew boy', he appeared in an embroidered Andalusian jacket, white trousers and a rainbow-coloured sash. He sailed to Corfu tricked out as a Greek pirate: red cap, blood-red shirt, shilling-sized silver buttons, a sash stuffed with pistols and daggers, blue-striped trousers and red slippers. In Turkey he wore a turban and smoked a six-foot-long hookah.

And his behaviour matched his dress. Everywhere he acted the foppish, epigrammatic, slothful and sybaritic young English milord. His sexual escapades were such that he was eventually obliged to undergo a mercury cure. 'Mercury,' as one of his disreputable travelling companions put it, 'had succeeded to Venus.'

Disraeli was dazzled by the Middle East. His letters home were full of the intoxicating sights and sounds of these sun-drenched lands: the domes, the minarets, the call of the muezzin, the camel trains, the gorgeous costumes, the narrow streets, the flaming sunsets, the rustling, spiky, elegant palms. All made an indelible impression on that romantic mind.

Climax of this journey was the week he spent in Jerusalem. The view of the walls and towers of the distant city, across a desolate and stony plain, was dramatic in the extreme. 'I was thunderstruck,' he writes. Here, in this crowded, tumbled city, in the heart of the land from which his ancestors had sprung, his imagination was stirred to its depths. 'His exultation,' says one of his biographers, 'was supreme.'

After a stay of several months in Egypt, at the end of which Meredith suddenly died, Disraeli returned home.

This mammoth journey to the East was to colour Disraeli's thinking for the rest of his days. Again and again he re-created its exotic atmosphere in his novels and romances. In public life, too, he remained obsessed with the East. He frequently professed to be following some sort of Eastern philosophy; he seemed always to be moving in an aura of Oriental colour, intrigue and, said some, duplicity. The tour certainly affected his attitude towards foreign policy. The most spectacular achievements of his premiership would all be concerned with the East.

And perhaps the journey gave him a renewed belief in his destiny. The tour may have restored his health, his tranquillity and have given him a deeper appreciation of the complexities and mysteries of life, but it had made him no less certain that he would one day achieve great things.

'I believe,' he was to write in one of his novels, 'in that Destiny before which the ancients bowed. Modern philosophy, with its superficial discoveries, has infused into the heart of man a spirit of scepticism, but I think that ere long science will again become imaginative, and that as we become more profound we may become also more credulous. Destiny is our will, and our will is our nature. . . All is mystery; but he is a slave who will not struggle to penetrate the dark veil.'

Refreshed, the twenty-six-year-old Benjamin Disraeli plunged headlong into the social and literary life of London in the 1830s.

It was his friend, Lytton Bulwer, who first introduced him into this world of fashion, but it was by his own colourful qualities that he remained there. As always, he was immediately taken up by older women. Ill at ease in exclusively masculine society ('I have not gained much in conversation with men . . .' he claimed with that characteristic blend of affectation and sincerity), he glittered in the company of matrons. In the *salons* of such hostesses as Lady Blessington, Mrs Norton and Lady Cork, he was eminently at home.

His literary activities were hardly less hectic than his social. Publications poured forth in a torrent; none of them particularly good but none of them valueless. His most noteworthy book was a four-volume work entitled *Contarini Fleming* but, like all his books, it won him rather more acclaim than cash. His debts remained unpaid and his creditors became more pressing.

Inevitably, the question of a good marriage for this handsome, talented but insolvent young man came up. But Disraeli was in no hurry to get married. And he certainly did not intend to marry for love. 'By the bye,' he once wrote to his devoted sister Sarah, 'would you like Lady Z. for a sister-in-law, very clever, £25,000 and domestic? As for "love", all my friends who married for love and beauty either beat their wives or live apart from them. This is literally the case. I may commit many follies in life, but I never intend to marry for "love", which I am sure is a guarantee of infelicity.'

None of this is to say that he was living without love. By 1832 he was entangled with yet another married woman, a doctor's wife by the name of Clara Bolton, and a year later he embarked on the most important love affair of his long bachelorhood: his liaison with Henrietta, Lady Sykes.

Once again his mistress was a married woman and older than himself. And once again the relationship was half-erotic, half-maternal. Henrietta was the wife of Sir Francis Sykes and the mother of four children, the youngest of whom was three at the time of her meeting with Disraeli. If she was not exactly beautiful, Henrietta Sykes was a voluptuous-looking woman, assertive, possessive and strong-minded. As such, she had the motherly qualities he always needed. One would imagine, from some of her letters to him, that he was her son rather than her lover. He must not neglect to comb his hair or brush his teeth. She would scold him if he smoked too much. He must remember to keep his shoulders back. She would be 'such an affectionate old Nurse to my child, and kiss and soothe every pain'. She would even sign herself 'your Mother'.

But she could satisfy, rather more wholeheartedly, his other needs. For Henrietta Sykes was a passionate woman, vigorous and highly-sexed. She loved him desperately; rather more, in fact, than he loved her. Once Sir Francis Sykes had accustomed himself to the situation (actually, he was busy consoling himself with Disraeli's most recently discarded mistress, Clara Bolton) the lovers lived together quite openly.

They were invited everywhere together—to river parties, to garden parties, to theatre suppers. In the frivolous, easygoing society of the 1830s, the dashing young Disraeli and his handsome mistress moved quite freely. Every season saw the young man take yet another step up the social ladder. He was received by the great Tory hostess, Lady Londonderry. He met Lord Hertford, Lord Durham and the Duke of Wellington. (No longer could old Isaac D'Israeli ask what Ben knew of dukes.) He became very friendly with the former Tory Lord Chancellor, Lord Lyndhurst. Through the slightly tarnished figure of Lyndhurst, Disraeli was drawn into the inner world of politics and power. It was a heady experience. At Mrs Norton's *salon* he met Lord Melbourne, one of the leading lights in the Whig cabinet and a future Prime Minister.

'Well now, tell me what you want to be?' asked the worldly Melbourne of this equally worldly young man.

'I want to be Prime Minister,' answered Disraeli unblinkingly.

The exchange, in the light, not only of the political futures of both men but in their relationship with Queen Victoria, is a fascinating one.

And a no less fascinating first meeting took place the following year. At yet another gathering Disraeli met the serious-minded young Tory M.P. for Newark, W. E. Gladstone. This time there was no significant exchange. Disraeli pronounced the dinner 'rather dull'; they ate a 'swan very white and stuffed with truffles' which the flippant Disraeli judged to be 'the best company there'.

Inevitably, after three years, Disraeli's affair with Henrietta Sykes began to wear a little thin. He found her too demanding, too distracting, too stiflingly possessive. If she had been able to do something spectacular about his ever more persistent creditors (one of them the husband of the rejected Sara Austen) Disraeli might have put up with her a little longer. But the little she was able to do was no more than a drop in the ocean of his debts. In any case, Henrietta seemed to be seeking consolation elsewhere. By the autumn of 1836 she had yielded to the charms of a handsome painter named Daniel Maclise; by that Christmas the affair between her and Disraeli was over.

One tangible result of this celebrated liaison was the publication of yet another novel by Disraeli. He called it *Henrietta Temple*. Financially, it was the most successful of his books since his first, *Vivian Grey*. Its publication brought him his last letter from the real Henrietta.

'I am not very eloquent in expressing my feelings,' wrote she, whose impassioned love letters to him had only too eloquently expressed her feelings, 'therefore I must fail to convey to you a tythe part of the extreme gratification I have in your brilliant success. Your complete triumph is echoed by everyone I come near.'

That was the kind of letter he liked to receive.

6

Disraeli was thirty-one at the time of his break with Henrietta, Lady Sykes in the autumn of 1836. Although he enjoyed a certain amount of social and literary success (and not a little notoriety) he was still far from being the famous figure of his aspirations. There was only one way, he had by now decided, to win such fame. He must enter politics.

His own political philosophy was rather hazy. When he made his first attempt to get into Parliament, as the member for High Wycombe in the by-election of 1832, he stood as an independent Radical. It seemed to be the smartest thing to do. The Radicals of the period were a kaleidoscopic group, cheerfully lacking in any coherent political creed. This suited the unconventional Disraeli perfectly. He did not wear, he assured the crowd gathered around the Red Lion Inn in the main street of High Wycombe, the badge of any party. But he was wearing everything else. His listeners were astonished at the sight of this black-ringleted, lace-cuffed, velvet-coated candidate who had chosen, as his campaign colours, pink and white.

'When the poll is declared,' he cried, pointing first to the head and then the tail of the lion pictured above the portico, 'I shall be there and my opponent will be there.'

He was proved wrong. At the final count, he was at the tail.

Nothing daunted, Disraeli stood again in the general election of December the same year. Again he stood as an independent Radical. 'Englishmen . . .' he this time urged the crowd, 'rid yourselves of all that political jargon and factious slang of the Whig and Tory—two names with one meaning, used only to delude you—and unite in forming a great national party.'

But few were swept along by his oratory. Again Disraeli was beaten.

In 1835 he stood a third time. Again he was the most colourful, the most eloquent and the most original speaker. And again he was bottom of the poll.

This third defeat taught him a lesson. If he wanted to win a seat he would have to ally himself with one of the two great political parties—Whig or Tory—on which he had recently heaped such scorn. He chose the Tory party. Already he was friendly with that one-time Tory Lord Chancellor, Lord Lyndhurst and, as Disraeli's Radicalism had always been of a rather fanciful variety, he did not find it too difficult to adjust himself to his no less fanciful interpretation of Toryism.

In later years Disraeli's apologists would go to great lengths to trace a consistency in their hero's political philosophy. They could have saved themselves the trouble. The truth was that Disraeli's craving for renown far outweighed his political convictions.

In the spring of 1835 Disraeli fought his fourth election. He was the official Tory candidate for Taunton. The campaign did little to enhance his reputation. His conversion to Toryism seemed a little too pat; his appearance—all those glittering rings and chains—was too showy; a highly publicized quarrel with the Irish leader Daniel O'Connell, which all but ended in a duel, was distasteful. He was not a man, they said, to be trusted. Once more, Disraeli was defeated.

The long-fought battle was finally won in the summer of 1837. The death of King William IV and the accession of Queen Victoria meant a general election. Disraeli was nominated, along with another Conservative, Wyndham Lewis, in the two-member constituency of Maidstone, in Kent. Together, the two Tories beat their Radical opponent. At last, after four defeats in as many years, Disraeli was in the House.

Victoria's accession to the throne had made possible Disraeli's entry into parliament.

He was now thirty-two years old. His youth—that unorthodox, flamboyant, extravagant, theatrical youth—could be protracted no longer. Count d'Orsay, that no less colourful dandy, scribbled a few lines of sage advice to the new Member of Parliament. 'You will not make love! You will not intrigue! You have your seat; do not risk anything! If you meet with a widow, then marry!'

Chapter Three

With Queen Victoria's accession began her celebrated association with her Prime Minister, Lord Melbourne. Melbourne had become Whig Prime Minister for the second time in 1834, and he thus became the Queen's chief adviser as well as her unofficial Private Secretary. Their relationship has become a classic example of the first love of an unsophisticated young girl for an urbane older man. It is no less an illustration of the Queen's taste for the unorthodox.

At eighteen, the new Queen was a charming creature. By no means beautiful, she had a prettiness, a freshness and a sparkle that served her almost as well as beauty. Her skin was clear, her eyes were bright, her voice was beautiful. She was, admitted a surprised Lord Holland, 'a very nice girl and quite such as might tempt.' He had emerged from his meeting with her 'quite a courtier and a bit of a lover'. Despite her smallness of stature, Victoria was extraordinarily dignified; yet her self-possession never became stiffness and her composure could be tempered by the most winning of blushes. She might be conscientious and full of common sense, but she was also an effusive, artless and affectionate girl. 'She has great animal spirits,' wrote Charles Greville, 'and enters into the magnificent novelties of her position with the zest and curiosity of a child.'

As such, the little Queen was clay in the experienced hands of Lord Melbourne. Neither could have hoped for a more suitable partner at this stage of their respective careers.

In the year of Queen Victoria's accession, William Lamb, Viscount Melbourne, was fifty-eight years old. About his greying head there still clung much of the glamour of his youth; of the days when, as a rich, clever and strikingly handsome young man, he had married the beautiful Lady Caroline Ponsonby. The marriage had been disastrous. The eccentric Caroline Lamb, having flung herself at an unresponsive Lord Byron, finally went mad. Their only son, an epileptic, died in his twenties.

These domestic tragedies seem to have added an air of melancholy to Melbourne's many other charms; women found him irresistible. At fifty-eight, with his grey-blue eyes, his dark lashes, his arched nose and his still luxuriant grey hair, Melbourne remained a handsome man. His air was sophisticated, *insouciant*, seductive; his conversation was witty, entertaining, shot through with cynicism; his views were detached, philosophic and, it must be admitted, a shade too easygoing.

To the young Victoria, Lord M, as she called him, was perfection. And one can understand her attitude. She had passed—quite literally overnight—from the unsympathetic and intimidating authority of her mother's comptroller and ally, Sir John Conroy, into the bland and deferential care of this highly civilized statesman. Here, moreover, was exactly the romantic, unconventional and somewhat mysterious sort of man to whom she would always respond. From their very first meeting, on the day of her accession, she took to him. She pronounced him, with rather more enthusiasm than perception, to be a 'very straightforward, honest, clever and good man.'

The better she came to know him, the better she liked him. Time and again she would make note of his physical attractions: of how handsome he looked in his dark blue 'Windsor uniform' with its red facings, of how appealingly his silver curls were ruffled by the breeze. His talk was a delight; his tutoring (and he did a great deal) was done in the kindest, wittiest, most interesting way imaginable. In his skilful hands, she became more confident, less headstrong and fired with an enthusiasm to do her best. Victoria could hardly have hoped for a wiser and more devoted mentor.

'I have seen him in my Closet for Political Affairs,' she wrote happily, 'I have ridden out with him (every day), I have sat near him constantly at and after dinner, and talked about all sorts of things, and have always found him a kind and most excellent and very agreeable man. I am very fond of him. . . .'

They were in constant communication. When he was not talking to her, he would be writing to her; sometimes he wrote as often as three times a day. Her journal—written in her candid, detailed, dashing, inimitable style—was full of him. Every observation, every piece of advice, every epigram, whether understood or not, was dutifully noted down by the enraptured young Queen.

Together they went riding in Windsor Great Park; side by side they sat in her little sitting room at Buckingham Palace; with his silver head bent towards her blonde one, they paged through illustrated books or played chess. Eventually, she could hardly bear to have him out of her sight. It was noticed that her eyes followed him wherever he moved; when he left the room, she would give a slight, involuntary sigh. If he were ill for a day, she would pronounce herself *'quite annoyed* and *put out'*. If she thought that one of her ladies was monopolizing him at the dinner table, she would become extremely jealous. When she considered that he was spending too much time in the company of the famous Whig hostess, Lady Holland, she accused him of finding the aged Lady Holland more attractive than herself.

'Lord Melbourne dines with Lady Holland tonight,' she complained to her journal. 'I WISH he dined with me!'

2

Inevitably, there was a great deal of speculation about the exact nature of the association between this ageing man of the world and his starry-eyed pupil. 'Take care,' the disgruntled Duchess of Kent told her daughter, 'that Lord Melbourne is not King.' There was no fear of that; not even in the sense that the Queen's mother meant it. Lord Melbourne was an honest man with a scrupulous regard for the Constitution; he would never have made use of the Queen to further his own ends. He may not have been above taking advantage of any royal breeze that happened to be blowing his way, but he would not have originated it.

But what of their more intimate relationship? Among cynics it seemed almost inconceivable that the close friendship should not have a physical basis. Melbourne was known to have a taste for artless young women, and they were no less attracted to him. 'I hope you are amused,' wrote Lady Grey to Thomas Creevy, 'at the report of Lord Melbourne being likely to marry the Queen.' But not everyone was so ready to be amused. On one occasion, disapproving cries of 'Mrs Melbourne' greeted Victoria as she appeared on a balcony beside her Prime Minister.

The Queen, wrote Charles Greville, 'could not endure the thought of parting with Melbourne, who is everything to her. Her feelings, which are *sexual* though She does not know it, and are probably not very well defined to herself, are of a strength sufficient to bear down all prudential considerations. . . .'

Greville may well have been right. If her feelings were sexual, then they were unconsciously so. Victoria was, on her own admission, 'naturally very passionate', but she was passionate in an emotional rather than in an erotic sense. She had a fiery temper, she was given to fierce loyalties, she was capable of an all-consuming love. There is no doubt that she was titillated by Melbourne's light-hearted approach to questions of sexual morality but this did not mean any slackening of her own high moral code. Her undoubted affection for Lord M was a frank, unknowing and innocent emotion. She loved him, certainly, but she thought of him as 'a dear friend' and would even refer to him as 'Father'. Like her Uncle Leopold, Lord Melbourne became a second father.

And how did Lord Melbourne regard her? The young Victoria had precisely the qualities that were needed to set his own cool and rational being aflame: a combination of passion and *naïveté*. But just as she thought of him as a father, so did he look upon her as a daughter. 'I have no doubt that he is passionately fond of her,' writes the ubiquitous Charles Greville, 'as he might be of his daughter if he had one; and the more because he is a man with a capacity for loving without anything to love. It is become his province to educate, instruct and inform the most interesting mind and character in the world.'

But, of course, in the final analysis, there was rather more to this famous partnership than that. No relationship between a father and a daughter could have been as exciting, as explorative, as unclouded and as rich in sexual undertones as was the one between Lord M and Queen Victoria. 'At once his sovereign, his daughter and the last love of his life,' writes Lord David Cecil, 'Queen Victoria inspired Melbourne with a sentiment tenderer if not more vehement than he had ever felt before.' She, on the other hand, was playing—in the most innocent way imaginable—with fire.

For the two of them—Lord M in the sunset of his career and Queen Victoria at the dawn of hers—it was an idyllic time.

3

Unfortunately, not all Lord M's advice was good. Those droll turns of phrase, so dutifully noted down by the admiring Victoria, did not necessarily make good sense. Melbourne might be civilized but he was not really enlightened. He tended to be lackadaisical, to let things drift, to be too suspicious of social change. The impressionable young Queen was only too ready to believe that one should not concern oneself overmuch with reform; that appalling poverty, overcrowding, child labour and rebellious Irishmen were the natural order of things and not to be tampered with. The scant concern that Queen Victoria was always to pay to the conditions in which the majority of her subjects lived can partly be attributed to the influence of Lord M.

Melbourne was lax, too, when it came to personal relationships. In the continuing feud between the Queen and her mother Lord Melbourne should have taken a firmer line. With Victoria's accession, the relationship between mother and daughter had worsened. They bickered even more at Buckingham Palace than they had at Kensington Palace. Melbourne should have encouraged Victoria less in her criticism of her admittedly difficult mother ('I never saw so foolish a woman,' says Melbourne; 'Which', notes the Queen, 'is very true, and we both laughed') and taken advantage of the Duchess's occasional efforts at reconciliation.

Things came to a head, and revealed Melbourne at his least resolute, during the regrettable Flora Hastings affair.

Lady Flora Hastings was one of the Duchess of Kent's ladies-in-waiting. This, and Lady Flora's friendship with the Duchess's comptroller, Sir John Conroy, was enough to set the Queen against her. When the unmarried Lady Flora began to show a suspicious thickening around the waist, the scandalized young Queen decided that she was pregnant, moreover, by 'the Monster and Devil Incarnate'—Sir John Conroy.

This possibility made the Queen, egged on by her even more excitable governess, Baroness Lehzen, determined that something must be done. She consulted Lord Melbourne and he, as was his way, advised her to do nothing. But this was not Victoria's way. Nor could it be Lady Flora's. With the court seething with gossip, she was obliged to undergo a medical examination to prove her innocence. The result of the examination was an exoneration of Lady Flora. She was still a virgin. Whatever it was that was wrong with her, she was certainly not pregnant.

By now, however, the story of Lady Flora's persecution had reached the ears of her family. They demanded of Lord Melbourne that the scandal be traced to its source and the instigator exposed. This he refused to do for fear that the Queen's part in promoting, or possibly originating, the slander would become known. Incensed, the family made the matter public. In the clamour that followed, Victoria's popularity was considerably diminished. Only on the intervention of the old Duke of Wellington did the outcry begin to die down. In the meantime, poor Lady Flora became progressively more ill and in July 1839 she died. A post-mortem revealed that she had been suffering from a tumour of the liver.

The whole unfortunate incident had shown Victoria and Melbourne at their worst: she at her most headstrong, he at his most indecisive. The root of the trouble lay in the Queen's dislike of her mother, Conroy, and their circle but, as a man of the world, Melbourne should have seen to it that this antipathy did not lead the Queen into a compromising position. And the *fracas* was an illustration of Victoria at her most partisan: as strong in her dislikes as she was in her likes. The facts had to be made to fit her preconceived notions. She was not dishonest, she would never tell a lie or simulate a feeling, but once she believed something to be true, or right, it took a great deal to change her mind.

4

This partisanship, this blind loyalty on the part of Queen Victoria was again illustrated in the spring of 1839. On 7 May, Lord Melbourne's government fell on some colonial issue. He sent the Queen a letter to say that he had no alternative but to resign. She was appalled.

'The state of agony, grief and despair into which this placed me may be easier imagined than described!' she wailed. '*All, all* my happiness gone! That happy peaceful life destroyed, that dearest kind Lord Melbourne no more my minister. . . . I sobbed and cried much; could only put on my dressing gown. At 10 minutes past 12 came Lord Melbourne. . . . It was some minutes before I could muster up courage to go in—and when I did, I really thought my heart would break; he was standing near the window; I took that kind, dear hand of his, and sobbed and grasped his hand in both mine and looked at him and sobbed out, "You will not forsake me!"'

He had no choice. The Queen was obliged to send for Sir Robert Peel to ask him to form a new, Tory government. She hated doing so. Throughout the audience she remained, she claimed, 'very much collected, civil and high'. Not only could she not bear the thought of losing Lord M but she disliked Peel intensely. She found him stiff, gauche, unattractive; his smile was said to resemble the silver plate on a coffin. A 'cold, unfeeling, disagreeable man,' is how she described him. In fact, in many ways, Peel was a more admirable man than Melbourne. The Queen's description of Lord M as 'a most truly honest, straight-forward and nobleminded man' would have suited Sir Robert Peel much better. But lacking Melbourne's charm, good looks and slightly raffish air, Peel could not hope to please the Queen.

For exactly the same reasons, forty years on, would Victoria prefer the seductive Disraeli to the more upright Gladstone.

She did not have to put up with Peel for long. Melbourne's parting advice that the Queen should not allow the new Prime Minister to replace her Whig with Tory ladies-in-waiting, put an idea into her head. She dried her tears and prepared to do battle. When Peel suggested that a few of the more important posts be changed, Victoria dug in her heels. She refused to give up *any* of her ladies. When the disconcerted Peel asked if she meant to retain them all, her reply was unbending. '*All*,' she snapped. Unless she surrendered *some* of them, countered Peel, he could not accept the premiership.

This was exactly what she wanted. In a foam of excitement, she scribbled a note to Lord Melbourne, telling him to hold himself in readiness. The impasse was resolved at a hastily convened meeting of the Whig ministers. Melbourne read out his letters from the Queen on the subject of her ladies. At the sound of the imperious phrases ('they wished to treat me like a girl, but I will show them that I am Queen of England') the Cabinet was overwhelmed. How could they possibly desert 'such a queen and such a woman'? A letter was drafted to the effect that the Queen was not prepared to give up her ladies. This Victoria was only too ready to sign. On 10 May, the fourth day of the crisis, Peel declined office.

Lord M, with a no less precarious majority to back him up, resumed office and the triumphant Queen was in her seventh heaven. As always, her heart had run away with her head.

As Lord Melbourne's influence waxed, so did Uncle Leopold's wane. Bolstered, both by her new status and by the fascinating Lord M, Queen Victoria no longer needed to rely quite so heavily on the King of the Belgians for advice and affection. Their letters still criss-crossed the Channel and Uncle Leopold and Aunt Louise were still welcome at Windsor ('It is an inexpressible *happiness* and *joy* to me to have these dearest beloved relations with me in *my own* house,' ran the effusive phrases) but the relationship had subtly altered. Victoria's tone had become slightly more imperious, Leopold's slightly more deferential. Uncle Leopold now discovered that when he wrote to his niece on political matters, it was as the Queen of England that she answered. Uncle Leopold's influence, as the Queen herself assured Lord Melbourne, was now '*very* small'.

Lest it become smaller still and lest Victoria, already at daggers drawn with her Coburg mother, gradually loosen all her Coburg ties, King Leopold decided to act. The proposed marriage between Victoria and her cousin Albert must be hurried on.

But Victoria, who had been so ecstatic about Albert in 1836, was no longer anything like as enthusiastic about the idea of marrying him. In fact, she was not really anxious to marry at all. She admitted to Lord Mebourne that although both Uncle Leopold and Uncle Ernest (Albert's father, the Duke of Saxe-Coburg-Gotha) had been urging her to marry Albert, she was hesitant about it. Perhaps Albert would gang up with her mother against her; perhaps she was too accustomed to having her own way ('Oh! but you will have it still . . .' countered the knowing Lord M); perhaps she was still too quick-tempered, too emotionally unstable to share her life with anyone. She was prepared to wait, she announced, for three or four years before coming to a decision.

But Uncle Leopold was not. Knowing his niece, he felt sure that one glimpse of the handsome young Albert was all that would be necessary to overcome her reservations. He therefore set about arranging for Albert and his elder brother Ernest to visit their cousin in the autumn of 1839. At this Victoria took fright. She was determined not to be rushed into marriage.

'I can make *no final promise this year*, for, at the *very earliest*, any such event could not take place till *two or three years* hence. . . .

'Though all the reports of Albert are most favourable, and though I have little doubt that I shall like him, still one can never answer beforehand for *feelings*, and I may not have the *feeling* for him which is requisite to ensure happiness. I may like him as a friend, and as a *cousin*, and as a *brother*, but not *more*; and should this be the case. . . . I am very anxious that it should be understood that I am not guilty of any breach of promise, for I *never gave any*. . . .'

Some, at least, of Victoria's disinclination to be rushed into an arranged marriage was due to the fact that she was basking in the unaccustomed glow of masculine attention. Lord M was not the only one to be paying her court. One of her gentlemen, the dashing Lord Alfred Paget, made no secret of his admiration for her, and when the young Tsarevich, Grand Duke Alexander, visited England in the spring of 1839, he was no less attentive. Indeed, the little Victoria was so taken with this tall, smiling, masterful young man that she pronounced herself 'quite in love' with him. To this she hastily added that she was 'talking jokingly'.

It was no wonder then, that Uncle Leopold's letters were becoming increasingly grumpy. But the astute Belgian monarch knew better than to press his candidate's claim too strongly. He agreed that his niece need not give Albert an immediate answer; all he asked was that the proposed visit of his nephews take place. To this Victoria acquiesced.

In truth, Uncle Leopold was submerging his niece in a veritable flood of Coburgs that autumn. In September came her Uncle Ferdinand with her cousins Augustus, Leopold and Victoire. With them was yet another cousin, Alexander Mensdorff-Pouilly, whose mother had been a Coburg. The family party was then joined by King Leopold and Queen Louise.

Victoria, as warm-hearted, as sentimental, as effervescent as ever, found herself responding to the *gemütlichkeit* of this family gathering; in no time she was half in love with the lot of them. Their departure left her, as did most partings, feeling desolate.

Uncle Leopold had taken advantage of Victoria's new-found sense of family solidarity to finalize arrangements for the visit of Prince Ernest and Prince Albert. On the morning of 10 October 1839, a page came racing up with a letter from King Leopold: it told Victoria that her cousins would arrive at Windsor that very evening.

At 7.30 p.m. the Queen was standing at the head of the great stone staircase to receive her cousins. She had been prepared for Albert to be goodlooking but at the sight of this tall, well-built, astonishingly handsome young man, she was overwhelmed. In a flash, she fell in love.

'It was with some emotion that I beheld Albert,' she afterwards wrote, 'who is *beautiful*.'

6

It was Prince Albert's beauty, and that alone, that caused Queen Victoria to fall so instantly in love with him. She had always responded to masculine good looks and at the sight of this handsome twenty-year-old, all hesitations about their marriage were swept away. Within a couple of hours, and without getting to know him any better, she had made up her mind.

For the first four days of his stay (by the end of which she had proposed to him) almost all her thoughts were of his physical attractions. 'Albert really is quite charming, and so excessively handsome,' she wrote, 'such beautiful blue eyes, and exquisite nose, and such a pretty mouth with delicate mustachios and slight but very slight whiskers; a beautiful figure, broad in the shoulders and a fine waist; my heart is quite *going*. . . .' To see him dance was a pleasure: 'he does it so beautifully, holds himself so well with that beautiful figure of his.' A gratified Uncle Leopold was treated to a paean on Albert's '*most striking*' looks, and again and again in her journal the enraptured Queen made note of his manifold attractions: his bewitching eyes, the colour of his 'dear lovely face', his muscular legs in 'tight cazimere pantaloons (nothing under them) and high boots'.

'Oh! when I look in those lovely, lovely blue eyes,' she sighed, 'I feel they are those of an angel.'

That dearest, dearest Albert was a trifle overcome by this surge of passionate admiration was only to be expected. His life, hitherto, had been singularly lacking in feminine attentions. When he was four years old, his parents separated: his father, Duke Ernest of Saxe-Coburg-Gotha, to continue his debaucheries, his mother to console herself elsewhere. A rumour has persisted, to this day, that Albert was illegitimate: that his father was a Jewish chamberlain at the little court of Coburg. Giving weight to the story was the fact that Albert in no way resembled his father or brother; neither in looks nor in the looseness of their morals. To some, he seemed to have a slightly Jewish cast of face and a definite Jewish air of melancholy. The allegation has never been proved and is relevant only in that it was Albert's type of beauty—romantic, *triste*, un-English—that made a particular appeal to Victoria.

Yet there were those who were ready to believe that, in later years, a Jewish Albert had been succeeded by a Jewish Disraeli.

The young Albert had been fashioned in a world of men. Even as a child he is said to have shown a 'great dislike to being in the charge of women'. He grew up in the company of his father, his brother Ernest and his adored tutor, Herr Florschütz. He was educated in the all-male atmosphere of Bonn University. The Coburg family factotum, Baron Stockmar, shepherded him on a tour of Italy. His uncle, King Leopold of the Belgians, subjected him to a tireless course of grooming for his role as Queen Victoria's future husband. Neither during these years, nor in later life, did any woman other than Queen Victoria play a significant part in Prince Albert's life. Feminine beauty stirred him not at all. His attitude towards women was always chivalrous but unemotional. No breath of sexual scandal ever touched him.

It was no wonder then, that he confessed to being bewildered by the suddenness and intensity with which Victoria fell in love with him. But he was well enough satisfied. This was what he was here for. Before arriving at Windsor he had not known whether the marriage would take place at all; now he could only be pleased and flattered by the ardour of Victoria's feelings for him. And if he was not quite as besotted by her as she was by him, one could never have imagined it from her impassioned outpourings.

'He was *so* affectionate, *so* kind, *so* dear,' she wrote, 'we kissed each other again and again and he called me "Darling little one, I love you *so* much" and that we should have a very fortunate life together. Oh! what *too* sweet delightful moments are these!! Oh! how *blessed*, how happy I am to think he is *really* mine; I can scarcely believe myself to be *so blessed*. I kissed his dear hand and do feel *so* grateful to him; he is such an Angel, such a *very* great Angel! We sit so nicely side by side on that little blue sofa; no two Lovers could ever be happier than we are!'

She was even prepared to delight in his somewhat backhanded compliment that he could hardly believe that her little hands *were* hands, as the only hands he had hitherto held were those of his brother Ernest.

Yet even now, when Victoria seemed to be taking all the initiative, Albert was emerging as the tutor and she the pupil. The Queen might have been stubborn, headstrong, determined to have her own way and deeply conscious of her position but she was still in search of a father figure. She still craved guidance.

And in Albert, no less than in Uncle Leopold and Lord M, she had an only too willing mentor. This, after his beauty, was what made him so attractive to her. She sensed that he was morally and intellectually her superior. He was more earnest, more conscientious, more controlled than she. 'I intend to train myself to be a good and useful man,' he had once written and it was this moral strength in him that appealed to her. Before long, she was promising to cure herself of bad habits, to try and control her temper, even to improve her handwriting. 'Dearest beloved Albert,' she wrote, 'I pray daily and nightly that I may be more worthy of you, dearest, dearest Albert.'

Not quite everyone shared the Queen's obsession for her husband-to-be. With the wedding date set for 10 February 1840, Albert returned to his beloved Coburg in the middle of November, and during the time that he was away, opposition to the match began to manifest itself. Many Englishmen felt that they were simply having another penniless German princeling foisted on them. There were quarrels about his future title, about his rank, about his annual allowance (Parliament cut the proposed £50,000 down to £30,000), about his religion (the fact that some Coburgs were Catholics was used to sow doubt about his own beliefs), and about his future household. Albert wanted his household to be made up of both Whigs and Tories but Victoria, backed up by Melbourne, insisted that they be Whig. Indeed, the Prime Minister's own private secretary, George Anson, was assigned to the Prince.

On this question Victoria revealed herself to be unexpectedly resolute; she, not he, would choose his household. Not for the last time did Albert catch a glimpse of that steeliness which was at the core of the Queen's extremely complex character. She, who was so anxious to be led, was no less anxious to be obeyed.

It would need a very astute man to give her the leadership she wanted while at the same time giving her the impression that he was carrying out her wishes.

Victoria blamed all this opposition to Prince Albert fairly and squarely on the Tories. As her wedding day approached, so did her indignation against them gather force. She was, she admitted, perfectly frantic. The Tory Duke of Wellington she described as 'this wicked old foolish Duke'; Sir Robert Peel was a 'nasty wretch'; the Tories were all 'vile, confounded, infernal'.

'Poor dear Albert,' she wrote, 'how cruelly are they ill-using that dearest Angel! Monsters. You Tories shall be punished. Revenge! Revenge!'

But on 8 February 1840, the sight of Albert's *dear, dear* face (even if still a little green from a frightful Channel crossing) put her, she says, 'at rest about everything'. Two days later they were married. The ceremony took place at the Chapel Royal, St James's Palace. The little Queen, in a white satin dress trimmed with lace and a wreath of orange blossom on her fair hair, looked suitably composed. Prince Albert, in the skin-tight uniform of a Field Marshal in the British Army, looked superb. After a gargantuan wedding breakfast, they set out on a jolting, three-hour-long drive by coach to Windsor.

It needed a rush of underlinings and capital letters for Victoria to do justice to the delights of that evening when, at long last, the two of them were left alone together. *Never, never* had she spent such an evening; how *could* she ever be thankful enough to have a husband of such beauty, such sweetness, such tenderness; it was all 'bliss beyond belief!'

Chapter Four

Disraeli, by now, was also married. His election, as a Tory Member of Parliament for Maidstone, had given him a wife as well as a seat in the House: for he married the widow of his running mate, Wyndham Lewis. Lewis had died, very suddenly, in March 1838, less than a year after the election.

Disraeli had first met Mrs Wyndham Lewis in 1832. It had been at a *soirée* given by his friend Edward Lytton Bulwer. At the sight of this attractive and vivacious woman, with her skittish clothes and her elaborately ringleted hair, he had asked to be introduced to her. 'She shook her ringlets at him,' runs Philip Guedalla's unforgettable pen-picture of the meeting, 'and he might, by way of repartee, have shaken his.' To his sister Sarah, Disraeli had reported her as being 'a pretty little thing, a flirt and a rattle; indeed gifted with a volubility I should think unequalled, and of which I can convey no idea. She told me she liked silent, melancholy men. I answered that I had no doubt of it.'

And, on a subsequent occasion, he is said to have sighed, 'Oh, anything rather than that insufferable woman,' on being asked to take her into dinner.

But then Disraeli did not always mean what he said and there is no doubt that he was attracted to Mrs Wyndham Lewis. At that first, and at later meetings, she proved herself to be gay, coquettish and gratifyingly interested in everything that the conceited young man had to say. She was quite obviously ready to become yet another worshipper at the shrine. And, more important still, she was twelve years older than he.

Within a matter of weeks after their first meeting, he was sending her one of his flowery notes.

Mary Anne Wyndham Lewis was forty at the time of her first meeting with Disraeli. She had been born Mary Anne Evans in Devon in 1792, of respectable but far from affluent middle-class parents. What she lacked in riches, however, she more than made up for in looks and personality. Mary Anne Evans was slight and seductively proportioned, with large dark blue eyes set in a fashionably oval face. She radiated a refined sensuality. To these alluring looks she brought a no less alluring effervescence of manner: she was frivolous, flirtatious, intensely feminine. She might not have been especially intelligent but she was entertaining, practical and a good deal more sensible than many gave her credit for.

It was no wonder that when Wyndham Lewis first met this fascinating creature at a ball in Clifton, near Bristol, he fell in love with her. Nor was it any wonder that she accepted his proposal of marriage. He might have been a shade too serious and a shade too old for her taste (he was twelve years her senior) but he was gratifyingly rich. Once married to him, Mary Anne moved into a world far removed from her modest beginnings. When he entered Parliament, and they moved to London, she developed into a lavish and accomplished hostess.

Yet Mary Anne always retained something of her Devonshire upbringing. Under the flighty social manner and the tinselly clothes was a warm-hearted, shrewd, almost earthy countrywoman; she remained an efficient housewife and good organizer.

Nor did she outgrow her coquettishness. Throughout her years of marriage to Wyndham Lewis, Mary Anne conducted a series of flirtations. Whether or not they went beyond a titillating exchange of notes, or sighs, or kisses, one does not know but there is no doubt that Mrs Wyndham Lewis revelled in an aura of slightly *risqué* romanticism.

As such, she was made for someone like Disraeli. He was no less addicted to amorous intrigue. Once they were thrown together during the parliamentary election at Maidstone in 1837, their relationship quickly developed into something far warmer than might have been expected between the thirty-two-year-old candidate and the forty-four-year-old wife of his senior colleague. This silver-tongued and exotically-dressed young man ('What *is* the meaning, Ben, of all those chains?' he was once asked. 'Are you practising for Lord Mayor, or what?') quite dazzled her.

'Mark what I say—mark what I prophesy,' wrote Mary Anne to her brother John Evans. 'Mr Disraeli will in a very few years be one of the greatest men of his day.' They were calling him, she claimed proudly, her parliamentary protégé.

And he, with his *penchant* for attractive, and adoring, older women, was hardly less drawn to her. Before long, a series of archly-worded little notes were flitting between the Wyndham Lewises' elegant home in Park Lane and Disraeli's rooms in Duke Street, St James's.

A flirtation that might have developed into a full-scale liaison or have petered out after a few weeks, was suddenly brought to a head in the spring of 1838. On 14 March, Wyndham Lewis died of a heart attack. In her grief and confusion, Mary Anne turned to Disraeli. He lost no time in comforting her. After all, the pretty Mrs Wyndham Lewis was now a rich widow with a house in Park Lane. Within weeks of her husband's death, rumours of a marriage between the two of them were circulating London; it was a rumour which neither was prepared to refute. Indeed, by July of the same year, Disraeli was proposing marriage.

Why should the debonair young Disraeli have been so eager to marry this talkative, forty-five-year-old widow? Firstly, because she was rich, although she was not anything like as rich as he at first imagined. Wyndham Lewis had left her with an income of between £4,000 and £5,000 a year as well as the house in Park Lane. But this was a life interest only: both the annual income and the house would go to her husband's relations after her death. This, Disraeli did not at first realize. But when he did, it made no difference. He pursued her just the same.

Then, she was certainly pretty. Like so many childless, skittish women, Mary Anne had retained the look of youth. At forty-five, with her glowing complexion, her lustrous eyes and her abundant brown ringlets, she looked at least ten years younger. Her dresses, too, with their low-cut bodices and their wealth of lace and ribbons and flounces, were youthful to the point of eccentricity; but then Disraeli was never one to mind a little eccentricity. He might not, in fact, have known exactly how old she was. She was purposely vague about her age. Even on her husband's tombstone, Mary Anne took care to extol their seventeen—rather than their twenty-three—years of 'unbroken happiness'. Mourners, totting it up, would have been led to believe that she was thirty-nine at the time of his death, not forty-five.

Not that Disraeli would have minded her age: this, as always, was part of the attraction. Once again, she had soon become his 'mother' and he was calling himself 'your child'. Once again, it is a quasi-maternal quality that he is seeking.

And of course, she was prepared to give him, in full, all the admiration, adoration and sympathy he needed. Before long, she seems to have been giving him even more than this. In one of his many notes to her, he mentions his uneasiness at the thought that she might be embarrassed by her servants finding the watch, the seal and the chain that he has left in her bedroom. 'My dearest love,' he writes more frankly on another occasion, 'I have been obliged to take myself to bed and wish you were with me there.'

Moreover, Disraeli had reached the age, and stage, where he felt the need to be married. He had had enough of amorous escapades. The advice of his friend, Count d'Orsay, had been sound. Now that Disraeli was a Member of Parliament, he needed a more settled, a more secure, a more respectable background. He needed a home and a hostess.

All these factors led him towards marriage with Mary Anne Wyndham Lewis. But there was something more. He had fallen in love with her. Cynics might sneer at the possibility of this handsome, rakish and debt-ridden young man marrying a rich and middle-aged widow for any other than mercenary reasons, but there is no doubt that Mary Anne had set his always unaccountable and unconventional heart aflame. Even on discovering that he would inherit nothing on her more-than-likely predeceasing of him, he pressed on.

It was she who was holding back. She loved him, certainly, but for convention's sake she felt that they must wait a year before marriage. During that wait, she began to have second thoughts; or rather, friends began to put second thoughts into her head. Was she not perhaps making a spectacle of herself? Already she had lent him money; would anyone believe that he was marrying her for any other reason? When, in February 1839, the impatient Disraeli pressed her to marry him immediately (his position, he maintained, was becoming impossible: everyone was assuming that he was her paid lover) they had a furious row. He slammed out of the house and, on reaching his lodgings dashed off a 1,500-word letter to her.

It was a most extraordinary letter—cruelly frank, self-justifying, theatrical, insulting. 'Farewell,' ran the closing lines. 'For a few years you may flutter in some frivolous circle. But the time will come when you will sigh for any heart that could be fond and despair of one that could be faithful. Then will be the penal hour of retribution; then you will recall to your memory the passionate heart that you have forfeited and the genius you have betrayed.'

Almost any other woman would have ripped up the letter and sent the young man packing. But Mary Anne was not altogether foolish. She loved him, and she could recognize the love for her that throbbed on every page of Disraeli's harsh and impassioned letter. 'For God's sake come to me,' she answered. 'I am ill and almost distracted. I will answer all you wish. I never desired you to leave the house, or implied a thought or word about money. . . .'

He came back, they kissed and made up, and they set a date for the wedding. On 28 August 1839, at a quiet ceremony at St George's, Hanover Square, they were married. Meticulous housewife that she was, Mary Anne recorded the day's events in her account book.

'Gloves 2s 6d. In hand £300. Married 28.8.1839. Dear Dizzy became my husband.'

2

Dear Dizzy's parliamentary course was running no more smoothly than was his amorous course. His maiden speech in the House was a fiasco. The sight of this ringleted, beruffled, and be-chained young man mouthing extravagant metaphors was too much for the assembled members; he sat down amid a cacophony of catcalls, hoots and hisses. But above the clamour he was heard to shout a prophetic sentence: 'I will sit down now but the time will come when you will hear me.'

That time seemed to be a long time coming; certainly too long for Disraeli. In May 1841, after Dizzy had been in Parliament for almost four years, Lord Melbourne's Whig administration finally fell. It had been Queen Victoria's stand on the Ladies of the Bedchamber question that had kept the Whigs in office ('Madam,' the disapproving Disraeli had written anonymously to *The Times* during the crisis, 'it cannot be . . .') but this time there could be no royal rebuffing of Sir Robert Peel and the Tories.

In the election that followed, the Conservatives were returned with a sizeable majority. Disraeli, who had been keeping in with Peel in the hopes of a future cabinet post, imagined that his hour had now struck. He seemed to be the only one under that illusion. When no offer came from the new Prime Minister, Disraeli wrote a supplicating letter. It was backed up by another from Mary Anne. 'Do not destroy all his hopes,' she begged, 'and make him feel that his life has been a mistake.' But Peel remained unsympathetic. There was no reason why he should be anything else. As yet, Disraeli counted for very little.

It might well have been Sir Robert Peel's coolly expressed rebuff that finally turned Disraeli away from the sort of Conservatism that Peel represented. Disraeli had never been an orthodox Tory: the creed of men like Sir Robert Peel was too mundane, too middle-class, too unemotional for his taste. He yearned for something more colourful. He wanted to be associated with, or in the forefront of, an altogether more inspiring movement: something more romantic, more patriotic, more rooted in what he imagined to be the glorious past.

Gradually, Disraeli had come to see Conservatism, not as the philo-sophy of privilege, but as a noble alliance between the aristocracy and the people. Toryism should be a popular movement: a working together of the nobility and the masses in support of the monarchy and the church. It should be a revival of the loyal, chivalrous, idealistic spirit of the days before the Whig triumph in the revolution of 1688. He maintained that the liberal-seeming Whigs, in their stand against the power of the Crown and the Church, were actually destroying, rather than safeguarding, popular liberties. He wanted an unfettered but enlightened triumvirate—of monarchy, clergy and aristocracy—to dedicate itself to the general good of all the people. What Disraeli dreamed of, in fact, was a type of aristocratic paternalism.

There were two main ways in which he set about trying to imple-ment his somewhat fanciful ideals. The one was through writing; the other through politics.

Disraeli's pen had almost never been still ('When I want to read a novel, I write one,' he once quipped) and during the early 1840s he wrote two of his most significant political novels. The first was *Coningsby; or the New Generation*, which was published in 1844; and the second was *Sybil: or The Two Nations*, published a year later. In each of these three-volume works, Disraeli expounded his interpretation of Conservatism. It was in the second of these books (in which he drew attention to the miseries of the industrial and agricultural workers) that he invented one of his most famous catch-phrases: that Britain was a country of two nations, 'the rich and the poor'.

In the House of Commons he was actively concerned with the emergence of a group of idealistic young Tories that became known as 'Young England'. For the most part its members—and they constituted a mere handful—were the scions of aristocratic families. What they were looking for was a noble cause, an ideal that would transcend the crass materialism of the times, a return to the glories of a largely mythical past. 'Young England' was, in truth, a lost cause but it gave its members the chance to make their presence felt in the House. They became a persistent thorn in the side of Peel s government. Disraeli, particularly, benefited from the opportunity it gave him to speak out. For it was during his years as a member of 'Young England' that Benjamin Disraeli first earned his reputation as a brilliant orator.

3

By the year 1845 Disraeli was in open revolt against Sir Robert Peel. As yet, he had no sizeable following in the Tory party but in the autumn of that year he was given an opportunity to rally support. The issue was the Prime Minister's proposed repeal of the Corn Laws.

Peel, to help ease the situation created by the Irish famine, was anxious to do away with the protection duties on foreign imported grain. He had become, in the phrase of the time, a Free Trader. Against Peel's Free Trade policies, Disraeli was now able to drum up support. He drummed it up, not only from the starry-eyed Young Englanders, but from amongst those conservative country squires who made up the bulk of the Tory party.

Not yet highly regarded enough to lead the rebellious Tories against their Prime Minister, Disraeli was able to conduct his campaign under the nominal leadership of Lord George Bentinck. His speeches were outstanding. The time had indeed come, as he had prophesied it would, when the House was ready to listen to him.

Disraeli could not actually prevent the repeal of the Corn Laws (the opposition Whigs voted with Peel on this issue) but he was determined to get the better of Peel. The opportunity came in June 1846. On yet another issue (the Irish Coercion Bill) Bentinck, Disraeli and their followers voted with the Whigs, and the government was defeated.

Peel was forced to resign. The Queen sent for Sir John Russell to head a Whig administration and the Disraeli-rent Conservatives went into opposition.

For Disraeli, the crisis meant a turning point in his career. There now seemed to be every possibility that from out of the disunited state of the Conservative opposition, he would emerge as leader. 'Health, my clear brain, and your fond love;' he once said to the concurring Mary Anne, 'and I feel that I can conquer the world.'

4

Disraeli was forty-one at the time of Sir Robert Peel's resignation, and of his emergence as the leading light in the Conservative party. Although he was always to remain young at heart, he began cultivating an image more in tune with his increased political stature. No longer did he look, or act, the foppish man-about-town. The ringlets—although a little sparser on the temples—remained, but the lace cuffs and the coloured waistcoats and the myriad chains had gone. He now dressed sombrely if hardly less dramatically, in dark colours; the affected mannerisms had been replaced by an even more telling immobility. He had perfected a detached, hooded, sphinx-like look. The no less dazzling epigrams, witticisms and metaphors were now delivered in the most controlled fashion. Things sounded no less flamboyant, no less lush, but they took a more disciplined form. He was obviously a person to be taken seriously.

Socially, too, Dizzy had increased in stature. The house at Grosvenor Gate had been altered and refurbished to serve as a more impressive background for the rising politician. The hallway was hung with rose-coloured silk to resemble a Persian tent. The walls of the drawing room were regally red, the curtains richly gold; bric-à-brac, often Eastern in origin, crowded every available surface. On the vast dining table, set for forty, the damask and crystal and silver gleamed in the light of scores of candles. Mary Anne was an excellent hostess. Guests might smile at the youthfulness of her clothes—lace looped over pink satin, wreaths of flowers in her hair—but they had to admit that she was disarmingly good-natured. She never put on airs; in fact, she could be almost embarrassingly natural.

Before long, all society was repeating her racy but apparently artless stories. One never knew what she was likely to come out with next. To someone who was extolling the paleness of some beauty's skin, Mary Anne exclaimed, 'Ah, I wish you could only see my Dizzy in his bath! Then you would know what a white skin is.'

At a country house party, the Disraelis' bedroom was next to Lord Hardinge's: to the startled company at breakfast, Mary Anne boasted of having slept between the greatest statesman and the greatest soldier of the day. And at yet another country house breakfast she announced that she had been obliged to keep awake half the night to distract Dizzy from a particularly suggestive painting of Venus and Adonis in the bedroom.

That she adored him was only too obvious. There were no extra-marital flirtations now. A sure way of pleasing her was to praise him. An appreciative word about him and her eyes would fill with proud and grateful tears. And he was equally devoted to her. Mary Anne's joking remark that Dizzy had married her for her money but that, given the chance again, he would marry her for love, was not inaccurate. In the dedication of his novel *Sybil*, he referred to her as one 'whose taste and judgement have ever guided its pages; the most severe of critics but—a perfect Wife!'

They quarrelled about one thing only—his debts. She had had no conception of their size when she married him and he always tried to keep the alarming truth from her. But every now and then she would find out something more and there would be a scene. However, she was not ungenerous: in the end she paid something like £13,000 toward settling them.

Although some of the grander hostesses, like Lady Londonderry and Lady Jersey, were less anxious to entertain a Disraeli married to a middle-class widow than a Disraeli single, the couple moved in elevated enough company. They were entertained in several great country houses. One of the most significant of these visits was early in 1845 when they were guests at Stowe, the grandiose home of the Duke of Buckingham. For it was on this occasion that the Disraelis were presented to Queen Victoria and Prince Albert.

This was not, of course, the first time that Dizzy had been in the Queen's company. As a Member of Parliament he had attended her Coronation (the Queen had played her part, he told his sister Sarah, with 'great grace and completeness') and, with the other members of the House of Commons, he had gone to Buckingham Palace to deliver an address on the occasion of her marriage. While admitting that the little Queen looked 'well' and Albert, 'in high military fig', impressive, Disraeli's most appreciative comments were for his own appearance.

'It is generally agreed,' he reported to Sarah, 'that *I* am never to wear any other but Court costume; being . . . a very Charles II.'

But this was to be the first time that they would meet, in a sense, socially. While Dizzy was gratified enough, Mary Anne was all agog. Her hostess showed her over the apartments in which the royal couple were being accommodated. Suitably impressed by the furnishings, Mary Anne was astonished to discover that the royal couple slept *without pillows or bolster* and that they were obliged to share a lavatory hidden behind a red curtain; *there was no second convenience*, she reported.

The presentation was a stiff affair. The room was freezing; Dizzy, in knee breeches and stockings, was shivering with cold (but 'in his best looks' declared his loyal wife); Mary Anne was in an elaborate dress of black velvet with trailing sleeves looped up with knots of blue ribbon and with more blue velvet bows in her hair; as the company passed the royal couple, the Duke of Buckingham called out their names 'exactly the same as an ordinary groom'; each made a bow or a curtsey and passed on.

But all became bliss for the Disraelis when they learnt, from their hostess later that evening, that the Queen had pointed Dizzy out, saying 'There's Mr Disraeli.'

'Do you call all this nothing?' asked an exultant Mary Anne.

Chapter Five

The Disraelis' excitement at their first meeting with Queen Victoria was not echoed at the Palace. The Queen, in her journal, did not even mention meeting Disraeli, although she did have something to say about the 'singularity' of Mary Anne's appearance.

The truth was that the royal couple detested Disraeli. The Queen had been incensed to hear of his asking Sir Robert Peel for a cabinet post: 'Mr Disraeli(!) *high office*' she had snorted. To her Uncle Leopold, she had complained of the foolish recklessness of the 'Young England people'. And when, during the debates on the Corn Laws, Disraeli attacked Peel, his own leader, Victoria was furious. He was 'unprincipled, reckless and not respectable'; his attacks had been 'dreadfully bitter'. She fully agreed with Peel's report that Disraeli and Bentinck had concocted a 'foul conspiracy' against him.

For by now the Queen had quite overcome her own initial antipathy towards Sir Robert Peel. It had taken Prince Albert to open her eyes to Peel's many good qualities. What Disraeli considered to be Peel's shortcomings—his dull, unemotional, middle-class worthiness—looked more like strengths to Prince Albert. Like Peel, the royal couple were ardent Free Traders. Albert had even gone so far as to attend a session in the House of Commons in order to display royal sympathy for Peel's Free Trade cause. So the fact that it was Disraeli who finally brought Peel down did nothing to endear him to the Queen.

What Victoria's attitude towards Peel might have been without Prince Albert to guide her, one does not know. By now she was ready to be instructed by her husband in all things. Gradually, year by year, Albert had been increasing his influence over his adoring wife. At first it had not been easy. Victoria had not always been able to abide by her sworn resolution 'to make this beloved Being happy and contented'. Albert's complaint to a friend that he was 'only the husband, and not the master in the house' had been fully justified. The poor Prince had to battle against his wife's imperiousness, stubbornness and violent temper. There had been countless scenes. After several particularly stormy ones, Albert had been able to get rid of Victoria's confidante, the possessive Baroness Lehzen. While this meddlesome creature was still in the Palace, Albert felt that he would never command his wife's complete confidence.

With the fall of the Whigs and the departure of Lord Melbourne, Albert had been able to get rid of yet another, albeit more benevolent and by now less influential, competitor. Lord M's parting advice to the Queen was that she should put her trust in her husband. 'The Prince understands everything so well and has a clever able head,' he said. Victoria was only too ready to follow the advice. Never again, during Albert's lifetime, would the Queen come under the sway of a prime minister. Instead of Lord M, Prince Albert now became the Queen's unofficial private secretary.

And because she not only adored and admired Albert but because she must always be guided by a man, Victoria allowed him greater and greater authority. From being trusted to blot her signature on official documents, the Prince graduated to reading despatches; from reading despatches, he graduated to giving advice, and from giving advice to making decisions. He was entrusted with the keys to the boxes of confidential State documents. At ministerial audiences, he was always by her side. There were few subjects on which he was not prepared to write a long, solemn but eminently sensible memorandum. From now on Victoria spoke as 'we', not as 'I'. In her absence (and her recurring pregnancies made them frequent) he held levees; presentations to him were said to be considered equal to presentations to the Queen herself. 'We women,' she would even go so far as to protest, 'are not *made* for governing.'

'He is become so identified with her that they are one person,' wrote Greville, 'and as he likes, and she dislikes, business, it is obvious that while she has the title, he is really discharging the functions of the Sovereign. He is King to all intents and purposes.'

Although both Victoria and Albert had a strict regard for the limits of constitutional monarchy, they felt that the powers and prestige of the Crown should be somehow enhanced. By the blamelessness of their private life and the high moral tone of their court, the monarchy came to command more respect than had been the case for many a long year. In addition to this, Prince Albert encouraged the Queen, not only to take a greater interest in foreign—which at that time meant European—

affairs, but to insist on her right to be consulted on them. Foreign affairs became her particular province, just as, in the years ahead, imperial affairs were to hold a special interest for her. Domestic politics would never be able to fire her imagination to the same extent.

Another of Prince Albert's achievements was to lift the Crown above party politics. At the time of his marriage to Victoria, she had been an ardent Whig; her predecessor, King William IV, had been an ardent Tory. Gradually, Albert convinced her that she must give allegiance to neither party; that the Crown must stand high above the political *mêlée*. It was one of his most significant contributions to British political life. After his death, his more emotional wife could not adhere to it with quite as much conviction.

Albert's influence spread to other spheres as well. He set about filling the gaps in Victoria's education. He introduced his hitherto unappreciative wife to the wonders of art and science. Under his guidance, her reading became more serious. People were invited to Court because of their accomplishments rather than because of their lineage: to a certain degree, the Court became more democratic. He developed in her a taste for the beauty and the quiet of the countryside as opposed to the clamour of London. Windsor became more dear to her than Buckingham Palace.

To ensure greater privacy, the couple bought a property on the relatively remote Isle of Wight and another in the even more remote Highlands of Scotland. Albert designed an Italianate palace, Osborne House—to suit the moderate, if not exactly Mediterranean, climate of the Isle of Wight. And for the Highlands, which were the closest that he could get to the romantic scenery of his beloved Coburg, he designed Balmoral Castle. Buckingham Palace, too, benefited from his Teutonic attentions. First he carried out a thorough reorganization of the running of the palace and then he badgered the government into enlarging and improving it.

With the birth of each child (they had no less than five during the first seven years of marriage) Albert's position was strengthened. Early on in their marriage, a Bill had been passed by which, in the event of the Queen's death, the Prince would become Regent for their eldest son. ('Three months ago they would not have done it for him,' claimed Melbourne. 'It is entirely his own character.') Yet the wretched question of his precedence remained unsolved. Victoria's surviving uncles were quite likely to elbow him out of the way on official occasions and on the Continent, he was expected to give precedence to mere archdukes.

All this infuriated Victoria. So passionately in love with him, so appreciative of his many talents, so convinced of his moral and intellectual superiority, she could not bear the thought of his taking second place to any man.

'Oh!' she once exclaimed, 'if only I could make him King.'

2

Their intimate marital life seems to have been very happy. On sexual matters Albert was prudish. He loathed coarse conversation. Masculine, after-dinner talk, as the port went round and the stories became smuttier, was a nightmare to him. He lost very little time in joining the ladies. In this, he closely resembled Benjamin Disraeli. But, on the other hand, he did not share Dizzy's preference for female company. Albert was not one for flowery compliments or attentive gestures or flirtatious remarks. He was at his most comfortable in the company of men like himself—earnest, idealistic, conscientious.

Yet his relationship with Victoria was affectionate and tender. She was his 'own darling', his 'little wife', his *Fräuchen*. His letters to her were full of endearments. If he could not quite match the fervour of Victoria's love for him there was no one that he loved more. Inevitably, they had rows. Albert's method of coping with them was to leave the room until such time as she regained her composure; her method was to follow him from room to room, upbraiding, accusing, complaining until she had worked herself up into a state bordering on hysteria. The scene over, he would write her one of his wordy, compassionate, closely-reasoned letters to which she would reply in her altogether more emotional style.

Yet such quarrels were rare. They were born, not only out of what Albert calls her 'fidgety nature' and her 'feverish eagerness' but out of her deep, possessive love for him.

Greville's jibe that their short wedding night was 'not the way to provide us with a Prince of Wales' was wide of the mark. Just over nine months after their wedding the Queen gave birth to her first child, a daughter who became the Princess Royal. The Prince of Wales was born a year later. After that the children came thick and fast. There was hardly a year in which the Queen was not pregnant. All in all, the couple had nine children.

During the times that the Queen was laid up, Albert could hardly have been more attentive. 'The Prince's care and devotion,' she wrote, 'were quite beyond expression. He refused to go to the play, or anywhere else. . . . He was content to sit by her (the Queen) in a darkened room, to read to her, or write for her. No one but himself ever lifted her from her bed to her sofa, and he always helped to wheel her on her bed or sofa into the next room. For this purpose he would come when sent for instantly from any part of the house.' His care of her, she said, 'was like that of a mother, nor could there be a kinder, wiser, or more judicious nurse.'

It was as well that he was so attentive for Queen Victoria loathed the whole business of childbearing. Each time that she discovered that she was pregnant, she was miserable. When a delighted King Leopold wrote to congratulate her on the birth of the Princess Royal and to say that he hoped that she would become the 'Mamma d'une *nombreuse* famille', he earned the sharp edge of her tongue. 'Men never think, at least seldom think,' she answered, 'what a hard task it is for us women to go through this *very often.* . . .'

Queen Victoria would always refer to childbearing as *die Schattenseite*—the shadowy, negative, less pleasant side—of the marital union. 'You men are far too selfish!' she was later to write to her son-in-law, Prince Frederick Wilhelm of Prussia. 'You only have the advantages in such a case, whereas we poor women have to bear all the pain and suffering (of which you can have no conception).'

To her tirades, the long-suffering Prince Albert would answer with admirable patience. Trust in God whose 'wisdom and goodness should lift you above the feelings of degradation, indignation etc. etc. which you describe,' he once wrote. 'That relationship is sacred, in spite of the pains and trials which women have to suffer. My love and sympathy are limitless and inexhaustible.'

This dread of childbearing (only during the birth of her later children was she given chloroform) may partly explain Queen Victoria's somewhat lukewarm attitude towards babies. She was not exactly indifferent towards her children when they were very young but she was certainly not ecstatic about them. Of the two, Prince Albert was the more affectionate parent. Queen Victoria was always a wife first, a mother second. She was to love none of her children to the extent that she loved her husband. Nor was she ever to be as emotionally involved with her children as she was with men like Lord Melbourne, John Brown and Benjamin Disraeli.

A legend has taken root to the effect that Queen Victoria was a highly-sexed woman, positively Hanoverian in her appetites and that, by the fervour of her love, she wore poor Prince Albert out. There is no possible way of proving this. In any event, the assumption runs counter to what one knows of the Queen. To her eldest daughter Vicky she once admitted that the sexual side of marriage was 'a complete violence to all one's feelings of propriety' and went on to complain that 'we poor creatures are born for Man's pleasure and amusement'.

Passionate Queen Victoria undoubtedly was, but her passions were not of the body: they were of the senses, and of the emotions, and of the heart.

3

Different from Victoria and Albert in almost every other way, Disraeli and Mary Anne resembled the royal couple in the felicity of their marital life. No less than Victoria did Mary Anne enjoy the security of a husbandly faithfulness; no less than Albert did Dizzy bask in the sunshine of a wholehearted wifely devotion. When, in later life, Victoria and Disraeli embarked on their romantic association, both would have known the bliss and the serenity of a happy marriage.

With every passing year Mary Anne's devotion for her husband deepened. In her eyes, he was perfection. To others he seemed already to have lost his once striking looks; with his hunched shoulders, dark skin, furrowed cheeks, drooping lower lip and saturnine expression he seemed positively ugly, but to his wife he was beautiful. When someone remarked on how splendid he was looking, Mary Anne was quick to agree. 'You think he looks splendid?' she purred. 'People think he is ugly, but he is not; he is very handsome. I should like them to see him when he is asleep.'

In public they behaved like young lovers. They would stroll along arm in arm; often he lifted her little hand to his lips or she would ruffle his improbably black ringlets. In the presence of his embarrassed secretary, Mary Anne would kiss and fondle him. When he returned from the House she would wait on him like a slave—or a mother—fetching a bowl of warm water, washing and drying his hands, and curling or smoothing his hair. 'One evening,' noted a friend, 'on coming up from dinner, he knelt before her and, as they say in novels, devoured both her hands with kisses, saying at the same time, in the most lackadaisical manner, "Is there anything I can do for my dear little wife?"'

Mary Anne had been quick to identify herself with her husband's Jewish background. Once, with ringlets swirling and skirts billowing, she came rushing into Baroness de Rothschild's drawing room. Scarcely coherent, she informed the Baroness that, in the event of Dizzy dying before her, she planned to leave all her personal property to the Baroness's little daughter. 'Besides my dearest husband,' she rattled, 'I care for no one on earth, but I love your glorious race, I am rich, I am prosperous. . . . I love the Jews.'

'Away rushed the testatrix,' reported the bemused Lady de Rothschild, 'leaving the testament in my unworthy hands.'

There was no sacrifice that Mary Anne would not make for her husband. Once, on her way to stay with the Salisburys at Hatfield House, she had a bad fall in which she bruised and scratched her face. Dizzy, who had followed after, knew nothing about her disfigurement. To save upsetting him, Mary Anne begged Lady Salisbury to place her at some distance from Dizzy at dinner: in the candlelight and without his monocle, he would never notice her battered condition.

On another occasion, she drove with him to the House. He was to take part in an important debate and she had come to see him safely off. After he had alighted from their carriage, the footman slammed the door shut, crushing Mary Anne's fingers. She made no sound but, smiling her gay smile, watched him enter the House. Nothing must be allowed to distract him. Afterwards, in recognition of her courage, Disraeli had the carriage door taken off and preserved.

Her conversation, which became scattier by the year, was almost all about him. When a young man told her that he was going up to Oxford, she answered, 'Oh yes, I love Oxford; they are all so fond of

Mr Dizzy there, they all applaud him so.' They had made him a 'D.T.C.C. or something of that sort', she added airily.

Asked if she cared for politics, she protested that she simply did not have time to take an interest in them. She was far too busy going through books and pamphlets to see if her husband's name was in any of them. 'I am sorry when he is in office for then I lose him altogether,' she sighed.

She had many people, she added, who called themselves her friends, 'yet I have no friend like him'.

It could almost have been Victoria talking about Albert.

4

To match his improved political standing (the hiving off of the Peelite group and the death of Lord George Bentinck in 1848 had left Disraeli as the only Conservative of any real ability in the House of Commons), Dizzy felt that he must do something to improve his social prestige. One could hardly expect to lead a party of landed gentry without being a landed gentleman oneself. A house in Park Lane, belonging to one's wife, was not nearly good enough a base from which to broadcast one's particularly rural version of conservatism: a party of benevolent squires, of enlightened country clergymen, of satisfied tenant farmers; of, in short, the whole carefully gradated pattern of pastoral England.

So Dizzy found himself a country house. It was a simple, white, stuccoed, three-storied mansion called Hughenden Manor, situated in deeply wooded country near High Wycombe, not far from Isaac D'Israeli's home, Bradenham.

To find it was one thing; to pay for it another. Its price was £35,000 and, at that time, Dizzy's debts still amounted to something like £20,000. Even the death of both his mother and father, within a few months of each other, did little to get him out of his financial morass. His inheritance of £11,000 was quickly swallowed up. In the end, the Bentinck family lent him most of the money. By the autumn of 1848, Dizzy was able to tell Mary Anne, 'It is all done, and you are the Lady of Hughenden.'

Mary Anne was delighted. With her uninhibited taste, she set about decorating it. To the sober pieces inherited from Bradenham, she added some distinctly more flamboyant furnishings. One visitor described the drawing room as being 'a terribly gaudy apartment, very lofty, and the walls all green paper, dotted with fleur-de-lys and adorned with large panelled brown carved wood—or composition—frames, which are the only relief to this green wilderness of wall.' But to Mary Anne's less aesthetic brothers-in-law, Ralph and James Disraeli, she seemed to have wrought wonders with her 'clever arrangements and magic touches'.

It was going to take a great deal more than the possession of a country seat, however, to render Disraeli respectable in the eyes of his fellow parliamentarians. The death of Lord George Bentinck had not automatically made him Conservative leader in the House of Commons. To many of his colleagues, he was still not a man to be trusted. His past—that flashy, frivolous, debt-ridden past—was not entirely hidden behind the sober clothes and the decorous manner. There remained Dizzy's undeniable foreign appearance and his dyed ringlets: 'My hair will be white as long as I live: While yours will be black as long as you dye,' ran a contemporary quip about the improbable glossiness of his curls.

He was suspect on other counts as well. Having toppled Peel because of the Prime Minister's championship of Free Trade, Disraeli promptly began to champion it himself. As the leader of the Conservative Party, Lord Stanley, was to say to the astonished Queen Victoria, 'he did not think Mr Disraeli had ever had a strong feeling, one way or the other, about Protection or Free Trade.'

Dizzy's stand on Jewish questions caused further embarrassment and distrust. In his three-volume novel, *Tancred*, published in 1847, Disraeli set out some highly unorthodox views on Judaism and Christianity. To Disraeli, Christianity was the logical and highest development of Judaism. A Christian, he maintained, was simply a completed Jew. It was, perhaps, the most convenient way of explaining away how he—who was so proud of his 'aristocratic' Jewish ancestry—had converted to the Christian faith.

While Dizzy's bizarre theory had been confined to the perfervid pages of *Tancred*, no one had much minded. But in 1847 Baron Lionel de Rothschild (to whose daughter Mary Anne had so impulsively decided to leave her 'personal property') was elected Liberal member for the City of London. As a practising Jew, he could hardly take the parliamentary path 'on the true faith of a Christian'. Lord John Russell, the Whig Prime Minister, therefore introduced a motion by which the civil disabilities on Jews would be removed.

To his credit, Disraeli spoke out in its favour. He need not have done so. He could simply have sat mum. He was a Christian, trying hard to win the Conservative leadership by presenting himself as a respectable, dependable, ordinary English country gentleman. Rothschild, moreover, was a Liberal: why should Disraeli make an effort to get him a seat in the House?

But he did. He did so, however, by putting forward his extraordinary thesis. Had he championed Rothschild from an accepted liberal standpoint—that of religious toleration—he would have been understood but Dizzy treated the House to all his high-flown theories about Christians being nothing more than completed Jews. The 'infallible throne of Rome', he reminded them, had been established by a Jew. It was as a Christian, he argued, that he could not take upon himself 'the awful responsibility of excluding from the legislature those who are of the religion in the bosom of which my Lord and Saviour was born'.

By his own followers—those rows of stolid country gentlemen—Dizzy's speech was considered highly objectionable.

The Jewish question was to concern Parliament for the next ten years. Each time a Jewish Emancipation Bill was passed by the Commons, it was rejected by the Lords. Not until 1858 would the matter be resolved. And throughout this long period, Disraeli would give it his unequivocal, if outlandishly-reasoned, support.

Such, however, was the force of Disraeli's personality (and so lacking was he in any competitors) that he was able to overcome all reservations on the part of his colleagues. By 1849, Disraeli was recognized as the Conservative leader in the House of Commons. It was a consisiderable achievement but, for one of his ambitions, it was not nearly enough. He was now forty-four years of age. How much longer would he have to wait for office?

Chapter Six

For Queen Victoria the delights of dearest Albert's most magnificent achievement to date—the Great Exhibition of 1851—were spoiled by the alarming prospect of having Mr Disraeli in her government.

In February 1851, Lord John Russell's Whig ministry was defeated on a franchise issue. Russell resigned and the Queen was obliged to send for the leader of the Conservative party, Lord Stanley. Poor Stanley was forced to admit that although his party could claim considerable numerical strength, it lacked men of stature.

'There was one certainly of great ability and talent,' ventured his Lordship, 'Mr Disraeli.'

But Victoria wanted none of him. In Prince Albert's view, and in hers, Disraeli 'had not one single element of a gentleman in his composition'. When Stanley began to propose him as one of the possible secretaries of state, Victoria interrupted. She had not, she announced, 'a very good opinion of Mr Disraeli'.

When Stanley persisted, Victoria gave way. As much as Lord Stanley, she appreciated the dearth of talent in the Conservative party. She would therefore not veto Disraeli's appointment. But one thing she must make quite clear. Lord Stanley must be responsible for Mr Disraeli's conduct; should he cause her 'any displeasure', she would feel free to blame Lord Stanley.

To this royal proviso, Lord Stanley was obliged to agree. Her Majesty should understand, however, that Mr Disraeli had had to make his own way in the world: not born to a position of importance, he had had to reach there by establishing a reputation for 'cleverness and sharpness'.

'That is true,' answered Victoria grudgingly. 'And all I can now hope is that having attained this great position, he will be temperate. I accept Mr Disraeli on your guarantee.'

But, in the end, she did not need to. Try as he might, Stanley simply could not scrape together enough Conservatives of sufficient ability to form a government. 'The material,' as Prince Albert put it, 'was certainly sad.'

Five days after the fall of Lord John Russell's government, Lord Stanley had to admit defeat. Russell resumed office as Prime Minister.

A year later, Victoria was going through the whole thing again. Russell's shaky Whig ministry was once more defeated. Again the Queen had to send for Lord Stanley (who, having succeeded to the earldom the previous summer, was now the Earl of Derby) to ask him to form a government. This time Derby was successful. By 27 February 1852 the matter was settled. Lord Derby was Prime Minister and Disraeli was Chancellor of the Exchequer and Leader of the House.

The achievement made him feel, said Disraeli, like a girl going to her first ball.

Why, though, had Disraeli been given the post of Chancellor of the Exchequer rather than the more important one of Foreign Secretary? He certainly did not want it. Whatever other Jewish traits there might have been in his character, Dizzy was utterly lacking in the most characteristic trait of his race: a flair for finance. When he protested to Derby about this lack of fiscal knowledge, the new Prime Minister brushed aside his reservations. 'They give you the figures,' he said airily.

Derby's real reason for his choice of Disraeli as Chancellor of the Exchequer would have hurt Dizzy considerably. It was Queen Victoria's dislike of him. She would not need to give as many audiences to the Chancellor as she would to the Foreign Secretary.

But if Disraeli knew nothing about finance, he knew something about women. He might not often see the Queen but he would often be writing to her; and, as writing was not the least of his many accomplishments, he was soon employing his pen with considerable effect. Now began his first advance along the road that was ultimately to lead him to the Queen's heart.

Within days of Disraeli's assumption of his post, Queen Victoria was receiving the most interesting reports from him. Never before had she had parliamentary debates presented in so colourful and entertaining a fashion. Here was Mr Disraeli writing of speeches being 'elaborate, malignant, mischievous'; he describes Lord Russell's speech as 'statesmanlike, argumentative, terse and playful'. It was all so delightfully different from the dry-as-dust accounts that she was normally obliged to read. She even went so far as to copy out a few of the more scintillating ones into her journal. By the end of March 1852 she was telling her Uncle Leopold that 'Mr Disraeli (*alias* Dizzy) writes very curious reports . . . much in the style of his books.' It was all very amusing. It helped take some of the drudgery out of politics.

That April, Victoria moved a step closer. She invited the Disraelis to dinner. This was the first occasion on which the Queen was able to study the couple at her leisure. Mary Anne, by then, was a few months short of sixty; it was an age to which she was not prepared to make the slightest concession. Her tinted hair would still be crowned with an extravagant wreath of diamonds, velvet leaves and feathers; her dress would still be an elaborate confection of white satin trimmed with looped-up flounces of gold lace and all glittering with diamonds and turquoises.

To Victoria, whose own taste in clothes was uncertain, such outlandishness might pass unremarked; it was Mary Anne's frank and colourful conversation that astonished her.

'*She* is very vulgar,' noted the Queen, 'not so much in her appearance, as in her way of speaking.'

The forty-seven-year-old Dizzy, Victoria pronounced 'most singular'. He was 'thoroughly Jewish looking, a livid complexion, dark eyes and eyebrows and black ringlets. The expression is disagreeable, but I did not find him so to talk to.'

He had, she said, 'a very bland manner, and his language is very flowery.'

3

Not for long, however, could Dizzy employ his bland manner and his flowery language on his Sovereign. Before the year 1852 was out, Derby's government had fallen. It had fallen, moreover, on the question of Disraeli's budget. And the man who was as responsible as any for bringing it down was William Ewart Gladstone.

At this time, Gladstone was forty-three years of age, some five years younger than Disraeli. In almost every way, the two men were opposites. Gladstone was a tall, upright, robust figure, with flashing eyes, strongly chiselled features and a commanding voice. To his champions, he was a man of exceptional piety, high principles and unblemished integrity. In the House, Gladstone was a Peelite: exactly the sort of earnest, high-minded, God-fearing man of whom the late Sir Robert Peel approved. Indeed, Peel had once prophesied that Gladstone would one day be Prime Minister.

And what, someone had then asked of Peel, would happen to Disraeli? 'We shall make him Governor General of India,' answered Sir Robert.

Between Gladstone and Disraeli there had never been much love lost. Gladstone saw Disraeli as a slippery, cynical, irreligious opportunist, while Disraeli saw Gladstone as a priggish and sanctimonious hypocrite. But only now, during the debate on Disraeli's budget, did the two of them cross swords in public. It was the start of a famous parliamentary duel that was to last for over a quarter of a century. It was a duel with which Queen Victoria was to be intimately involved.

In his study of Disraeli, Robert Blake has captured this first, significant clash of arms between the two future giants. 'The artist who wished to immortalize, as if upon a Greek vase, an instant of time that would illuminate the political history of the mid-Victorian era,' he writes, 'would have done well to choose the moment when Gladstone rose to answer Disraeli at one o'clock in the morning of December 17, 1852; the faces of the members, pallid in the flaring gaslight, contorted, some with anger, some with delight, arms gesticulating in hostility or applause; Gladstone on his feet, handsome, tall, still possessing the youthful good looks, the open countenance, which had charmed his contemporaries at Eton and Christ Church; Disraeli seated on the Treasury Bench, aquiline, faintly sinister, listening with seeming indifference to the eloquent rebuke of the orator. It was a scene which was not easily forgotten. It coloured the parliamentary life of a whole generation.'

This particular round went to Gladstone. The government was defeated. Disraeli retired from office with a good grace, not neglecting to write letters of thanks to the Queen and Prince Albert for their kindness and help.

'I may, perhaps,' he wrote to Albert, 'be permitted to say that the views which Your Royal Highness had developed to me in confidential conversation have not fallen on ungrateful soil. I shall ever remember with interest and admiration the princely mind in the princely person, and shall at all times be prepared to prove to your Royal Highness my devotion. I have the honour to remain, Sir, your Royal Highness's most obedient Servant, B. Disraeli.'

The princely mind in the princely person. The Queen could hardly have wished for better than this.

Chapter Seven

Queen Victoria might have been looking a little more kindly on Mr Disraeli but he would not be the next man to set her always susceptible heart a-flutter. It was Napoleon III, Emperor of the French. In some ways, though, the relationship between the Queen and the Emperor was in the nature of a dress rehearsal for her future, and even more romantic, association with Disraeli.

The two men—Napoleon and Disraeli—had known each other well in younger days. At that time Prince Louis Napoleon Bonaparte, as the active pretender to the throne of his uncle, the Great Napoleon, had been living in exile in England. The two of them, having met at the *salon* of the celebrated Lady Blessington, had moved in the same circles. Dizzy had been rather taken with the Prince. He admired him for 'that calm which is rather unusual in foreigners, and which is always pleasing to an English aristocrat.' He had even had a good word to say about his clothes. His dress, pronounced Dizzy, 'was in the best taste, but to a practised eye had something of a foreign cut.'

On one occasion, the two men had found themselves, quite literally, in the same boat. In the summer of 1839 Dizzy's friend Lytton Bulwer had given a breakfast party at his Thames-side home. Louis Napoleon, arriving late, discovered that the rest of the party had already set out on a steamer trip. The only other guests present were also latecomers— the newly-married Dizzy and Mary Anne. The Prince promptly suggested that they hire a rowing boat and follow the others. They agreed, and with Louis Napoleon rowing, set off. Before they had got very far, however, the Prince landed them on a mud bank. Nothing he could do could get them off.

Mary Anne was furious. 'You should not undertake things which you cannot accomplish,' she exclaimed. 'You are always, sir, too adventurous.'

Dizzy kept quiet. So did Louis Napoleon. 'Nothing,' noted

Disraeli, 'could be more good-natured than the Prince, and I could not have borne the scolding better myself.' They were rescued, eventually, by a passing boatman.

Mary Anne's castigations had been particularly pertinent. For the following year the Prince, who had already made one unsuccessful attempt to gain the French throne, made another, even more disastrous one. Heading a small invasion force, he landed at Boulogne; within hours he had been taken prisoner. 'Louis Napoleon,' announced Disraeli, 'who last year at Bulwer's nearly drowned us by his bad rowing, has now upset himself at Boulogne. Never was anything so rash and crude to all appearances as this "invasion". . . .'

The Queen would have agreed with her government that the attempt had been quite 'mad'.

But those days had long since past. The tenacious Louis Napoleon, having escaped from his French prison, had finally won this throne by less showy means. On the overthrow of King Louis Philippe in 1848 and the proclamation of a republic, Louis Napoleon had been elected President. 'The success of Louis Napoleon is an extraordinary event. . .' Victoria had written to her Uncle Leopold adding, with characteristic sagacity, that 'it will, however, perhaps be more difficult to get rid of him again than one at *first* may imagine.'

She had been right. Three years later Louis Napoleon had staged a *coup d'état* and the following year he had re-established the Empire, assuming the title of Napoleon III.

Having achieved his life-long ambition, this new Napoleon was determined to avoid the rock on which the First Empire had foundered: Napoleon I's rivalry with England. This was one feature of his illustrious ancestor's reign that he planned not to emulate. Subtly but surely, he set about courting England and with it, of course, England's Queen. Napoleon had always been one for the conducting of affairs on a personal rather than an official level.

But his approaches, for all their subtlety, proved unsuccessful. It needed the threat of a war to bring the sovereigns of England and France together. Their countries were drawn into a military alliance to defend Turkey against Russia. By March 1854 their combined armies were on their way to wage war against Russia in the Crimea. In September, a gratified Napoleon invited Prince Albert to visit him at his military camp at Boulogne. Albert accepted.

Napoleon, whose charm could be prodigious, used every ounce of it during Prince Albert's four-day stay. And Albert, by no means gullible and with a strong distaste of the flamboyant, found himself warming to this colourful adventurer. All in all, the visit was a great success.

While Prince Albert returned home to write a ponderous memorandum on his stay, Napoleon employed his time in a more advantageous fashion. He bombarded the Queen with praise of her husband. To Victoria such flattery sounded sweet indeed. Not since Mr Disraeli's delightful letter on relinquishing office had the Queen heard the Prince so highly spoken of.

Having prepared the ground, the Emperor moved in closer. He was determined to be received by the Queen. During the visit to Boulogne Prince Albert had said something about the possibility of the Emperor and Empress visiting Windsor; he now pressed for a more definite invitation. The Emperor would be 'delighted to avail himself of the Queen's gracious kindness; nothing would give him so much pleasure. . . .'

Finally, the matter was arranged. The Emperor Napoleon III and the Empress Eugénie would pay a State Visit from 16 to 21 April 1855.

'I cannot say what indescribable emotions filled me, how much it felt like a wonderful dream,' wrote Queen Victoria of the moment that she welcomed the Emperor, with his beautiful young Empress, to Windsor. 'These great meetings of sovereigns, surrounded by very exciting accompaniments, are always very agitating. . . .'

Her agitation did not last very long. In no time the Queen found herself responding to Napoleon's soothing but fascinating manner. With those hooded eyes, that hooked nose, those cat's-whisker moustachios and that top-heavy body, he might not be considered conventionally handsome, but his manner was certainly very engaging.

'We got on extremely well at dinner,' she wrote, 'and my great agitation seemed to go off very early; the Emperor is so very quiet; his voice is low and soft and *il ne fait pas de phrases.*' There was, admitted the Queen in a letter to her Uncle Leopold the following day, 'great fascination in the quiet, frank manner of the Emperor. . . .'

Not for the first, nor for the last, time in her life was Queen Victoria falling for an accomplished seducer.

There were many ways in which Napoleon III resembled Benjamin Disraeli. They were pretty much of an age, Napoleon having been born only four years after Disraeli. Both had what the Queen would have called a 'foreign' appearance: they were sallow-skinned, beak-nosed, with heavy-lidded eyes. In each case, their youth had been unconventional—rakish, glamorous, adventurous; indeed, something of the dashing, devil-may-care air of the early nineteenth century clung to them still. Both were exotics. Yet their manner was decorous, their expression impenetrable, their aura mysterious. They were enigmas. There was a duality in both their natures: neither Napoleon III nor Disraeli were straightforward men. Ruthless ambition went hand in hand with high romanticism; realism with idealism. Both could command unswerving loyalty; both had a reputation for duplicity. They were accused of being devious, Oriental, Machiavellian; too much concerned with showy gestures and too little with principles. There was too much dazzle, it was said, and not enough morality.

Both men had a perfect understanding of women. For them, feminine company was essential; their behaviour towards the opposite sex was confiding, attentive, flattering. Each radiated an undeniable air of sexuality. And, as far as Queen Victoria was concerned, each appreciated, to the full, the value of treating her as a woman first, a sovereign second.

It was no wonder then that Queen Victoria, with her marked taste for the *outré* in men, found the Emperor Napoleon III so fascinating. Both during his six-day visit to England and during Victoria and Albert's return visit to Paris in August, the Queen found herself becoming more and more enamoured of him.

The Emperor, Lord Clarendon afterwards told Charles Greville, 'with perfect knowledge of women, had taken the surest way to ingratiate himself with her, by making love to her. . . . As his attentions tickled her vanity without shocking or alarming her modesty, and the novelty of it (for she had never had any love made to her before) made it very pleasant, his success was complete.'

The worldly Lord Clarendon was a shade too glib in his assessment. Prince Albert had proved himself quite capable of making love to the Queen and Napoleon III did not make love to her in even the generally accepted nineteenth-century sense of the phrase. But he certainly set out to fascinate, flatter and indeed, flirt with her. It was not so much what he said as how he said it. With characteristic astuteness, he had made himself completely conversant with her past, her tastes and her personality. 'It is very odd,' she afterwards admitted with charming *naïveté* to an amused Lord Clarendon, 'but the Emperor knows everything I have done and where I have been ever since I was twelve years old; he even recollects how I was dressed, and a thousand little details it is extraordinary he should be acquainted with.'

'*Le coquin,*' thought Lord Clarendon to himself.

But Victoria was no fool. Her common sense was probably her most outstanding characteristic and had Napoleon III been nothing more than a charlatan, she would have lost no time in sensing it. The fact that he set out, consciously, to impress and captivate her does not mean that he was not impressive nor captivating. His advances to the Queen might have been carefully calculated but they were not forced. Naturally charming and considerate, Napoleon tended to treat every woman as though she were both beautiful and interesting. These things were second nature to him.

And once she had come to appreciate his real worth, Victoria allowed herself to meet him more than half way. She was ripe for the mild flirtation that he was offering her. In this spring of 1855 the Queen was thirty-five years old, quite young enough to believe that she was still a desirable woman. She had been married to Albert for fifteen years and although she still adored him, there must have been times when she found him a little too serious-minded, a little too matter-of-fact, a little too preoccupied. By now, he was taking her for granted. In any case, Albert was never one for the honeyed phrases of love-making. So when Napoleon, with his sleepy eyes and his dangerous reputation, began his subtle advances, Victoria abandoned herself to his attentions.

This skilful courtship was conducted along the most innocuous lines: it never went beyond an exchange of confidences. But then Victoria had never exchanged confidences with a man like Napoleon III; to the urbanity of a Lord Melbourne, he brought all the swashbuckling air of the man who had so thrilled her girlhood senses, Charles, Duke of Brunswick. Everything Napoleon spoke about seemed tinged with romance and adventure. The Emperor, she noted, 'is *very* fascinating;

he is so quiet and gentle, and has such a soft pleasant voice. He is besides so simple and plainspoken in all he says, and so devoid of all phrases, and has a good deal of poetry, romance, and Schwärmerei in his composition, which makes him peculiarly attractive. He is a most extraordinary, mysterious man, whom one feels excessively interested in watching and knowing. . . .'

In short, he was the sort of man to supply that flash of emotional colour that would always be so essential to the staid-looking little Queen.

On the last night but one of the State Visit to Paris, Victoria and Napoleon, having returned to the Palace of Saint-Cloud from a ball, sat up for another hour, loath to go to bed and so put an end to a magical evening.

'It's terrible that there's only one more night,' sighed the Emperor. In full agreement, Victoria begged him to come soon again to see her in England. 'Most certainly!' he answered.

'But you will come back, won't you?' Napoleon went on. 'Now that we know each other, we can visit each other at Windsor or Fontainebleau without any ceremony, can't we?'

Victoria assured him that this would give her great pleasure. Laughingly she told him that she would come back the following year as an ordinary traveller. With her bag in her hand, she would jump out of the train, take a cab and present herself at the Tuileries to beg some dinner. It was a delicious, if wistful idea. (And one, one may be certain, of which Albert would not have approved.)

Here was Queen Victoria at her most endearing: a frank, charming and happy young woman, very much in love with life and—unconsciously—more than half in love with Napoleon III. No one, seeing her flushed face, her bright eyes and her sweet smile would have doubted that she was enjoying herself to the full. It was so seldom that Victoria was able to relax with anyone other than the members of her family. And few were able to put her at her ease as completely as this softly spoken, worldly man sitting beside her.

But, of course, Napoleon's accomplishments did not end with this putting of the normally nervous Queen at her ease. As valuable was his ability to create a heady, almost erotic atmosphere; it was an atmosphere to which her passionate nature was quick to respond. No wonder that she claimed that she would always look back on this period as one of the most memorable of her life.

Not for another twenty years, during her close association with

Disraeli would she again experience the intoxication of such a relationship.

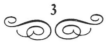

3

Side by side with Queen Victoria's infatuation for Napoleon III went a mounting chauvinism. For the Queen's emotions were almost as much involved with the background against which this royal friendship was being played out—the Crimean War—as with the friendship itself. The Crimean War revealed fully, for the first time, that bellicose patriotism which was to become so characteristic of the Queen in later life.

At first she had hoped for peace. But once it had become clear that the struggle against Russia could not be avoided, Victoria began to change her mind. By the time war was declared on 28 February 1854—with Britain and France supporting Turkey against Russia—the Queen was heart and soul for battle. Suddenly, she saw the times as 'stirring', the Tsar Nicholas I as an ogre, and herself as a latter-day Boadicea. The British army became 'my Army', the fleet 'my Fleet' and the troops 'my children'. It was as if the spirit of the great Queen Elizabeth I lived again in her dumpy little figure.

Braving the icy dawn she stood on the balcony of Buckingham Palace to see a battalion of Guards march off to war; they 'cheered us *very heartily* and went off cheering. It was a *touching and beautiful sight. . . .*' An equally 'splendid and never-to-be-forgotten sight' was the sailing of 'our noble Fleet' from Spithead. The Navy and the Nation, she assured her Uncle Leopold, 'were particularly pleased at *my leading them out*'.

Her emotions see-sawed between agony at the sufferings of her troops and elation at such scant military successes as there were. When, before meeting Napoleon III, the Emperor had announced that he was thinking of going out to the Crimea to take personal command of his armies, the Queen had been appalled. What if the French troops, led by their Emperor, were to win a glorious victory and so steal the British thunder? 'This?' she had exclaimed, 'we *never* could bear.'

In her new belligerent mood Victoria was even prepared to give her *bête noire*—her current Prime Minister, Lord Palmerston—his due. She was obliged to admit that by his courage and energy, the jaunty Palmerston was maintaining the 'honour and interests' of the country.

The longer the war dragged on, the stronger became what Greville called the Queen's 'military mania'. She graduated from knitting scarves and mittens for the men and from writing heartfelt letters of condolence to the widows, to visiting hospitals for the wounded. In mounting anguish she trailed through ward after ward, making gruesome note of the exact nature of the wounds. Dressed in a scarlet tunic and a navy-blue skirt, she sat astride her horse to review her troops. Looking distinctly less dashing in a lilac dress and a green shawl, she distributed medals to the returned and often cruelly maimed heroes. 'The rough hand of the brave and honest private soldier came for the first time in contact with that of their Sovereign and their Queen' ran her triumphant report of this medal-distributing ceremony at the Horse Guards. 'Noble fellows! I own I feel as if they were *my own children*; my heart beats for *them* as for my *nearest and dearest*. They were so touched, so pleased; many, I hear, cried. . . .'

It was all so '*beautiful and touching*'; it was all so glorious.

Here was a mood of exultation which Prince Albert, so dedicated to the arts of peace, simply could not share. Although this conscientious Prince might be working himself to death for the benefit of his adopted country, he could not be transported to the same extent by Britain's military glories. It would need a different sort of man to respond to this side of Queen Victoria's nature.

4

Disraeli—the man who would one day encourage the Queen's fervent patriotism—could not share her enthusiasm for the Crimean War either. The best that he could bring himself to say about it was that it was 'a just but unnecessary war'. Its mismanagement appalled him. More appalling still, for him personally, was the fact that during the course of the war the Conservative leader, Lord Derby, turned down the Queen's invitation to form a new government.

Lord Derby's timidity infuriated Disraeli. He was itching for office. Flushed, presumably by his moderate success with the Queen and Prince Albert, Disraeli had recently been claiming that he had received 'from the highest quarter' a hint that he, and not Derby, would be invited to form the next Conservative government. But now neither Derby nor himself—neither 'the Jockey' nor 'the Jew'—was in office, and Lord Palmerston reigned supreme.

Dizzy welcomed the Treaty of Paris that officially ended the Crimean War and not long after its signing he and Mary Anne visited Paris. Amid the tinselly splendours of Napoleon III's regime, Dizzy felt eminently at home. Second Empire Paris was like something out of the Arabian Nights; the Queen, the year before, had claimed that nothing was 'more *beautiful* and gay than Paris—or more splendid than the Palaces.' It was 'like a fairy-tale'. To the equally enraptured Dizzy, Paris was 'a city of palaces and glittering streets, and illimitable pleasure gardens, statues and gondolas, and beautiful birds and deer'; the newly-joined palaces of the Tuileries and the Louvre were 'worthy of Babylon'; the Bois de Boulogne had been converted 'into a Paradise'. Hospitality was on the most lavish scale; the Disraelis dined out eleven nights in succession.

Climax to this orgy of entertainment was a grand dinner at the Tuileries at which Mary Anne was placed beside the Emperor, and Dizzy beside the Empress. They might all four have been parvenus (the Empress had been a Spanish countess, born Eugénie de Montijo) but they were a no less remarkable group for that. The Empress Eugénie, who had earlier that year given birth to a son, the Prince Imperial, was looking particularly radiant. 'Round her swanlike neck the Empress wore a necklace of emeralds and diamonds such as might have been found in the cave of Aladdin,' enthused Dizzy, 'and yet, though colossal gems, for her they were not too vast.'

Mary Anne, in her honest-to-goodness fashion, reminded the Emperor of the time when he had run them aground in the rowing boat; and of how she had berated him for undertaking things which he could not accomplish. 'Just like him,' laughed the Empress.

Beneath the glittering chandeliers of the Tuileries they sat, these two strangely similar men: Napoleon III then fresh from his conquest of Queen Victoria, Disraeli with his days of conquest still ahead. Dizzy showed the keener understanding of the other's character. 'In dealing with this personage,' he said of the Emperor, 'we must remember that we are dealing with a mind as romantic as it is subtle.'

Napoleon, who could have said the same thing about Disraeli, dismissed him as being 'like all literary men . . . ignorant of the world, talking well, but nervous when the moment of action arises.'

If the Emperor had taken Queen Victoria's measure, he had sadly misjudged Disraeli.

5

Prince Albert was not nearly so enamoured of Napoleon III as was the Queen. Although he liked the Emperor well enough, he could not bring himself to trust him. For this serious-minded, methodical Prince, devoted to the ideals of peace and orderly progress, Napoleon's Second Empire was too showy, too militant, too loosely rooted. The harm which this new Napoleon might do to the peace of Europe was something which Albert greatly feared.

And as Prince Albert, despite Napoleon's charm, retained his hold on both the Queen's heart and mind, Victoria gradually came to share her husband's reservations. Away from the Emperor's seductive presence, it was easier for Victoria to appreciate his shortcomings. When he began acting in a manner prejudicial to Britain, Victoria quickly revised her opinion of him. Their next meeting, for four days at Osborne in 1857, was harmonious enough but after that, as Napoleon III launched his regime on a series of political and military adventures, Victoria became progressively more disenchanted. She even convinced herself that he was planning to invade England. By 1859 she was in full cry against him. There would be 'a *regular Crusade*,' she once exploded, 'against the *universal disturber* of the world. It really is monstrous!'

The truth was that no man, no matter how intelligent or fascinating, could hope to retain Queen Victoria's trust and affection if his political activities ran counter to what she considered to be the best interests of her country.

Chapter Eight

Just as Queen Victoria had been drawn to one of those apparently irresistible exotics in the person of Napoleon III so, during the 1850s, had Dizzy become involved with yet another of those indispensable mother-figures. This was an elderly widow by the name of Mrs Brydges Willyams.

In spite of her uncompromisingly British name, Mrs Brydges Willyams was a Jewess. Her father had been an Abraham Mendes da Costa but either before, or on, her marriage to Colonel James Brydges Willyams, she had converted to the Christian faith. It was their common racial and religious background that first prompted Mrs Brydges Willyams to contact Disraeli: she wrote him several adoring letters in which she made mention of their shared inheritance.

Disraeli ignored the letters ('Do any of you know an old madwoman at Torquay?' he would ask) but when she wrote to him about an altogether more tangible inheritance, he pricked up his ears. Would he, she wanted to know, consider becoming one of her executors as well as a residuary legatee? This was quite a different matter. Without showing any indecent haste, Dizzy accepted her offer and travelled down to Devon to meet her.

In 1851, Mrs Brydges Willyams was eighty years old: a rich, lonely, somewhat eccentric widow, obsessed with the splendour of her ancestry. She believed that she and Disraeli were related; related, moreover, through an aristocratic Spanish family named Lara. With this, Dizzy was only too ready to agree; he shared her views on the grandeur of his origins. However, her interest in him did not end in their alleged kinship. Once she had met him, she became besotted with him. From then on, he became the sun about which her world revolved. 'Dear Dizzi' was her god.

It was a situation in which Disraeli felt very much at ease. He had always been at his best with dowagers, particularly if they were adoring dowagers. Although Mrs Brydges Willyams seems never to have visited him at Grosvenor Gate or Hughenden, he—with Mary Anne—would go and see her at Mount Braddon, Torquay. He would accompany her on little drives, he would join her at little tea parties, he would sit beside her at dinner, he would partner her at cards and he would chat to her in his fluid, flattering, entertaining fashion. With her, Dizzy was part son, part beau.

And when they were not seeing each other, they would be writing. Hardly a week went by without a letter from her adorable Dizzy. Addressing her as 'My dearest,' he would write to her on every topic under the sun. Few things afforded him more pleasure than describing his daily life to doting elderly ladies and his letters to Mrs Brydges Willyams were masterly. Through them, the old lady in Torquay was transported into another world: a lush, romantic, exciting, animated world—half real, half imagined, yet always entertaining. Under his pen, any subject took fire. 'It is a privilege to live in this age of rapid and brilliant events,' he wrote on one occasion. 'What an error to consider it an utilitarian age! It is one of infinite romance. Thrones tumble down and are offered, like a fairy tale, and the most powerful people in the world, male and female, a few years back, were adventurers, exiles and demireps.'

Beside such effusions, her letters must have seemed very dull. But Disraeli was lavish in his praise. When, in her stilted language, she once described a dinner party, he answered, in his gallant fashion, that her style reminded him of Jane Austen.

With the letters came the gifts. To Mount Braddon went game; to Hughenden came seafood. He sent her cuttings; she sent him flowers. 'My delight this year were the roses which you sent Mary Anne. They lived in my room, and on my table, for more than a week. I think I never met with roses so beautiful in form, so lustrous in colour, and with a perfume so exquisite—without which latter charm the rarest and the fairest flowers have little spell for me. I really think your roses must have come from Cashmere.'

And if her roses had come from Cashmere, then her lobster must surely have come from the caves of Amphitrite. 'It was so fresh! It tasted of the sweetness—not the salt—of the Ocean, and almost as creamy as your picturesque cheese!'

For year after year Dizzy paid his gentlemanly court to Mrs Brydges Willyams. It was not, of course, that he was in love with her; or that he had tired of Mary Anne. It was simply that Disraeli could no more resist an entanglement with a mature and devoted female than could Victoria—despite her great love for Albert—withstand the attentions of a flamboyant man.

Mrs Brydges Willyams was well over ninety when she died in 1863. From her will, the faithful Disraeli received over £30,000. She requested that while he continue his efforts 'to vindicate the race of Israel', she be given a Christian burial in Hughenden Church. Today her body lies, beside those of Disraeli and Mary Anne, in a specially built vault next to the church.

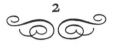

2

By March 1858, Queen Victoria was once more receiving those delectable reports from Mr Disraeli. Lord Palmerston's government had fallen the previous month and Lord Derby was again Prime Minister. As Chancellor of the Exchequer for a second spell, Disraeli lost no time in re-establishing contact with the Queen.

'Your Majesty once deigned to say that your Majesty wished in these remarks to have the temper of the House placed before your Majesty, and to find what your Majesty could not meet in the newspapers,' he wrote. 'This is the Chancellor of the Exchequer's excuse for these rough notes, written on the field of battle, which he humbly offers to your Majesty.'

Once again the Queen could have the proceedings in the Commons brought to vivid life. She could know when the house was 'tranquil and interesting' or when it was 'wild and capricious'. She could read that a statement had been 'clear, calm, courteous, persuasive, and full of knowledge' or when a speech had been 'apt, terse and telling'. She could smile at the story of the wife of the Governor of Singapore who insisted on employing convicts in her nursery; when asked whether she chose thieves or murderers, the lady's unhesitating reply was 'Always murderers'.

And there was closer contact than this. In April 1858 Dizzy was invited—without Mary Anne—to Windsor. He was able to assure her that the Queen was 'very gracious' and that Prince Albert 'talked to me a great deal'. September of the same year saw him at Osborne which, in his inimitable style, he described as 'a Sicilian Palazzo with gardens, terraces, statues and vases shining in the sun, than which nothing can be conceived more captivating.'

The parliamentary session of 1858 saw the passing of one measure on which the hearts of Victoria and Disraeli beat as one. This was the India Bill. The horrific Indian Mutiny of the year before had underlined the fact that the days of rule by the East India Company must end and that India should be transferred to the British Crown. With satisfaction the Queen had made note of the general feeling that 'India should belong to *me*. . . .'

This was Dizzy's view exactly. The people of the East had no understanding of things like chartered companies, he argued; one must appeal to their imaginations. He had no time for those who wanted to westernize and 'civilize' the gorgeous East. Its glamour should be enhanced, not minimized: it needed the mystique of a benevolent monarch, not the dreariness of a chartered company. The Indians should realize that their 'real Ruler and Sovereign' was Queen Victoria and that she would respect their laws, customs and religions.

There was even a moment, before the passing of the India Bill, when it was rumoured that Disraeli might become the first Viceroy of India. 'It is quite on the cards,' wrote the editor of *The Times* to a colleague. 'He wants the money and the high station. . . .' But a rumour it remained, and India was denied the reign of what would undoubtedly have been the most bizarre viceregal couple in its history.

The India Bill received the Queen's assent in August 1858. At once, she applied herself to her new responsibility with a customary sense of duty. Her Proclamation to her Indian subjects, drawn up in her name, she altered radically. In common with Disraeli, who had always spoken out strongly against any attempt to undermine the power of the princes or to convert the masses, Victoria was all for Indian traditions being respected and upheld.

Lord Derby must understand, she wrote, that she was 'a female sovereign who speaks to more than a hundred millions of Eastern people' and that, as such, her Proclamation 'should breathe feelings of generosity, benevolence and religious toleration.'

Her revised Proclamation was received by Lord Canning, the Viceroy of India, in October 1858. 'It is a source of great satisfaction and pride to her to feel herself in direct communication with that enormous Empire which is so bright a jewel in her Crown, and which she would wish to see happy, contented and peaceful,' she wrote to the Viceroy. 'May the publication of her Proclamation be the beginning of a new era, and may it draw a veil over the sad and bloody past.'

The passage could have been written by Dizzy himself.

Although, in fact, the India Bill was not Disraeli's creation (and was, as he described it to the Queen, 'only the ante-chamber to an imperial palace') it set the two of them—Victoria and Disraeli—on the road that was to end so triumphantly eighteen years later when he made her Empress of India.

3

The second important bill of Lord Derby's administration was not nearly as successful as the India Bill. This one was entirely Disraeli's brainchild.

For some years now Dizzy had been thinking in terms of electoral reform. He saw no reason why it should be left to the Whigs to champion extensions of the franchise. His dream had always been of popular Toryism: of an alliance between the aristocrat and the artisan. He felt sure that a wider electorate would vote Conservative; that it would uphold Queen and Empire. An extended franchise, granted by the Conservatives, would draw the teeth, not only of the revolutionaries, but of the Whigs.

Accordingly, after endless Cabinet wranglings, a Reform Bill was introduced in February 1859. It was defeated.

Derby, refusing to resign, dissolved Parliament. With the election giving no party a clear majority, the Whigs, Peelites, Liberals and Radicals decided to bury their differences and work together. Their decision marked the birth of the Liberal Party. In the reassembled parliament this powerful combination again defeated Derby's government. At half-past two on the morning of 11 June 1859, Disraeli scribbled a doleful note to the Queen to announce a majority of 13 'against your Majesty's servants'.

Derby resigned and the Queen sent for Lord Palmerston. He was Prime Minister for the following six years.

To the bitterly disappointed Mary Anne, Dizzy's sister Sarah wrote a letter of condolence. 'Remember what great things you have seen, and that we have never known dear Dis experience a disappointment, or more than a disappointment, but that it has proved the very step to greater eminence.'

'The pear,' she said, 'is not yet ripe.'

Chapter Nine

I

Disraeli had always thought very highly of Prince Albert. Although the two men were very different types, there were some points of similarity. Both were looked upon as outsiders. 'No Englishman,' maintained Frederick Greenwood, the editor of the *Pall Mall Gazette*, 'could approach Disraeli without some immediate consciousness that he was in the presence of a foreigner.' And Albert, with his German accent and his German ways, had never been accepted as an Englishman. Although Victoria, on creating him Prince Consort in 1857, argued that 'the Queen has a right to claim that her husband should be an Englishman, bearing an English title,' to many he remained a foreign princeling.

Neither man felt at ease in the hard-drinking, fox-hunting, philistine society of so many members of the aristocracy; they were far more interested in things of the mind. Both were highly intelligent men; both had a thorough understanding of, and absorbing interest in, politics. Disraeli, even in private, claimed that the Prince Consort had 'great ability' and one of the 'most richly cultivated minds' he had ever come across.

Yet if Disraeli was quick to appreciate the Prince's many good qualities, the Prince Consort was slower in coming to an appreciation of Disraeli's. It was the Napoleon III story all over again. The charm and the wit and the flattery that were beginning to melt the Queen's previous hostility were cutting less ice with Albert. Disraeli, when in office, might be careful to keep the Prince fully informed and to be lavish in his praise of his painstaking memoranda, but Albert could never quite shake himself free of the notion that Dizzy was something of an opportunist. And, as Victoria's opinions invariably reflected Albert's, she, too, tended to distrust Disraeli.

By 1860 however, the relationship between the two men had improved. Disraeli's term as Chancellor of the Exchequer had caused no friction; and the Prince Consort, who always looked upon too much party squabbling as somehow unseemly, approved of the way in which Disraeli, now in opposition, refrained from attacking the government unnecessarily. Moreover, the royal couple were beginning to look more kindly on the Conservatives. With the old Whig Party having been absorbed into a more liberal combination, the Queen was convinced of 'the importance of a *really* strong Conservative Party, as a check upon the Liberals and *not* as it had been *now*, to a certain extent—competing with the Liberal Party.'

Early in 1861 Dizzy and Mary Anne were invited to spend a couple of nights at Windsor. They were delighted. 'It is Mrs Disraeli's first visit to Windsor,' wrote Dizzy to Mrs Brydges Willyams, 'and is considered very marked on the part of Her Majesty to the wife of the Leader of the Opposition when many Cabinet Ministers have been asked there *without* their wives.' When Lord Derby, intrigued by this show of royal favour, asked Dizzy about the visit, his reply was noncommittal.

'They were very gracious and very communicative,' he said.

Before many months had passed, however, the Prince Consort was finding it more and more difficult to be either gracious or communicative. He could hardly cope with the strains of everyday living. Prince Albert had never been strong; to his life-long gastric troubles were now added rheumatism, toothache, nausea and shivering. He slept very badly. Every bout of illness left him more exhausted still. Yet he refused to spare himself. As conscientious, as involved, as finicky as ever, he allowed himself—cried his anguished wife—to be 'torn to pieces by business of every kind.' He was working himself, quite literally, to death.

So many things seemed to be troubling him. He was apprehensive about increasing French aggression. A reasonable and analytical man, he was often upset by Victoria's highly emotional behaviour: by her possessiveness, her touchiness, her lack of impartiality. Her irrational grief on the death of her once-despised mother, the Duchess of Kent, 'well-nigh overwhelmed' him. He missed his beloved eldest daughter, Vicky, who in 1858 had married Prince Frederick Wilhelm of Prussia and had gone to live in Berlin.

But perhaps most upsetting of all was the problem of his eldest son Bertie, the Prince of Wales. Both Victoria and Albert had had such high hopes of their son. He was to be a man in his father's image: a diligent, intelligent, unsullied prince; a man of 'calm, profound, comprehensive understanding'. To this end they had subjected the boy to a rigorous course of training, Bertie's boyhood had been one long, grinding round of instruction.

It had all been to no purpose. Amiable and affectionate enough, Bertie had proved to be lazy, slow and stupid. He simply did not have the mental ability to cope with all this forced learning. With each passing year his parents became more disappointed. Clothes seemed to be the only thing in which the adolescent Bertie showed the slightest interest; for things of the mind he cared not a rap. In vain the Queen begged him to try and be more like his father—if only in *some* ways. She realized only too well that her son was developing into what she might have become had it not been for Albert's example; Bertie, she sighed, was her 'caricature'. Of any serious-minded Coburg characteristic he was showing no trace. He was all Hanoverian.

In November 1861 came undoubted proof of what Bertie's parents considered to be his bad blood. It was this blow by Bertie, the Queen afterwards maintained, that finally broke the Prince Consort's spirit. 'I do not cling to life,' said Albert to Victoria during this crisis. 'You do: but I set no store by it. I am sure that if I had a severe illness I should give up at once, I should not struggle for life. I have no tenacity of life.'

2

It was through old Baron Stockmar, now in Germany, that Albert first heard of what he looked upon as Bertie's fall from grace. Stockmar wrote to tell him that there was talk that the twenty-year-old Prince of Wales, while doing a spell of military training at the Curragh camp near Dublin, had slept with a woman. Stockmar's tale was confirmed by the gossipy Lord Torrington. It appears that Bertie's fellow officers had smuggled an easygoing actress by the name of Nelly Clifden into camp and that the Prince, not unnaturally, had had sex with her.

The Prince Consort was appalled. Rational in everything else, Albert was quite irrational when it came to sexual matters. The escapade, which most aristocratic fathers would have treated as perfectly natural and even commendable, was regarded by Prince Albert in the blackest possible light. Shocking in itself, it seemed like the final blow to Albert's dream of fashioning the perfect heir. What hope was there now of presenting the country with that paragon who, by his unimpeachable morals and high sense of duty, was going to win the respect and love of the people? Quite obviously, Bertie was about to go the way of Queen Victoria's unspeakable uncles.

The Queen, on being told the story (Albert assured her that he was sparing her 'the disgusting details'), was equally shocked. She would never again be able to look at Bertie, she declared 'without a shudder'.

With a heavy heart Prince Albert sat down to write his son a letter 'upon a subject which has caused me the greatest pain I have yet felt in this life'. It was one of the Prince Consort's longest, most sanctimonious and most anguished literary outpourings. In it he painted a horrifying picture of the possible repercussions of his son's misdemeanour: the loss of purity, the scandal, the ridicule, the almost inevitable lawsuit with Nelly Clifden naming him as the father of her child.

To this astonishing letter, Bertie wrote a suitably contrite reply. His father duly forgave him (although advising him to hide himself from the sight of a, presumably, less forgiving God) and then travelled down to see him. His spell of military duty over, Bertie was finishing his nightmarish education at Cambridge, and here father and son took a long walk in the chilly November weather. The Prince Consort was feeling desperately ill and tired, and the fact that Bertie, by taking a wrong turning, prolonged their walk, made the Prince feel more ill and tired still. He returned to Windsor exhausted. A week later he collapsed with typhoid fever.

For the following two weeks the Queen was in agony. For much of this time the Prince Consort was delirious; at other times there seemed to be a slight improvement. His wife see-sawed between wild hope and still wilder despair. Yet no matter how hysterical her tears and prayers when she was away from her husband, in his presence she always showed a calm and cheerful face.

On the morning of his death—14 December 1861—things seemed to be a little better. She was led to believe that the crisis might be over. But by afternoon hopes were fading. By nightfall it was clear that he was dying. '*Est ist das kleine Fräuchen*,' whispered the Queen as she leant over him. When she asked him for a kiss, he moved his lips. 'Two or three long but perfectly gentle breaths were drawn, the hand clasping mine, and (Oh! it turns me sick to write it) all all was over....'

The Prince Consort died at a quarter to eleven that night. He was only forty-two years of age.

Sir Charles Phipps, the Prince's private secretary, wrote to Lord Palmerston to announce the death. 'The Queen, though in an agony of grief, is perfectly collected, and shows a self-control that is quite extraordinary,' he wrote. 'Alas! she has not realized her loss—and, when the full consciousness comes upon her—I tremble—but only for the depth of her grief.

'What will happen—where can She look for that support and assistance upon which she has leaned in the greatest and the least questions of her life?'

3

'We have buried our Sovereign,' wrote Disraeli on the death of the Prince Consort. 'This German Prince has governed England for twenty-one years with a wisdom and energy such as none of our Kings have ever shown....'

This was certainly Victoria's view. To the question of to whom she would now turn for 'support and assistance' she had a ready answer. She would turn to no one. Or rather, she would continue to rely on Prince Albert. In an anguished letter to King Leopold (whom, significantly, she immediately started calling her '*own*, dearest, kindest *Father*') the Queen was emphatic in claiming that Albert's spirit *alone* would guide and inspire her. It was her *firm* resolve, her *irrevocable decision* 'that *his* wishes—*his* plans—about everything, *his* views about *everything* are to be *my law*! And no *human power* will make me swerve from *what he* decided and wished....'

She signed herself 'your wretched but devoted Child'.

But if Queen Victoria was prepared to carry out Albert's wishes in private, in public she was prepared to make no effort whatsoever. The thought of facing curious eyes appalled her. 'They wish to move the Queen [from Windsor] to Osborne,' reported Disraeli to yet another of his mature female correspondents, Lady Londonderry, 'but she puts it off every day, dreading the sight of the glaring daylight, it being impossible for the yacht to bring up under Osborne after dark. . . .'

She had assured Lord Palmerston, continued Dizzy, that he would 'always find her mindful of her duty and of her people, but that her worldly career was at an end. . . .'

The trouble was that she was not being particularly mindful of her duty. At first, she even refused to grant personal audience to her ministers. They were forced to communicate through her second daughter, Princess Alice, or the late Prince's secretary, General Grey. During a meeting of the Privy Council, the Queen sat in one room, the councillors in another, while the Clerk, acknowledging her nods through an open door, would solemnly pronounce 'Approved' to each item under discussion. Any attempt to involve the Queen more closely in the day-to-day business of State she firmly resisted.

In the matter of immortalizing Albert's memory, however, the Queen was extraordinarily active. She saw to it that the Blue Room at Windsor, in which he died, was kept undisturbed; his bust dominated the two wreath-strewn beds; his clothes, fresh towels and hot water were laid out each evening. She slept with his nightshirt clutched to her breast; she had a cast of his hand within reach.

'*What* a dreadful going to bed!' she wailed. '*What* a contrast to that tender lover's love! *All alone! Yet*—the blessings of 22 years *cast* its reflection. . . .'

She lost no time in arranging for the building of a grandiose Mausoleum to house his remains. She distributed engravings of his likeness, she presented bound copies of his speeches, she organized the setting-up of countless memorials.

No praise of the Prince could be too fulsome for her ears. Every tribute was scrutinized and analysed; every politician assessed by his particular peroration. And of all the paeans that poured in, few were more fulsome than Disraeli's. It was not long, therefore, before his tributes to the Prince Consort were winning the Queen's gratitude. Indeed, it was Dizzy's publicly expressed reaction to the death of the Prince Consort that first changed Victoria's feelings into something more than mere official civility.

A few weeks after Albert's death, the leaders of the various political parties paid formal tribute to the late Prince. Disraeli's was particularly moving. He spoke of Prince Albert as the 'prime counsellor of the realm'; he drew attention to his great services towards cultural affairs, where 'a want of culture had been a great deficiency in the national character.' Albert, he declared, had been no mere figurehead. 'His contributions to the cause of the State were more powerful and far more precious. He gave it his thought, his time, his toil; he gave to it his life.'

The Queen devoured every word. In a letter to Lord Derby, she wrote that 'The Queen would be glad that Mr Disraeli should also be made aware of H.M.'s grateful sense of his testimony to the worth and character of the Prince—perhaps as discriminating in the characteristics pointed out, and certainly as eloquent in the language employed, as any of those beautiful and glorious orations. . . .'

Disraeli wasted no time in following up this lead. 'What I attempted to express on Thursday night I deeply felt,' he answered. 'During these conversations with which, of late years, the Prince occasionally honoured me, I acquired much, both in knowledge and in feeling, which will ever influence my life.'

This tribute brought him still further royal favour. The Queen sent him two engravings of pictures of herself and Albert. These Dizzy acknowledged as 'a hallowed gift'. It might all have beeen a little overdone but, as always with Disraeli, the froth of flattery concealed a core of sincerity. It certainly paid dividends.

'Mr Disraeli,' Victoria is reported to have said, 'was the only person who appreciated the Prince.'

Through his extravagantly expressed reaction to Albert's death, Disraeli took a giant stride along the road that would end in him all but taking Albert's place.

Chapter Ten

I

What Disraeli regarded as proof positive of Queen Victoria's newly-found esteem for him came early in the year 1863. He was invited to the wedding of the Prince of Wales to Princess Alexandra of Denmark on 10 March 1863. This apparent mark of royal favour left him exultant.

'I listen hourly to the lamentations of the great ladies who are not asked,' he wrote triumphantly to the hardly less gratified Mrs Brydges Willyams. 'The Duchess of Marlboro in despair! The Duchess of Manchester who was Mistress of the Robes!!! Mme de Flahaut only a month ago Ambassadress of France and a host of others as eminent. None of my late colleagues are invited except Lord Derby and he would go as a matter of course as Knight of the Garter.

'*But I am invited!*

'And what is still more marked Mrs D too and this by the Queen's particular command. . . .'

But Dizzy was being far too cock-a-hoop. Although he might believe that his invitation was by the express wish of the Queen, it was to Lord Palmerston that he owed his inclusion. The Prime Minister had suggested that Disraeli be asked in recognition of his sympathetic attitude towards a Bill concerning the Prince of Wales's allowance. For the sake of her children's grants, the Queen was always prepared to make an extra effort.

But however the invitation had come about, few could have appreciated it more than Dizzy. Nothing, he enthused, could have been 'more brilliant and effective' than the ceremony in St George's Chapel, Windsor. 'It is the only pageant which never disappointed me. The beautiful chapel, the glittering dresses, the various processions, first the Knights of the Garter, of the Royal Personages, of the Bridegroom, of the Bride: the heralds, the announcing trumpets, the suspense before the procession appeared, the magnificent music, the Queen in widowed garments in her Gothic cabinet. . . .'

Queen Victoria, who had agreed to the marriage mainly on the grounds that the late Prince Consort had given it his sanction, had none the less refused to play any part in it. She merely watched the proceedings from a dimly lit gallery—that 'Gothic cabinet'—high above the altar. The short-sighted Disraeli, insatiably curious, raised his quizzing glass to look at her. Unfortunately, at that very moment the Widow, glancing down, caught him staring up. 'I did not venture to use my glass again,' says the disconcerted Disraeli.

They met, face to face and in less embarrassing circumstances, a few weeks later. The wedding over, the Queen began granting audiences to a few selected ministers and politicians. When she received the Conservative leader, Lord Derby, who was suffering from the most agonizing attack of gout, Victoria was all sympathy. She feared, she sighed, that standing must be a torture for him. But she did not ask him to sit down.

To Lord Derby Victoria made the significant observation that the Prince Consort had had no will to live. 'He died,' she said frankly, 'from want of what they call pluck.'

The Queen received Disraeli, as Conservative leader in the Commons, on 23 April 1863, at Windsor.

He was ushered into the late Prince Consort's study. The room was exactly as Albert had left it; even his writing materials were laid out on the desk. Could Disraeli have realized, as he stood waiting for the Queen, how often, in the future, he would be received by Victoria in this very room?

After a five-minute wait, the Queen entered. In her black crinoline and veiled widow's cap, she looked plumper than when he had last seen her and her face was folded in sadness. Dizzy bowed. In her astonishingly sweet and musical voice, the Queen said, 'It is some time since we met.'

They discussed various topics: the current parliamentary session, the situation in North America, the insurrection in Poland. She hoped that no parliamentary crisis would topple Lord Palmerston's Liberal government; 'in her forlorn condition,' she sighed, 'she hardly knew what she would do.' (Indeed, this audience with Disraeli might have been designed to ensure that he would not make trouble in the House.)

Lord Palmerston, continued the Queen, had grown very old.

'But his voice in debate, Madam, is as loud as ever,' replied Dizzy.

'Yes!' she exclaimed with sudden animation, 'And his handwriting! Did you ever see such a handwriting? So very clear and strong! Nevertheless I see in him a great change, a very great change. His countenance is so changed.'

Perhaps the Queen was implying that if only Disraeli would bide his time and not harass Palmerston unduly, his chance of political power would eventually come.

They spoke of other things, amongst them Mary Anne, and then the Queen dismissed him. Dizzy gave one of his extravagantly low bows and Victoria, with a sad rustling of her black skirts, left the room.

The one thing the Queen had not mentioned was the subject which must have been uppermost in her mind: a suitable memorial for the Prince Consort. The matter was to be raised in the House that very afternoon. Earlier, when the Queen had written to Lord Derby on the subject, she had said that she 'had no objection' to him conferring with Disraeli about it; she would 'always entertain feelings of gratitude for the support which [Disraeli] had always given to the Prince.' But now, though knowing that Disraeli would be taking part in the debate she, 'with great delicacy', avoided the topic.

Typically, during that afternoon's debate, Disraeli pleaded for a monument rather than any more utilitarian structure. The memorial should be something dramatic, not a school or a hall or a hospital. 'It should be something direct, significant and choice,' cried Dizzy, 'so that those who come after us may say: "This is the type and testimony of a sublime life and a transcendent career, and thus they were recognized by a grateful and admiring people!" '

Lest the report of his speech miss out any of his eulogizing, Disraeli sent the Queen a memorandum of his actual words. It brought an instant response. From Windsor came a copy of the Prince Consort's speeches, bound in white morocco and inscribed in the Queen's own handwriting: 'To the Right Honourable Benjamin Disraeli. In recollection of the greatest and best of men, from the beloved Prince's broken-hearted widow. Victoria R.'

Accompanying this gift was a letter, tied up with black silk ribbon. 'The Queen,' wrote Victoria, 'cannot resist from expressing, personally, to Mr Disraeli her deep gratification at the tribute he paid to her adored, beloved, and great husband. The perusal of it made her shed many tears, but it was very soothing to her broken heart to see such true appreciation of that spotless and unequalled character. . . .'

Disraeli's reply was equally speedy and even more fulsome. In what one of his biographers calls a 'somewhat hyperbolic eulogium' Dizzy paid a tribute to the late Prince's qualities. 'The Prince,' ran the honeyed phrases, 'is the only person, whom Mr Disraeli has ever known, who realized the Ideal. None with whom he is acquainted have ever approached it. There was in him an union of the manly grace and sublime simplicity, of chivalry with the intellectual splendour of the Attic Academe.' On flowed the sentences to detail the Prince's 'high tone, his universal accomplishment, his blended tenderness and vigour, his rare combination of romantic energy and classic repose.'

With royalty, as Dizzy was the first to admit, one had to lay it on with a trowel.

No music could have been sweeter to Victoria's ears. The letter ('on a subject which so engrosses her Majesty' sighed one of her long-suffering ladies) was shown round the court. 'I need not tell you,' wrote Lady Augusta Bruce with just a hint of amusement as she passed the letter on, 'how her Majesty has been affected by the depth and delicacy of these touches, or how soothing it is to the Queen to have this inexhaustible theme so treated. . . .'

The subject which had given rise to this heartfelt exchange of letters—the proposed monument to the late Prince—eventually took tangible shape in Kensington Gore: it was that riotously mock-Gothic confection, the Albert Memorial.

2

If Hughenden suited Disraeli in his guise as an English country gentleman, it was not nearly impressive enough for his role as *grand seigneur*; or as a favourite—as he liked to imagine—of the Sovereign. He needed something altogether more palatial than a simple Georgian manor house, no matter how charming. Egged on by Mary Anne, Dizzy engaged the fashionable neo-Gothic architect, E. B. Lamb, to restyle the house. The result was an elaborate, red-brick, vaguely seventeenth-century building, all urns and arches and clustered chimneys. The couple were delighted with the result.

'We have realized a romance we have been many years meditating;'

wrote Dizzy in 1863 to Mrs Brydges Willyams (whose legacy, eventually, was to go towards paying for the realization of this particular romance), 'we have restored the house to what it was before the Civil Wars, and we have made a garden of terraces in which cavaliers might roam and saunter with their ladye loves!'

Be that as it may, the renovated house—both inside and out—perfectly reflected the personalities of its owners: it was ornate, romantic, slightly spurious. The rooms were a cheerful clutter of flowered carpets, papered walls, tapestried chairs, family portraits, marble busts and decorative vases. Colours were uninhibitedly bright. On the Italianate terraces peacocks trailed their magnificent tails; no terrace, claimed Dizzy, could do without peacocks. On the lake in the park glided two swans, Hero and Leander. Unlike his rival Gladstone, who was seldom happier than when chopping down trees, Disraeli was seldom happier than when planting them. He adored trees. Each year the woods that surrounded the great lawns became denser and denser. He loved to hear the nightingales singing in the woods. Once, when the Prince of Wales wanted to know what nightingales ate, Disraeli could tell him that it was glow-worms. Glow-worms, said Dizzy, were 'exactly the food which nightingales should require'.

At seventy, Mary Anne was a tireless gardener. Dressed in uncharacteristically sensible clothes, but with her hair riotously curled and her face gaily painted, she worked side by side with her gardeners, planning, laying out, planting. Her taste was for massive urns, marble figures and brilliantly coloured flowers. Any amount of fatigue was worth a word of praise from her beloved husband. He had only to say that her latest gardening achievement was her best yet for her to feel 'quite intoxicated for the moment and quite rewarded'.

Although the couple were perfectly content with each other's company, they were obliged to do frequent entertaining. Mary Anne, as a prudent housewife married to an extravagant man, could be penny-pinching (a local tradesman grumbled that she had ordered only six rolls for breakfast on the occasion of a visit by the Duke and Duchess of Teck) while Dizzy complained that entertaining was like running a playhouse or keeping an inn.

He liked paying visits to great country houses even less. Mary Anne might be happy enough to dress herself up and to divert the company with her frank and spirited chatter (she once told Lady Waldegrave's latest husband that she had heard him highly praised: when he asked where, she answered 'In bed.') but Dizzy was bored. He could neither digest the gigantic meals nor take the obligatory exercise. It was all too hearty for his taste. 'Whenever we go to a country house the same thing happens:' said Mary Anne. 'Dizzy is not only bored, and has constant ennui, but he takes to eating as a resource; he eats at breakfast, luncheon and dinner; the result is, by the end of the third day he becomes dreadfully bilious, and we have to come away.'

If Dizzy accepted invitations it was to keep up his association with the aristocracy that he was defending. And to derive a certain wry amusement from the enthusiasm with which his one-time detractors now welcomed 'this miserable, circumcised, soi-disant Christian' into their homes.

3

Yet even Disraeli's lukewarm approach towards entertaining or being entertained seemed positively enthusiastic when set against Queen Victoria's attitude. Nothing would induce her to lead a more active social and public life. Year succeeded year without the Queen showing the slightest sign of emerging from her mourning for the Prince Consort.

The court remained deadly dull. The Queen, who wore only black, insisted that her ladies do the same. Her maids-of-honour were allowed half-mourning: white, grey, mauve or purple. For days on end no one, other than her dressers or a single lady-in-waiting, would set eyes on her. Even with members of her household she would communicate by letter; and these always carried a half-inch mourning border.

An appearance at the dinner table was about as much effort as she was prepared to make towards entertaining her guests. Not that this did anything towards enlivening the atmosphere; on the contrary, it became gloomier still. The rooms were always ice cold (the Queen had a passion for fresh air), no one spoke above a whisper and any sound of merriment, no matter how subdued or distant, was likely to bring a strongly-worded rebuke from Her Majesty. Her secretary, Henry Ponsonby, describing one such dismal dinner, claims that 'there were prolonged silences, broken by the Queen's, Leopold's and

C's respectable coughs, Cowley's deep cough, S's gouty cough and all the servants dropping plates and making a clatteration of noise.' Smoking, of which the Queen strongly disapproved, had to be confined to certain times in the smoking room.

Not until three years after Prince Albert's death did the Queen show herself in London; and that was for the length of a carriage drive from Buckingham Palace to Paddington Station. She pronounced the experience 'very painful'. In 1866 she agreed to open Parliament, but only because she was anxious to secure adequate allowances for two of her children from the House. She agreed to it, however, with the worst possible grace. 'The Queen must say that she feels *very bitterly* the want of feeling of those who *ask* the Queen to go to open Parliament . . . why this wish should be of so *unreasonable* and unfeeling a nature as to *long* to *witness* the spectacle of a poor widow, nervous and shrinking, dragged in *deep mourning* ALONE *in* STATE as a *Show* where she used to go supported by her husband to be gazed at, without delicacy of feeling, is a thing *she cannot* understand, and never could wish her bitterest foe exposed to.'

The following year, at the Prime Minister's request, she did it again and hated it even more.

On such occasions, the Queen might spend one night at Buckingham Palace but more often than not she would hurry back to the seclusion of Windsor Castle. So, for most of the time, Buckingham Palace stood empty. 'These commanding premises to be let or sold in consequence of the late occupant's declining business,' read a prankster's notice outside the Palace; and the joke was not entirely good-natured.

The Queen spent only fifteen or sixteen weeks of the year at Windsor. Here a great deal of her time was passed in the Blue Room, where Albert had died or in the Mausoleum where he lay buried. 'Mausoleum Day', her less reverent relations called the anniversary of the Prince's death. Any members of her family neglecting to observe that sacred day would earn the sharp edge of her tongue. On hearing that her daughter Vicky had spent the anniversary travelling by train to Vienna, Victoria exploded. 'Even now I can hardly believe it!' she wrote. 'I should have thought that you would have preferred remaining in the smallest wayside inn and going to pray to God to support your broken-hearted mother rather than do that.'

The winter (part of December, January and February) the Queen spent at Osborne. As Osborne could be reached only by sea, and as a sea crossing, in the depths of winter, was something which her ageing ministers would do anything to avoid ('Not a pleasant day for crossing to Osborne,' sighed Dizzy on one occasion), the Queen felt relatively safe from her Cabinet. She always imagined that they were going to force her to undertake more than she was capable of; that they wanted to push her beyond her limits. Any suggestion, no matter how tactfully put, that she fulfil some public duty, was immediately countered by a letter from her complaisant doctor forbidding that she do any such thing. For by now her need for seclusion and her self-pity had been joined by hypochondria: she had convinced herself that her health was in a precarious state. It was most important, she told her Uncle Leopold, 'that I should have *no* excitement, *no* agitation, IF I am to live on.'

Even the most sympathetic visitors to Osborne were far from welcome. In the summer of 1867 the Empress Eugénie, of whom Victoria was very fond, spent three days with her. The Queen found the period exhausting. 'Greatly relieved the visit was over,' she afterwards wrote, 'as I am feeling far from well, and everything tires me so.'

At Balmoral she was least unhappy. Here she could get right away from any public contact; no one could expect her to carry out any public engagements. In spite of the fact that the weeks which she spent at Balmoral in May and June were during the parliamentary session, she would never dream of changing her dates of arrival and departure. It needed the most serious political crisis to induce her to alter her plans by a day or two.

Life within the tartan-walled rooms of Balmoral Castle was even drearier than in the south. 'Stagnation,' claimed one member of the household, 'dulled everyone's wits'. Only the Queen showed any sign of enjoying herself. No matter how tempestuous the weather she would venture out. With a gillie by her side she would go riding across the desolate hillsides or driving at a brisk pace along the lonely roads. For even greater seclusion there were little lodges hidden among the pine trees, where she would take tea or sit sketching.

Yet any criticism of the Queen's withdrawn life she airily dismissed as '*ill natured* gossip . . . caused by dissatisfaction at not forcing the Queen *out*.'

'It is very wrong of the world to say that it is merely her *distaste* to go out and about as she could when she had her dear husband to support and *protect* her,' she cried out, 'when the *fact is* that her shattered nerves and health *prevent* her doing so.'

She flatly refused to receive any visitors in state. A private audience was as far as she was prepared to go. And only then if it happened to suit her cast-iron arrangements. Her poor Prime Minister went through agony when Abdul Aziz, the Sultan of Turkey, was due to arrive on a State Visit. Apologizing profusely for raising so distasteful a subject, the Prime Minister hinted that the Queen's plan to receive the Sultan at Osborne *five* days after his arrival simply would not do; particularly after the magnificent reception given to the Sultan by the Emperor Napoleon III in Paris. Could she not possibly see her way clear to postponing her journey to Osborne by three days and give the Sultan a mere *ten minutes* at Buckingham Palace on his arrival?

The answer was No. Not only would this plan be inconvenient but it would be positively 'disadvantageous to the Queen's health'. (With the Queen's answer went Dr Jenner to back it up.) Let the Sultan arrive earlier and so save her the bother of postponing her departure. She was being driven to a state of desperation, she declared, 'by the want of consideration shown by the *public* for her health and strength'. She could see, before long, 'a *complete breakdown* of her nervous system'.

In the end, and only because of the government's threat that any royal slight would fling the Sultan 'into the arms of France', the Queen postponed her journey and received the Sultan. But she must have done so with the satisfaction that they would think twice before trying to force her hand again.

As the 1860s progressed, so did public sympathy for the widowed Queen begin to wear thin. A year or two of this seclusion might have been understood and forgiven but as year followed year so did dissatisfaction begin to mount. Only, it seemed, when the Queen was anxious to secure yet another annuity for one of her children was she prepared to bestir herself. Few believed her when she cried out that she was 'working and drudging . . . from morning till *night*, and weighed down by the responsibility and cares of her most unenviable position'; they simply presumed that she was shirking her duties. Was the monarchy really worth what it cost the country? Many thought not. By the end of the decade, republicanism was gathering force.

To some, it looked as though nothing short of a miracle would force the Queen out of her retirement and so save the monarchy.

Chapter Eleven

During the second half of the 1860s, the forces which would eventually lead to Queen Victoria's revival were beginning to muster. In the first place, Disraeli regained office.

In June 1866 the Liberal government (due, largely, to Dizzy's masterly tactics) was brought down. Lord Russell, who had succeeded the late Lord Palmerston as Prime Minister, resigned and the Queen sent for Lord Derby. For the third time Derby formed a Conservative government. And for the third time Disraeli became Chancellor of the Exchequer.

At once Disraeli applied himself to the most controversial issue of the day: Reform, or an extension of the parliamentary franchise. In this, he had the sympathy of the Queen. Victoria was all for Reform. Her conviction came partly from the shade of Prince Albert and partly from an ever-growing distaste for the frivolity of the aristocracy. 'The Lower Classes,' she maintained, 'are becoming so well informed—are so intelligent and earn their bread and riches so deservedly that they cannot and ought not to be kept back. . . .' There was a growing feeling for Reform, she noted, 'amongst all respectable classes'.

Nor, the Queen soon realized, was this growing feeling restricted to the respectable classes. When at a mass meeting in favour of Reform, the gates of Hyde Park were closed against the crowd, what Victoria called 'the worst sort of people' promptly tore up the railings and went rampaging about the Park. But if the Queen was shocked by this behaviour, Mrs Disraeli, who witnessed the rioting, was not. Through Dizzy's new secretary, young Montagu Corry, Mary Anne sent her worried husband a message to say that the people ripping up railings within sight of her windows in Park Lane seemed to be 'thoroughly enjoying themselves' and that she was not at all alarmed. Indeed, she rather sympathized with them.

Disapproving as the Queen might be of these particular Reform tactics, she feared a more orthodox battle—a parliamentary debate—almost as much. Convinced that Reform must come, she was all for taking it out of the sphere of party politics. The thing should be arranged on a non-party basis. To the new Conservative Prime Minister, Lord Derby, Victoria proposed that the matter be dealt with by a special committee of the Privy Council. She offered to mediate with the Liberal opposition.

But Disraeli was having none of it. Reform must be used to the advantage of his party: the Bill must be carried by a Conservative government. So he dismissed the royal offer of mediation out of hand. Usually so quick to enhance the prestige of the Crown, Dizzy pooh-poohed the idea of court intervention. 'Murmurings of children in a dream,' he wrote to Lord Derby. 'The royal project of gracious interposition with our rivals is a mere phantom. It pleases the vanity of a Court deprived of substantial power. . . .'

Such sacrilege was not, of course, for the royal ears. The Queen would have been astonished to hear such views from dear Mr Disraeli.

Dizzy flung himself into the Reform Bill battle with gusto. All the qualities that made him such a brilliant parliamentary tactician—his eloquence, his intuitiveness, his adaptability, his powers of impro-visation and persuasion—were brought into play. He had intended the measure to be a sweeping one, with definite safeguards, but in order to gain Liberal support, he was obliged to accept various amendments and so lose almost all his original safeguards. His performance, as he moved from crisis to crisis, was superb. In his verbal clashes with Gladstone who was, of course, his chief opponent, Dizzy invariably emerged victorious.

On 13 April 1867 the Second Reform Bill was passed with a majority of twenty-one. Gladstone described his defeat as 'a smash, perhaps, without example'. The Bill, which doubled the existing electorate, was far more radical than most Conservatives had intended. Not without reason could Lord Derby refer to it as 'a leap in the dark'.

But the Queen was not anything like as apprehensive. She fully agreed with Mr Disraeli's convincingly argued theory that the extended franchise would win still more adherents to the cause of Crown and Empire. She had even allowed Derby and Disraeli to talk her into opening the session of parliament which saw the passing of the measure. The Reform Bill might well prove to be the shock which she considered necessary to bring the idle upper classes to their senses and so avoid some 'dreadful crash'.

For Disraeli personally, the passing of the Second Reform Bill was a great triumph. He might not have been anything like as dedicated to an extension of the franchise as he was to the advancement of his own party (and with it, himself) but he had certainly given a dazzling display of parliamentary skill. That he would be Derby's successor as Prime Minister there was now no shadow of doubt.

At the Carlton Club, on the night of the passing of the Bill, Dizzy was uproariously acclaimed. But when his colleagues urged him to join them for supper, he declined. Instead, he hurried home to celebrate his success with his wife. 'I had got him a raised pie from Fortnum and Mason's, and a bottle of champagne,' said a proud Mary Anne, 'and he ate half the pie and drank all the champagne, and then he said, "Well, my dear, you are more like a mistress than a wife." '

She was in her seventy-fifth year at the time.

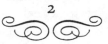

2

It was neither her concern for Reform nor the fact that she was once more in contact with the colourful Mr Disraeli that initially revived Queen Victoria's interest in life. It was her obsession with an altogether different sort of man: her Highland gillie, John Brown.

At the height of the John Brown scandal, in the year 1867, Queen Victoria was forty-eight and Brown forty-two. If the Queen looked the very picture of drab and heartbroken widowhood, John Brown epitomized the rude health and unashamed heartiness of the Highlander. He was handsome in a particularly Scots fashion: rugged, muscular, with clear blue eyes, a resolute chin and riotously curly red-gold hair and beard. He always wore a kilt. His manner was honest, straightforward, brusque; there was no hint of deceit or guile in his nature. Nor was Brown anyone's fool. All in all, he was what the Queen's secretary, Henry Ponsonby, called 'a child of nature': blunt, canny, stalwart and undeniably masculine.

John Brown had been in the Queen's service—as a gillie at Balmoral—for many years. Her first mention of him in her journal had been in 1849, almost twenty years before. During the last three years of the Prince Consort's life, John Brown had become the Queen's special gillie, combining, as Victoria told her Uncle Leopold, 'the offices of groom, footman, page, and *maid*, I might almost say, as he is so handy about cloaks and shawls. . . .' So the dependable Brown had accompanied Victoria and Albert on all those rides and drives and picnics and excursions that were such a feature of their life in the Highlands. He had been closely associated with some of the Queen's happiest and most carefree times.

In the first year or two after the Prince Consort's death, Brown continued to attend the Queen at Balmoral (and once in Germany) but it was not until late in 1864 that he was brought down to Osborne. The Queen's doctor was anxious for her to continue her riding and as Brown was the only groom whom she would trust, it was decided that he must attend her permanently.

Within months John Brown had become the Queen's favourite. He was quickly promoted from chief gillie to 'The Queen's Highland Servant'—a position that made him part-servant, part-secretary, part-confidant. He was responsible to her only; he took orders from no one else. In time, she could hardly bear to be parted from him. She relied on him more and more, not only for his services but for his support, sympathy and companionship. He was constantly at her elbow. When she sat working, he kept guard over her; when she drove out he sat, sturdy and impassive, on the box of her carriage.

To the despair of her family and her household (for Brown was becoming increasingly officious) the Queen used him for the issuing of her commands. 'The Queen says certainly not!' Brown once growled in answer to a request by a mayor that she attend some or other function. His wishes were considered before those of her family; a complaint from Brown that he had been overworked or overlooked or insulted would earn the culprit Her Majesty's grave displeasure. She would not hear a word against him. If her ministers planned to exclude Brown from some ceremony, she would explode in indignation. Even to a Prime Minister, whom he thought had detained the Queen too long, Brown snapped, 'You've said enough.'

Inevitably—given the Queen's seclusion and Brown's constant presence—rumours about the exact nature of their relationship began to filter through all levels of society. Few were prepared to believe that this solid, handsome, increasingly confident Highlander, who treated the Queen in so irreverent a manner, was not more than a servant. They would have been even less inclined to believe it had they been able to hear him address her or to see some of the Queen's almost skittish messages to him. 'What's this ye've got on today?' he would grumble if he disapproved of her dress. 'Hoots, then, wumman,' a startled tourist once heard him shout as he pinned together the Queen's cloak, 'can ye no hold yerr head up?' Indeed, when alone, he almost always called her 'wumman'.

And the words she used to him were even more revealing. She would inscribe herself as his 'true and devoted one' and refer to him as her 'best friend'.

What, it was wondered, kept this ill-matched pair so close together? Some claimed that Brown had second sight; that he was a spiritualist medium through which the Queen kept in touch with her late husband. Others said that she had gone mad and that he was her keeper. There was a theory that he was the power behind the throne; that the Queen was like putty in his hands. And, of course, a great many people were only too ready to believe the relationship was sexual: that John Brown was not only the Queen's lover but her husband. As Victoria had been called Mrs Melbourne earlier in the reign, so was she now referred to as Mrs Brown. By the year 1867 it was widely claimed that Queen Victoria was passionately in love with her gillie.

What was the truth? That Victoria was infatuated with, indeed almost besotted by, John Brown there is little doubt. She never made any secret of her devotion to him; even to members of her family she would refer to him as her '*dearest* best friend who no one in *this world* can *ever* replace'. But the very fact that she was so ready to admit this would seem to prove the innocence of the relationship. Like Brown himself, the Queen was without guile; she never dissembled, she could never live a lie. Indeed, one of her failings was that her nature was too open, too honest. Brown was many things to her, an intimate certainly, but he was neither a lover nor a husband. As always, her cravings were emotional, not physical.

There were many factors to account for her obsession. In the first place John Brown was a link—a tangible and not a spiritual link— with Prince Albert. Although there were many others who had been even more closely associated with the late Prince Consort, Brown had known him only in his happiest periods; in the Queen's beloved High-lands. When Brown came south in 1864, he came as a living reminder of those relaxed, unclouded days.

He brought with him, too, all those virtues which Victoria was coming to appreciate more and more. John Brown was an honest, simple, trustworthy, dependable man; a man sprung from those lower classes whom the Queen was championing ever more ardently. How sterling he seemed when set against the frivolity and the immorality and the self-indulgence of the upper classes: the people who were leading the Queen's own son so sadly astray. His bluntness was like a breath of fresh air in the affected, hot-house atmosphere of the aristocracy.

The Queen, who was shy in aristocratic or intellectual company (her ladies noticed how she gave a quick, nervous laugh on meeting anyone new), always felt at ease among the poor and the unsophisticated. With the Highland peasants she was particularly relaxed. For her, it was a tremendous comfort to have one of these rough-hewn, plain-spoken, industrious men by her side; someone with whom she could be utterly natural and whom she could trust implicitly. It is never easy for royals to make friends; they can never be quite certain of their disinterestedness. In Brown, the Queen felt that she had a friend who appreciated her for herself alone.

His good looks were an asset; there was no denying that. The Queen had always responded to masculine attractions and if John Brown had been an ugly man, it is doubtful that he would ever have enjoyed his privileged position. His physical strength, too, was an advantage. For by now the Queen, who had experienced several attempted assassinations and who had suffered several carriage accidents, was nervous about driving out. With Brown sitting four-square on the box, she felt more secure. Time and again he saved her from danger or even death: by grabbing pistols from the hands of madmen, by steadying runaway horses, by rescuing her from toppled carriages.

There were other ways in which he protected her. He saved her from being unduly pestered, he saw to it that she was warmly wrapped up, he took care that she did not tire herself. 'I feel I have here always in the House a good, devoted Soul . . .' she admitted to her daughter Vicky, Crown Princess of Prussia, 'whose only object and interest is my service, and God knows how much I want to be taken care of.' Like Albert, Brown could be almost motherly in his attitude to her.

But, when all is said and done, it was the masculine attention that he gave the Queen that rendered him so attractive. Brown was simply another of that long line of whom Victoria had always looked for either support or guidance or gallantry. He was another of her father-figures. Brown was invaluable, explained the Queen to Vicky, because the House had 'no Male head now'. The year 1865 had seen the death of the Queen's oldest mentor and confidant, King Leopold of the Belgians; there was now no one other than Brown, she decided, to whom she could turn for disinterested help and advice. Without a man by her side, Queen Victoria felt only half a woman.

And it was as a woman that Brown treated her. This, perhaps, was the real secret of his success. He was not overawed by her status; he was not afraid of her. In common with those other men in Queen Victoria's life—King Leopold, Lord Melbourne, Prince Albert and Napoleon III—John Brown treated her as a woman first and a queen second. Each had done so in a different fashion—Leopold in his role as uncle, Melbourne as ageing gallant, Albert as husband, Napoleon III as seducer—but each had appreciated that in that dumpy and increasingly intimidating figure there beat an intensely feminine heart. Brown's approach might have been less calculated and his manner less polished, but his instincts were no less sure. She was simply a woman who needed cherishing. Elderly courtiers or eminent statesmen, committing some slight breach of etiquette, would earn one of the Queen's most thunderous frowns; Brown, when he addressed her as 'wumman' and ordered her about, would be rewarded with one of her rare smiles.

There was one way only in which this dearest friend fell short: he could not set fire to the Queen's romantic imagination. Their relationship lacked one essential ingredient—magic.

3

There was magic in abundance during the year 1868. For from February to November that year Disraeli was Prime Minister.

The Queen was all approval. 'Mr Disraeli is Prime Minister,' she wrote to Vicky. 'A proud thing for a Man "risen from the people".' The description might not have been accurate (Dizzy certainly did not consider himself 'risen from the people') but the fact that he had gained this eminent position helped bolster the Queen's belief in the worth of the lower, and the uselessness of the upper, classes. Like good, honest Brown, Mr Disraeli had proved his worth.

It was, in fact, the Queen who had been responsible for Dizzy's elevation. Since the beginning of 1868 it had become clear that the Conservative Prime Minister, Lord Derby, would not be able to carry on much longer. His attacks of gout had become more severe and more prolonged. He could not hope to remain on the political scene much longer. And so, in January, the Queen had decided to act. She invited Disraeli to spend a couple of days at Osborne. There, in confidence, she asked him if he would be prepared to succeed Lord Derby as Prime Minister. She did not need to ask twice.

'The most successful visit I ever had: all that I could wish and hope,' wrote a triumphant Dizzy to Mary Anne. 'I was with the Queen an hour yesterday. She spoke of everything without reserve or formality.'

It was, he said, 'a brilliant day here'.

However, for a few weeks longer, the brilliance had to be kept subdued. Derby had not yet resigned. Late in February he wrote to the Queen, recommending Disraeli as his successor. He assured Victoria that Disraeli 'would not shrink from undertaking the duty; and that he, and he only, could command the cordial support, *en masse*, of his present colleagues.'

But still Derby did not resign. With admirable, if agonizing, patience, Dizzy waited. The deadlock was finally broken by the Queen herself. She asked Derby to resign immediately. By 25 February 1868 Disraeli was Prime Minister.

The news sent a ripple of disapproval through the stiffer-backed sections of society. 'We are all dreadfully disgusted at the prospect of having a Jew for our Prime Minister,' wailed Lady Palmerston. And Lord Clarendon, who had always disliked Disraeli, reported to the Duchess of Manchester that 'Mrs Dizzy is wild with delight and says to everybody "you know Dizzy always was the Queen's pet". That would be a strange tale if it was true, which it is not.'

Lord Clarendon was wrong. Or, at least, he would soon be proved wrong. Dizzy was well on his way to being the Queen's pet.

On 26 February, Disraeli wrote one of his courtly letters to the Queen. All he could offer, he said, was devotion. It would be his delight and duty to render the Queen's work as easy as possible. Even had the Queen not been gifted with great ability ('which all now acknowledge') her experience had given her a judgement which few living persons, and probably no living prince, could rival.

In her answer, the gratified Queen was hardly less complimentary. 'It must be a proud moment,' she wrote, 'for him to feel that his own talent and successful labours in the service of his Sovereign and country have earned for him the high and influential position in which he is now placed.'

On 27 February Dizzy went down to Osborne. 'All is sunshine here,' he wrote ecstatically, 'moral and material'. Hardly had he arrived than the Queen sent for him. With 'a very radiant face' she came into the room, holding out her hand and saying, 'You must kiss hands'. The sixty-three-year-old Disraeli, his sparse ringlets carefully arranged across his brow, went down on one knee. Taking the Queen's plump and beringed little hand in both of his, he kissed it and, like some medieval knight, pledged his 'loving loyalty and faith'.

'Yes,' he would afterwards say, 'I have climbed to the top of the greasy pole.'

Chapter Twelve

The Queen was delighted with her new Prime Minister. While admitting to her daughter Vicky that Mr Disraeli was 'very peculiar', Victoria described him as being 'full of poetry, romance and chivalry'. Audiences, which had hitherto been such a trial, suddenly became something to look forward to. Mr Disraeli seemed to be concerned solely with what the Queen called her 'comfort'. He was so attentive, so considerate, so obliging. He never lectured her, nor badgered her, nor tried to push her beyond her limits. He never even seemed to disagree with her. ('I never contradict; I never deny; but I sometimes forget,' was how Dizzy once summed up his political discussions with the Queen.) There was something very soothing about his manner. With the Queen he employed none of the actorish tricks for which his parliamentary performances were so famous—the meaningful pauses, the flourish of the pocket handkerchief, the deadly languor with which his *bons mots* were delivered. On the contrary, his attitude was an engaging mixture of deference and intimacy. In his comforting presence, the Queen found her own shyness disappearing. Mr Disraeli seemed to be so interested in everything she had to say. And he was so ready to discuss things other than what was strictly business. Quite often, audiences overran their time while the Prime Minister diverted her with the latest political, or even social, titbit.

And when he was not chatting to her, he would be writing to her. Those letters which had so entertained her during his terms as Chancellor of the Exchequer now came thicker and faster and more diverting than ever.

'Dizzy writes daily letters to the Queen in his best novel style,' reported Lady Augusta Stanley to the disapproving Lord Clarendon, 'telling her every scrap of political news dressed up to serve his own purpose, and every scrap of social gossip cooked to amuse her. She declares that she has never had such letters in her life, which is probably true, and that she never before knew *everything*!'

Dizzy describes the new Chancellor of the Exchequer, Ward Hunt, as 'more than six feet four inches in stature, but doesn't look so tall from his proportionate breadth; like St Peter's at Rome no one is at first aware of his dimensions. But he has the sagacity of the elephant as well as its form.'

The Opposition is compared to 'a company, a *troupe*, like one of those bands of minstrels one encounters in the sauntering of a summer street.' Although it was highly unlikely that Her Majesty would ever be found sauntering along a street, summer or winter, she was enchanted.

Disraeli took care to coat every possibly unpalatable suggestion in the most sugary language. When he ventured that the Prince of Wales should visit Ireland on the grounds that Ireland 'yearned for the occasional presence and inspiration of Royalty', she could hardly refuse. The 'inspiration of Royalty' was such a splendidly novel way of putting it. 'There for the first time,' says one of Victoria's biographers, 'like some Oriental Pan in the thicket, he sounded that flute-like note which she found irresistible.'

But she was not completely mesmerized. She insisted that, as the Prince's visit would be *official*, it must be paid for by the government (no one, she declared, would go to Ireland for *pleasure*), and when Disraeli proposed that the Prince spend a longer period there, she flatly refused. Dizzy promptly dropped the subject. He knew better than to press things too far.

For the first time, that spring, Victoria sent him flowers. She had heard him say that he was so fond of 'may and of all those lovely spring flowers' and was therefore sending him some from Windsor to brighten his rooms. Back came the letter, in Mary Anne's hand, to say that he was 'passionately fond of flowers, and their lustre and perfume were enhanced by the condescending hand which had showered upon him all the treasures of spring.' She promptly sent him more. To Grosvenor Gate, in their moss-lined boxes, came primroses from Windsor and violets from Osborne.

He presented her with a set of his novels; she gave him her recently published *Leaves from the Journal of our Life in the Highlands*. 'There is a freshness and fragrance about the book like the heather amid which it was written,' he declared and, in future conversation with the Queen, Dizzy would delight her by speaking of 'We authors, Ma'am'.

No wonder that a disgruntled Lord Clarendon was now forced to admit that 'the Jew, the most subtle beast in the field, has, like Eve's tempter, ingratiated himself with the Missus!'

Although it would be inaccurate to claim that Dizzy, at this stage, was drawing Victoria out of her seclusion in the way that John Brown was drawing her out of her mourning, this was certainly the first time for many years that the Queen ventured abroad on holiday. She decided to spend a few weeks in Switzerland that summer. She chose the Pension Wallis at Lucerne, travelling there *incognita* under the improbable name of the Countess of Kent. The alias (which allowed Disraeli to refer to her as 'our dear Peeress') fooled no one: her black-clad shape was unmistakable, particularly as the by now highly controversial figure of John Brown, kilted and uncompromising, was to be seen everywhere with her. He was 'insufferably bored and made himself intensely disagreeable,' complains Henry Ponsonby.

There was a slight *contretemps* when the Queen passed through Paris on her way to Switzerland. Although she made no effort to see Napoleon III, with whom she had long since become disenchanted, Victoria did receive the Empress Eugénie at the British Embassy. But she did not, as protocol demanded, return the Empress's visit. She simply did not feel up to it. Immediately there was an outcry in the French press. By not returning the Empress's visit, the Queen had insulted France. Disraeli was all sympathy. In private he might deplore the Queen's neglect of her duty but he assured her that she had acted 'quite rightly'. A return visit, he agreed blandly, would have been 'quite inconsistent' with her *incognita*. Perhaps though, he ventured, on her return through Paris, her Majesty, with her Majesty's happy judgement, 'might by some slight act gracefully dissipate this malaise.'

Her Majesty did nothing of the sort. She merely wrote to the Empress to say that she had given up paying all visits, even to her own relations. In answer to this politely worded snub, the Empress telegraphed 'most kindly'.

In September Dizzy went to Balmoral. Although, in confidence, he complained about the difficulties of 'carrying on the government of a country six hundred miles from the metropolis,' the visit had its compensations. The Library, in which they dined, was as cosy as a room at Albany; a carriage expedition to Braemar was 'sublime'; the falls at Garrawalt, seen through the relentless rain, were 'magnificent'; the view from the Queen's windows, across acres of closely-trimmed lawn, was 'exquisite'.

The Queen could hardly have been more attentive to his needs. When a party set out on one of those damp but obligatory picnics, Victoria insisted that all the ladies be included: 'to make it amusing to Mr Disraeli'. Greatest amusement on this occasion, however, was provided by a lady not of the party. Calling in on Lady Fife at Mar Lodge on the way back, Dizzy encountered Lady Sylvia Doyle: with her cheeks painted like a clown's and her golden hair piled 'as high as the neighbouring hills' she looked, decided Dizzy, 'more absurd than any human being I can well remember.'

The Queen was highly satisfied with her Prime Minister's visit. He 'seemed delighted with his stay and was most grateful,' she noted in her journal. 'He certainly shows more consideration for my comfort than any preceding Prime Ministers. . . .' When he left, she loaded him with presents: two books of views of Balmoral, a box of family photographs, a shawl for Mary Anne and—inevitably—a full length portrait of the late Prince Consort. In his adroit letter of thanks, Dizzy assured her that, because of those books of views, 'he will be able to live, as it were, in your Majesty's favourite scenes.'

That, in fact, was as near as he ever wanted to get to her Majesty's favourite scenes. For all its attractions, remote and rain-swept Balmoral did not suit Disraeli. Only once again did he visit it. During his second term as Prime Minister Dizzy would make every excuse to steer clear of its all too bracing delights.

2

If on a personal level Victoria and Disraeli were in accord, politically there was still a gap between them. The gap might have been narrowing but it was a gap none the less. The Queen's views were still coloured by those of the late Prince Consort and however sweetly Dizzy might pipe his tune, she was not yet ready to be enticed down his particular political path. He simply did not fit into that gallery of upright, earnest, liberally-minded men like Peel, Aberdeen and the Prince Consort himself.

But then with the man who did—with the direct political descendant of these worthies—William Ewart Gladstone, the Queen felt distinctly ill at ease. She had not yet come to loathe Gladstone but even now, given the choice between Gladstone and Disraeli, she would have plumped for the latter.

The parliamentary session of 1868 saw the two giants more closely locked in battle than ever. As the resignation of Lord Derby had made Disraeli Conservative Prime Minister, so had the retirement of Lord Russell ensured that Gladstone would be the next Liberal Prime Minister. They now fought as equals. The session had hardly begun before Gladstone attacked. He moved a series of resolutions in favour of disestablishing the Church of Ireland which was, at that stage, Anglican. Ireland was going through a particularly torrid period, with Fenian outrages being committed almost daily. The best way to cool this overheated situation, reckoned Gladstone, was to separate Church and State. By so disestablishing the Protestant Irish Church, at least one serious cause of Irish discontent would be removed.

This put Disraeli in an awkward spot. The truth was that he did not really feel very strongly about religious matters. A born Jew who was now a practising Christian, Dizzy seemed to belong to neither world. 'I am the blank page,' he once quipped to Queen Victoria, 'between the Old and the New Testament.' His extraordinary theory that Christians were merely completed Jews won favour with neither Jews nor Gentiles. His religious beliefs, like his political, were hazy, eccentric, inconsistent. He simply could not bring himself to be as earnest about religion as was the bulk of Victorian Englishmen; he could not be bothered with all those ecclesiastical arguments that so absorbed his contemporaries. Typically, to a collection of serious-minded dons and undergraduates, he once airily dismissed the entire controversy about Darwin's *Origin of Species* by declaring that he was 'on the side of the Angels'.

So, when Gladstone proposed a disestablishment of the Protestant Church of Ireland, Disraeli's reaction was political rather than ecclesiastical. To best exploit the situation, he raised a 'No Popery' cry. The Church of England, particularly its Low Church and violently anti-papal section, must be roused to fight for the retention of the Protestant Church of Ireland.

With this controversy, the Queen moved a step closer to Disraeli. Victoria could hardly relish the disestablishment of a Church of which she was the Head. And she certainly had no great love of the Catholics. Had not dear, wise Albert always said that the Reformation had still to be completed? Surely this proposed weakening of the Protestant Church of Ireland would have been contrary to the late Prince's wishes?

By coincidence, several important ecclesiastical posts fell vacant during Disraeli's term of office. These he attempted to fill with candidates sympathetic to his cause. In this instance, however, he did not have the Queen's wholehearted support. Unlike Disraeli, Victoria was deeply interested in, and knowledgeable about, Church affairs. Occasionally their views clashed. Where Disraeli saw the appointments in purely political terms, she took a broader view. He wanted the most politically suitable men; she wanted those who were best, ecclesiastically.

Invariably, it was Dizzy who gave way. Queen Victoria was never his puppet to the extent that many imagined. When it came to a choice between her enthusiasms and her common sense, the Queen's common sense usually won the day.

By using some rather suspect delaying tactics, Disraeli managed to postpone Gladstone's disestablishment issue and by the time the House rose at the end of July 1868, it was known that a general election would be held in November. Dizzy would fight the election on a 'No Popery' cry. The electors would include all those newly enfranchised by the Second Reform Bill and Disraeli was able to assure the Queen that 'generally speaking there appears to be nothing to dread from this franchise'. She could only hope that he was right.

3

By now the seventy-five-year-old Mary Anne Disraeli was seriously ill. During the previous year, both she and Dizzy had been laid up: she with gastric trouble, he with gout. The two of them lay in separate rooms: Grosvenor Gate, as Dizzy put it, 'has become a hospital', but he assured his wife that being in hospital with her was worth being in a palace with anyone else. They wrote little notes to each other. 'You have sent me the most amusing and charming letter I ever had,' reads one of Dizzy's pencilled scribblings. 'It beats Horace Walpole and Mme de Sévigné.'

Both recovered from this particular bout of illness but by then Dizzy knew that Mary Anne's gastric troubles were caused by stomach cancer. Imagining that she did not realize this, Dizzy said nothing to her about it. And she, in turn, imagining that he did not know, kept it from him. Just as Mary Anne had never made any concessions to old age, so did she now refuse to make any to illness. She simply added more rouge, wore even brighter colours, and pinned on a few more curls. When Dizzy became Prime Minister early in 1868, the couple held a great reception at the Foreign Office. For them both, it was a moment of supreme triumph. With Mary Anne on the arm of the Prince of Wales and Dizzy escorting Princess Alexandra, they moved amongst the brilliant crowd. But not even the splendour of the occasion or the sumptuousness of her dress could hide the fact that Mary Anne was looking 'very ill and haggard'.

The couple hated being separated. When Dizzy went up to Balmoral in the autumn of 1868 he wrote to her every day. 'I was greatly distressed by our separation,' he wrote from Perth. 'Nothing but the gravity of public life sustains me under this great trial, which no one can understand except those who live on the terms of entire affection and companionship like ourselves: and, I believe, they are very few.'

'The joy of our soon meeting again,' he wrote on the day he left Balmoral, 'is inexpressible.'

Even Lord Clarendon had to admit that Dizzy's kindness to what Clarendon called 'the old woman' was a redeeming feature.

Of considerable comfort, to both Disraeli and Mary Anne during this period, was the presence of Dizzy's new secretary, young Montagu Corry. Thirty years old during Disraeli's first premiership, Corry suited him perfectly. 'Male society is not much to my taste,' admitted Dizzy to a friend, but 'I like [Corry] very much better than any man.' For although Corry had all the attributes of a successful private secretary—discretion, loyalty, efficiency and lack of personal ambition—he was far from dull. That, Disraeli could never have tolerated. What Dizzy liked, almost as much as his secretary's abilities, were his good looks, his amusing talk, his warm heart and his worldliness. Queen Victoria's reservations about Corry on the grounds that he was a 'man of pleasure' would never have been entertained by Disraeli. It was precisely because Corry was a man of pleasure—gay, gossipy and a Lothario—that Dizzy approved of him. In time Corry, who never married, was to become like a son to the older man.

Hardly had Disraeli arrived back at Grosvenor Gate that autumn than he was plunged into the turmoil of the general election. Despite his optimism, the Conservatives were soundly beaten. The Liberal Party won over one hundred seats more than the Conservatives. Gladstone—'The People's William'—was to be the next Prime Minister. Dizzy's term had lasted for a mere ten months.

Yet during this term, Disraeli had laid the foundations for his next premiership. The 1868 term had been in the nature of a prelude: a prelude to his more spectacular premiership half a dozen years hence and a prelude to his romantic partnership with Queen Victoria. With the Queen still tied, politically to Prince Albert and emotionally to John Brown, Dizzy had had to move with circumspection. All he had been able to do was to ingratiate himself with Victoria; he had yet to bring their association into full flower.

4

Before resigning, Disraeli had a favour to ask of the Queen. As he was anxious to remain leader of the Party in the House of Commons, he wanted no honours for himself; but he asked the Queen to confer a peerage on his wife. He wanted Mary Anne to become Viscountess Beaconsfield. This would be his tribute to his wife's loyalty, courage and devotion.

The proposal embarrassed the Queen. Despite Dizzy's well-worded justifications for his request—an historical precedent, Mary Anne's personal fortune—Victoria was reluctant to grant it. Mary Anne had performed no political services; she was an exceedingly odd creature; she might well become 'the subject of endless ridicule'. None of these royal reservations, however, reached Disraeli's ears. The Queen discussed them with her secretary, General Grey, and in the end, she granted Dizzy's wish. The truth was that she simply could not bring herself to refuse it.

Mary Anne was overjoyed. The once impoverished, middle-class Miss Mary Anne Evans of Exeter was now Viscountess Beaconsfield. The College of Heralds designed her a coat of arms, and on writing paper, boldly embellished with a coronet and the intial B, she would sign 'your devoted Beaconsfield' on her letters to Dizzy.

And once the thing was done, Queen Victoria was hardly less pleased. After all, had not the elevation of Prince Albert into Prince Consort once been her dearest wish? 'The Queen,' she wrote to Dizzy, 'can truly sympathize with his devotion to Mrs Disraeli, who in her turn is so deeply attached to him, and she hopes they may yet enjoy many years of happiness together.'

Dizzy's letter of thanks was in his most florid style: 'Mr Disraeli, at your Majesty's feet . . .' ran the perfervid phrases.

Chapter Thirteen

I

As Disraeli bowed himself gracefully out of the royal Presence, so did Gladstone come marching into it. Although there was a certain lack of rapport between the two of them, both the Queen and her new Prime Minister were determined to make the best of the situation. But during the following five years, from late 1868 until early 1874, their relationship deteriorated drastically. Even if Queen Victoria had not already preferred Disraeli to Gladstone, she would certainly have done so by the end of Gladstone's term of office.

Fifty-nine years of age, tall, robust, craggy-featured and clear-eyed, Gladstone had come fully armed with advice on how to treat the Queen. His wife had urged him to 'pet' her; Dean Wellesley had been more explicit. 'Everything depends upon your manner of approaching the Queen,' he wrote. It was impossible to show her too much regard, gentleness and tenderness. Where they differed, the Prime Minister should not try to reason with her: he must simply 'pass the matter lightly over' and reserve discussion for a more opportune moment. He must never argue.

Although the advice did not exactly fall on deaf ears, it was being given to the sort of man who found it almost impossible to follow. Gladstone's intentions might have been of the best, but his manner—as far as Victoria was concerned—was of the worst. Honest, humourless, self-righteous, graceless, Gladstone could hardly have been in greater contrast to Disraeli. Where Dizzy was courtly, he was blunt; where Dizzy was romantic, he was pedestrian; where Dizzy simplified, he complicated; where Dizzy cajoled, he lectured; where Dizzy encouraged, he undermined; where Dizzy sympathized, he bullied. Where Dizzy treated the Queen like a woman, Gladstone is said to have treated her like a public meeting.

Mr Disraeli, noted one witness, 'used to engage Her Majesty in conversation about water-colour drawing and the third cousinships of German princes. Mr Gladstone harangues her about the policy of the Hittites, or the harmony between the Athanasian Creed and Homer. The Queen, perplexed and uncomfortable, tries to make a digression—addresses a remark to a daughter, or proffers a biscuit to a begging terrier. Mr Gladstone restrains himself with an effort till the Princess has answered or the dog has sat down, and then promptly resumes. "I was about to say——". Meanwhile the flood has gathered force by delay and when it bursts forth again it carries all before it.'

Victoria and Gladstone clashed on many issues but the one on which they clashed most seriously during his first term of office was on what he called 'The Royalty Question'. This question could only be solved, reckoned the Prime Minister, by getting the Queen out of her seclusion.

The monarchy was going through a particularly bad patch just then. It had reached a nadir of unpopularity: the air was thick with talk of a republic. Republican clubs were being established throughout England and even Members of Parliament—Sir Charles Dilke and Joseph Chamberlain—spoke to cheering crowds of the inevitability of a republic. The Prince of Wales was hissed in public and when the Queen's third son, Prince Arthur, came of age in 1871, a gathering in Trafalgar Square demonstrated against the granting of an allowance to this latest 'princely pauper'.

Several factors contributed towards this feeling against the monarchy. In 1870 France ditched its sovereign, Napoleon III, after his defeat at the hands of Prussia, and declared itself a republic. The subsequent aggression of the victorious German armies against the French reflected badly on Britain's very German royal family. The appearance of the profligate Prince of Wales in the witness box during the course of the scandalous Mordaunt divorce case further tarnished the image of royalty. But it was the Queen's own behaviour that most seriously damaged the throne. She was accused of hoarding her vast wealth, of shamming ill health, of not being prepared to make the slightest effort to carry out either her private or her public functions. Some of the accusations might have been groundless but they were being made none the less.

The only way to counteract this antagonism, decided Gladstone, was for the Queen to be seen to be doing more. She must shake herself out of her lethargy, she must make more public appearances, she must spend less time at Osborne and Balmoral, she must establish a residence in Ireland, she must allow the Prince of Wales to play a more active

LEFT: Queen Victoria in 1838, at the age of nineteen
RIGHT: Benjamin Disraeli at the age of thirty in 1834, sketched by the Count d'Orsay
BELOW: Queen Victoria with her first Privy Council, as described by Disraeli in his
novel, *Sybil*

Leopold I, King of the Belgians, Victoria's 'Dearest Uncle' and first mentor

Beruffled, ringleted and romantic—
the dandified young Disraeli

Disraeli's mistress, Henrietta, Lady Sykes,
as painted by Daniel Maclise

The urbane Lord Melbourne, object of Queen Victoria's youthful infatuation

This highly romanticized painting of Prince Albert as a knight in shining armour was Queen Victoria's favourite

LEFT: The forty-seven-year-old Disraeli at the time when, as Chancellor of the Exchequer, he first became closely associated with Queen Victoria

RIGHT: Queen Victoria in court dress at about the time of her first meeting with Napoleon III

BELOW: Napoleon III, the seductively mannered Emperor of the French

Hughenden Manor after its conversion

LEFT: The highly idealized portrait of Mary Anne Disraeli by J. G. Middleton
RIGHT: Selina, Countess of Bradford, another of the mother-figures in Disraeli's life

LEFT: Queen Victoria with her Highland gillie, John Brown
RIGHT: Millais's portrait of Disraeli, altered on the Queen's instructions

Queen Victoria and Princess Beatrice in the sitting room at Osborne House

ABOVE: 'New Crowns for Old Ones!' The famous *Punch* cartoon (1876) of Disraeli offering Victoria the crown of India

BELOW: Queen Victoria, newly proclaimed Empress of India, on an ivory throne presented by the Rajah of Travancore

Victoria on Disraeli's arm after her visit to Hughenden in December 1877

Disraeli, sketched on the terrace at Hughenden during the last few months of his life

part in public affairs. In letter after letter, each one longer and more pedantic than the last, Gladstone urged the Queen to play a more active public role. At audience after audience, he reminded her of the need for 'putting forward the Royal Family in the visible discharge of public duty'.

It was all to no purpose. The more Gladstone insisted, the more firmly Victoria dug in her heels.

Things came to a head in the autumn of 1871. Gladstone's suggestion that the Queen postpone her journey to Balmoral by a few days in order to prorogue Parliament brought forth a flood of outraged letters from the Queen. She would do no such thing. 'What killed her beloved Husband?' she demanded. 'Overwork and worry! What killed Lord Clarendon? The same! What has broken down Mr Bright and Mr Childers and made them retire, but the same; and the Queen, a woman, no longer young is supposed to be proof against all and to be driven and abused till her nerves and health give way with this worry and agitation and interference in her private life.'

'*No earthly political* object can be *gained* by her remaining a week longer,' ran a subsequent tirade, 'except gratifying a *foolish and unreasonable* fancy.'

She even suggested that Gladstone was using her as a party political object.

Poor Gladstone, who was a dedicated monarchist, could only grit his teeth in anger. 'I think it has been the most sickening piece of experience which I have had during near forty years in public life,' he declared as the royal train carrying the obdurate Queen steamed northwards. '*Worse* things may easily be imagined but smaller and meaner cause for the decay of Thrones cannot be conceived. It is like the worm which bores the bark of a noble oak tree and so breaks the channel of its life.'

And if, by the third year of Gladstone's term of office, he was in despair about the Queen, she had come to dislike him intensely. On his arrival at Balmoral in the autumn of 1871 she kept him waiting for several days before granting him an audience. When she did, he was chilled to the bone.

'The repellent power which she so well knows how to use has been put in action towards me . . .' he declared.

How different, how delightfully different was dear Mr Disraeli's attitude during these years. At the very time that Gladstone was hectoring Victoria to make a greater effort, Disraeli was expressing public sympathy for her condition. At a Harvest Festival at Hughenden, he delivered a fulsome speech on the onerousness of her burdens. Gladstone was appalled. He was certain that Dizzy and the Queen's doctor had cooked it up between them. 'That speech of Dizzy's savours of his usual flunkeyism,' growled Gladstone. 'Its natural operation will be to increase her bias against visible public duties. . . .' And at a mass meeting at the Free Trade Hall in Manchester (during the three-hour course of which he sustained himself with two bottles of 'white brandy', indistinguishable from water) Disraeli rebuked Gladstone for not disowning his radical supporters who were working against the Crown.

In less direct ways, too, Disraeli was winning the Queen's approval. The theme of his latest novel, *Lothair*, published in 1870, bore out one of Victoria's most firmly held convictions: that by forgetting its sense of duty, the aristocracy was degenerating into an indulgent and worthless caste. At the same time, Disraeli was fashioning his Conservative Party into something after her own heart. As, in the Queen's eyes, Gladstone's Liberal Party seemed to be becoming more and more radical, so did Disraeli's Conservative Party seem to be developing along the lines of which she heartily approved.

In a series of great public speeches, Disraeli clarified Conservative policy. It supported the Monarchy, the House of Lords and the Church. It believed in a consolidation of the Empire. It recognized the importance of social reform. It stood for a strong foreign policy; for the greatness of Britain as opposed to Gladstone's 'Little England' theory. In contrast to the internationalism of the Liberals, the Conservatives were a truly national party. The working classes were conservatives in the best sense; they were 'proud of belonging to a great country, and wish to maintain its greatness'.

This was the sort of language which Queen Victoria was coming to understand.

Early in 1872, and on the same occasion, both the Queen and Disraeli—both the Monarchy and the Conservative Party—were given an unexpected fillip. In November of the previous year, the Prince of Wales had been struck down with typhoid fever. For several weeks he was dangerously ill. At one stage it was thought that he would die. But he recovered and, on his recovery, the country was suddenly engulfed in a wave of royalist emotion. In the face of the possibility of the Prince of Wales's death, all republicanism seemed to have been swept away.

On 27 February 1872 a Thanksgiving Service was held in St Paul's Cathedral to mark the Prince's recovery. When, at Temple Bar, the procession halted and the Queen raised her son's hand to kiss it, her dramatic gesture was greeted by thunderous applause. Not for years had she heard such a loyal ovation. No music could have sounded sweeter.

But similar music was sounding similarly sweet in Dizzy's ears. As the statesmen attending the Thanksgiving Service arrived at St Paul's, they were greeted by the watching crowds. Gladstone was given a cool, even hostile, reception but Disraeli found himself riotously applauded. This unexpected tribute not only delighted him but set him thinking. Sir William Fraser, seeing Disraeli at the Carlton Club later that morning, noticed that he was sitting staring vacantly into space, quite oblivious of another member talking to him.

'I will tell you what he was thinking about,' said Fraser afterwards to Disraeli's companion. 'He was thinking that he will be Prime Minister again.'

2

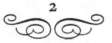

For many years an empty picture frame used to hang above the fireplace in the drawing room at Hughenden. When Disraeli was asked why it was there, he would explain that it was intended for a portrait of Mary Anne but that she had never sat for a picture other than for a miniature by William Charles Ross. He planned one day to have the miniature copied and placed in the frame.

Not only had Mary Anne not been painted for many years but it appears that she had never been photographed. So obsessed with looking young, she had never dared face the camera's merciless eye. Far better to leave behind an impression of beauty, colour and vivacity than some unflattering, static, sepia-tinted likeness. However, by the year 1872, during which Mary Anne turned eighty, there was precious little of her once celebrated beauty, colour or vivacity left. Only her unquenchable spirit kept her going. She still enamelled her wrinkled face, she still loaded her scraggy neck and arms with jewels, she still covered her shrunken, pain-racked body in brilliantly coloured, loosely flowing tunics. She gave dinner parties, she went to receptions, she attended Courts, she went out driving. Nothing would make her take to her bed. Eating very little, often in the most excruciating pain, she none the less astonished everyone by her smiles and her buoyancy.

Poor Dizzy was heartbroken. Not well himself, he could hardly bear to see her suffering. 'We have not been separated for three and thirty years,' he said to a companion, 'and, during all that time, in her society I never have had a moment of dullness. It tears the heart to see such a spirit suffer, and suffer so much!'

From the House, he still sent love letters to her. 'I have nothing to tell you, except that I love you, which I fear, you will think rather dull . . .' he once wrote. And from Grosvenor Gate she would answer that she missed him sadly. 'I feel so grateful for your constant tender love and kindness,' she would say.

By the middle of December 1872, it was clear that she was dying. They were at Hughenden then. When Disraeli's secretary, Montagu Corry, came in to see her, she told him that she had been persuaded to send for a clergyman. 'He told me to turn my thoughts to Jesus Christ,' she whispered, 'but I couldn't. You know *Dizzy* is my J.C.'

Some years before, Mary Anne had written Dizzy a farewell letter.

If I should depart this life before you, leave orders that we may be buried in the same grave at whatever distance you may die from England. God bless you my dearest, kindest. You have been a perfect husband to me. Be put by my side in the same grave. And now farewell my dear Dizzy.

And then, concerned only for his welfare, she added, 'Do not live alone, dearest. Someone I earnestly hope you may find as attached to you as your own devoted MARY ANNE.'

She died, sitting up in a chair, on Sunday 15 December 1872. In driving rain her coffin was carried from the house to Hughenden church. They laid it in a vault at the east end of the building, beside the remains of Mrs Brydges Willyams and Disraeli's brother James, who had died four years before. For a full ten minutes, bareheaded in the wind and rain, Dizzy stood staring down at Mary Anne's coffin before making his way back home.

The death of his wife brought additional losses for Disraeli; he now lost the house at Grosvenor Gate and Mary Anne's £5,000 a year income. These went to her family. Dizzy moved to rooms in Edwards'

Hotel in George Street, Hanover Square. For a man such as he, who relied so much on feminine company, hotel life was a desolation; he called the evenings a 'cave of despair'. To Queen Victoria who, throughout Mary Anne's illness, had shown heartfelt concern ('Poor Mr Disraeli has lost his faithful and devoted partner,' she wrote in her journal on Mary Anne's death) Dizzy complained of having to go to 'a homeless home, alone, every night'. This was something which the Queen understood only too well. Indeed, with the death of Dizzy's life's partner yet another link had been forged between him and the widowed Queen.

After Mary Anne's death, Disraeli had the Ross miniature copied by G. F. Middleton and placed in the frame over the mantleshelf at Hughenden. 'I am much pleased with the portrait . . .' he told Montagu Corry. 'He has succeeded in giving the countenance an expression of sweet gravity, which is characteristic.'

To this day Mary Anne stares out of the frame with those candid blue eyes, immortalized as she would have wished to be immortalized: seductive, beautiful, perenially young.

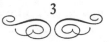

3

Those who imagined that Mary Anne's death would lead to Disraeli's retirement from active politics were soon proved wrong. Indeed, within three months of her death it looked as though Disraeli was about to take office. A combination of Conservatives and Irish Catholics defeated Gladstone's government on an Irish University Bill. Delighted, the Queen invited Disraeli to form a government.

He refused. For one thing, he had no wish to lead a minority government; for another, he felt certain that, given a year or two more, the electoral tide would turn in favour of the Conservatives. Better to bide one's time. But the Queen was not prepared to exercise the same patience. She sent her secretary, Henry Ponsonby, to Edwards' Hotel to discuss a possible dissolution of Parliament. Dizzy would not consider it: it was too soon for an election.

Colonel Ponsonby, who had not yet had a great deal to do with

Disraeli, found himself bemused by the stateman's part-florid, part-practical manner. 'There was something in his over-civil expressions about the Queen or "my dear Colonel" which made me think he was playing with me, and I felt once or twice a difficulty in not laughing; but when he developed the reasons for his policy he rose and stood much more upright than I had ever seen him, spoke in a most frank and straightforward manner, and with a sharpness and decision which was different from his early words. Yet probably he had measured the length of my foot, and had been more sincere and honest in his message to the Queen than when he made me to believe in his frank exposition of policy.

'He was far easier to speak to than Gladstone, who forces you into his groove while Disraeli apparently follows yours and is genial, almost too genial, in his statements. . . .'

Gladstone, put out by Dizzy's refusal to take office (a minority Conservative government would have suited him very well), was obliged to resume the premiership in a much weaker position. His action won no praise from the Queen. She complained to Vicky—now Crown Princess in a united and imperial Germany—that Gladstone's behaviour had been 'tactless, tiresome and obstinate,' and that he had done himself no good.

Dizzy, on the other hand, had done himself a power of good. By his restraint he had allowed his party more time to build up its strength, the Liberals more time to run into trouble and had proved to the world that he was no mere grabber of office.

4

'My nature,' Disraeli had once written, 'demands that my life should be perpetual love.' It did indeed. Hardly had Mary Anne been buried than the sixty-eight-year-old Dizzy was once more moving in an aura of high romance. Although Mary Anne could not have wished for a more faithful or devoted husband, once she was gone, he was drawn to that mature feminine society without which he could not live. And, in truth, this is exactly what Mary Anne had wanted for him.

But it was not always he who did the pursuing. Early in 1873, the dowager Lady Cardigan, who had been born Adeline Horsey de Horsey, began making advances. There was, in fact, more than a little of Mary Anne about the middle-aged Lady Cardigan: the same flamboyance of dress, the same eccentricity of behaviour, the same vivacity of manner. Lady Cardigan's reputation, however, was much more disreputable: among other things, she was known to have lived with the Earl of Cardigan—of the Charge of the Light Brigade fame—before the death of his first wife. According to her self-congratulatory memoirs, Lady Cardigan had always moved in a cloud of admirers. She claimed to have had eight proposals of marriage (including one from the Claimant to the Spanish throne) before her marriage to the Earl of Cardigan; and twelve since his death.

None of them, however, came from Disraeli. It was left to her, after a series of increasingly affectionate letters, to bring up the question of marriage. Quite clearly, she saw herself as exactly the sort of colourful and accomplished wife that was needed by this brilliant but unorthodox man. What could be more sensible, she asked, than an alliance between 'the greatest man we have in genius and intellect' and—she was shrewd enough to point out—the wealthiest widow of the 'staunchest Conservative Peer that ever lived'?

But Dizzy was not to be won over. He had no intention of marrying the bizarre Lady Cardigan; whether she be the wealthiest widow of the staunchest Conservative Peer or not. He merely asked her to stop writing to him. Spurned, she married the Comte de Lancastre instead. Dizzy was one of the first to be told the news of her triumph as he had always, she wrote, taken 'so kind an interest' in her welfare.

From then on the Countess of Cardigan and Lancastre, as she called herself, stoutly maintained that it was Dizzy who had proposed to her and she who had refused him. Luckily, Disraeli had kept her letter of proposal.

One reason why Dizzy could not be bothered with Lady Cardigan was that he was in love with someone else. Again it was with one of those mature, maternal creatures: a fifty-four-year-old grandmother by the name of Selina, Countess of Bradford. Their association started in the summer of 1873. Selina (the name, to Dizzy's delight, is the Greek for 'moon') was an attractive, vivacious and highly social creature. She had, ran his rose-coloured catalogue of her charms, 'a sweet simplicity, blended with high breeding; an intellect not overdrilled, but lively, acute and picturesque; a seraphic temper, and a disposition that is infinitely sympathetic. . . .'

Alas, Lady Bradford's disposition proved not nearly sympathetic enough. With Selina, Disraeli was indeed crying for the moon. For one thing, her husband was still alive; for another, she did not really return Dizzy's love. She was probably flattered by his attentions but embarrassed by his ardour. The torrent of his letters, sometimes as many as three a day, was enough to disconcert anyone.

But Dizzy refused to be put off. Unable to propose marriage to Lady Bradford, he did the next best thing. He proposed to her seventy-one-year-old sister, Lady Chesterfield, instead; but only for the reason that this would bring him closer to Lady Bradford. Not unnaturally, Lady Chesterfield refused. So Dizzy had to be content with writing his letters to both sisters and, as far as Lady Bradford was concerned, running 'the whole gamut of half-requited love—passionate devotion, rebuff, despair, resignation, renewed hope, reconciliation, ecstasy.'

Could this 'strange romance be, in very sooth,' asked the Marquis of Zetland, editor of Dizzy's impassioned letters to Selina, 'that of a nineteenth-century Prime Minister of Great Britain?' Could this figure, who hung about the Bradfords' house in Belgrave Square with all the persistence of a love-sick adolescent, be a man of almost seventy?

No wonder Disraeli could sigh that there must be no greater misfortune 'than to have a heart that will not grow old'.

5

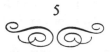

And all the while that other mother-figure, Queen Victoria, was battling with Gladstone. Beaten in his efforts to force the Queen out of her seclusion, Gladstone had turned his full attention to the Prince of Wales. If the Queen was not prepared to play her part, then her heir must be allowed to play his.

Now in his early thirties, Bertie was leading an utterly worthless existence. The chief reason for this was that he was not being given enough to do. The fault was his mother's. Victoria had a very poor opinion of her son's abilities. She considered him, and not without reason, to be irresponsible, immature and indiscreet. She would neither confide in him, nor entrust him with any State business. Her son must see nothing, she warned her ministers, of 'a very *confidential* nature'. He was kept in complete ignorance of the workings of the Monarchy.

The result of this exclusion was that Bertie lived in what his mother called 'a whirl of amusements'. And very happily he lived too. His life was devoted to racing, gambling, shooting, travelling, dressing up, eating out and making love. The Devil was indeed finding work for those idle hands. Yet, for all his frivolity, Bertie was not entirely foolish. He had considerable diplomatic gifts, great panache and exceptional vitality. These qualities could have been of real service to his mother. Given some active employment and some real responsibility, there was no reason why the Prince of Wales should not be a credit to the Monarchy.

This was certainly Gladstone's view. In March 1872, in one of his long-winded memoranda, Gladstone presented the Queen with his master plan for the Prince of Wales. He must become the Queen's permanent representative in Ireland; in other words, her Viceroy. This way the heir would be given 'manly' employment, the Monarchy would be given a boost and troubled Ireland would be given a treat.

The Queen would not hear of it. Nor, for that matter, would the Prince of Wales. But this did not deter the tenacious Gladstone. He retired to work out a still more elaborate plan. This he presented in July. Now, not only must the Prince represent the Queen in Dublin but he must deputize for her in London during the season. To this even longer and more insulting memorandum the Queen gave an even more crushing reply. She ended by saying that this was a question 'which more properly concerns herself to settle with the members of her family as occasion may arise.' In short, it was none of Gladstone's business.

By now anyone else—and certainly Disraeli—would have let the matter drop. But not Gladstone. He felt that he had not yet 'discharged his full responsibility in the matter.' So he drafted a third and even longer letter in which he set out to prove, under six separate headings, that the Queen's objections to his plan were unfounded. Victoria was astonished. Once again she gave him short shrift. 'The Queen therefore trusts,' she wrote firmly, 'that this plan may now be considered as *definitely* abandoned.'

Incredibly, it was not. Gladstone wrote a fourth time, this time reducing to five the number of headings by which he refuted the Queen's arguments. A brief note from the Queen informed him that it was 'useless to prolong the discussion'. Finally beaten, the unconvinced Gladstone contented himself by bemoaning the fact that his views had been 'so unequivocally disapproved by Your Majesty in a matter of so much importance, either way, to the interests of the Monarchy.'

The Queen's final verdict on the matter was that whenever she had a strong conviction about something, 'she generally found she was right'.

This series of exchanges destroyed the last shreds of the Queen's regard for Gladstone. 'She must say to General Ponsonby,' wrote the Queen to her secretary some time later, 'though he may hardly like to believe it, that *she* has felt that Mr Gladstone would have liked to *govern* HER as Bismarck governs the [German] Emperor. Of course not to the same extent, or in the *same* manner; but she always felt in his manner an overbearing obstinacy and imperiousness (without being actually wanting in respect as to form) which she never experienced from *anyone* else, and which she found most disagreeable. It is the same thing which made him so unpopular to his followers, and even to his colleagues.'

The Queen was right about Gladstone becoming more unpopular with his followers. An administration which had started well was running into trouble: it was being caught up in a tangle of mistakes and scandals. In by-election after by-election the Liberals were losing to the Conservatives. Early in 1874 Gladstone decided to dissolve Parliament and hold an election. The news which took Disraeli by surprise, did not find him unprepared. Not only had he used his years in opposition to define and popularize Conservative policy but he had overhauled the party machinery. The Conservative organization was now in an admirably efficient state.

The election was held early in February 1874. The results echoed, almost exactly, those of the previous election, but in the opposite direction: the Conservatives won just over a hundred more seats than the Liberals.

On 17 February Queen Victoria sent for Disraeli. Their meeting was ecstatic. 'He repeatedly said *whatever I wished* SHOULD *be done*,' declared the gratified Queen, and when Dizzy fell to his knees before her to kiss her little hand, his words could hardly have been more romantic. 'I plight my troth to the kindest of *Mistresses*.'

One really could not imagine Mr Gladstone saying that.

PART TWO

The Faery Queen

Chapter Fourteen

I

The idyll had begun. Victoria, at fifty-four, and Disraeli, at sixty-nine, were embarked on their six-year-long romantic partnership.

With Queen Victoria refusing to spend more than a night or two at Buckingham Palace, and with Disraeli refusing to expose himself to the vagaries of the Balmoral climate, it was against the backgrounds of Windsor Castle and Osborne House that the scenes of their close association were enacted.

Disraeli would travel down from London to Windsor in a special train; sometimes alone in a saloon carriage, 'like a wild animal in the *Jardin des Plantes*', sometimes accompanied by Montagu Corry. The Prime Minister invariably wore dark clothes. In winter he sported an ankle-length, astrakhan-collared black coat and, on his hat, he always wore a mourning band for his wife. Often he would stroll along the station platform with his arm through Corry's. To many, the uninhibited way in which the Prime Minister addressed Corry and other manfully bearded friends as 'Darling' or 'Dearest' seemed distinctly *outré*.

If the audience were to be a short one, he would be ushered directly into one of the Queen's overfurnished rooms. Cosiness and cheerfulness were what the Queen preferred in her surroundings; not by the wildest stretch of the imagination could her private apartments be considered elegant. In addition to the opulently upholstered chairs and sofas, the plush-covered tables, the inlaid desks, the velvet curtains, the patterned carpets, the papered walls, the screens and the palm stands and the hanging lamps, there would be innumerable paintings, busts and ornaments. The late Prince Consort would be portrayed in almost every conceivable medium and in almost every conceivable pose; wherever one turned, one came up against yet another oil painting or watercolour or photograph or statuette of dearest Albert. Yet, for all this clutter, the Queen's rooms were never stuffy or gloomy. They were fresh with the scent of orange flowers, which Disraeli would have loved, and their windows ever open to the winds, which Disraeli hated.

Sometimes Victoria would receive him in the more intimate Royal Closet, formerly the private room of the Prince Consort. This tiny room, no less crowded—with Meissonier paintings and assorted *objets*—boasted only one chair. Whenever Dizzy was received, however, the Queen would see that another small golden chair was brought in.

In the midst of this kaleidoscopic jumble, the Prime Minister would stand waiting for the Queen. To Disraeli, the cheerful lack of elegance would have been in no way offensive: the rooms at Hughenden looked very like this. The Queen seldom kept him waiting long. After a minute or two a liveried, low-bowing footman would open the door and Victoria would enter.

Small, plump, dressed in a black, elaborately bustled dress and with the veil of her white widow's cap cascading down her back, Victoria would greet her Prime Minister. To others she could be intimidating; to him she was invariably charming. Carlyle, meeting the Queen at this time, considered her attractive, and Disraeli would certainly have enjoyed the benefits of her more appealing features: her kindly, blue-grey eyes, her sweet smile, her beautiful voice, her silvery laugh, her graceful movements. Without losing a shred of her celebrated dignity, Victoria could be extremely animated, even gay.

That the Queen found Disraeli attractive there is no doubt. To others he might look old and odd and sphinx-like; to her he was merely Bohemian, exotic, interesting. The rouged cheeks, the single dyed curl on the forehead and the rings worn over the white gloves might look singular to some but to the Queen, says Ponsonby, any word of criticism was 'out of the question'. Indeed, so enamoured was Victoria of her Prime Minister's looks that she commissioned Jabez Hughes to take a series of photographs of Disraeli. In them—with his straggly imperial beard, his hooked nose and his hooded eyes—he looked astonishingly like that other figure who had once set her pulses pounding: the Emperor Napoleon III. He certainly did not look like any previous British Prime Minister.

She also had him painted. She had a favour to ask of him, she once wrote: as none of her ministers had 'ever shown *her* more consideration and kindness than he has,' would he allow his portrait to be painted for her by Joachim von Angeli? Although Dizzy hated having his portrait painted, he could hardly refuse. For several days he would go at noon to Buckingham Palace where he would sit on a gilt chair upholstered in crimson velvet in the Queen's private dining room, while Angeli painted and Corry read out the despatches. The room, filled with the bizarre 'Pagoda' furniture from the Brighton Pavilion, particularly appealed to Disraeli.

To the Queen, he reported the picture to be a great success, but to his friends, Dizzy was more frank. 'Oh,' he would say, 'is it not hideous—and so like.'

He was also painted by Millais. As the Queen was not entirely happy with the likeness she sent the painter some photographs of Disraeli. 'The photograph looking down at the newspaper gives the form and also something of the peculiar expression about the corner of the mouth, suggesting a keen sense of humour, which contrasts with the extreme seriousness of the upper part of the face,' ran the royal instructions. 'It prevents the whole expression being sad. . . .' When the picture had been changed to her satisfaction, Victoria was full of praise. 'Mr Millais has given the peculiar, intellectual, and gentle expression of his face.'

One Christmastime she honoured her Prime Minister by allowing him to wear the 'Windsor uniform': that special dark-blue uniform with red facings worn by the men of the royal family and the members of the household in personal attendance. Only very privileged outsiders, like Lord Melbourne and the Duke of Wellington, had been similarly honoured. She was giving it, wrote Victoria to Disraeli, 'as a mark of personal regard and friendship.'

With her other Prime Ministers, and certainly with Gladstone, the Queen would keep her audiences as short as possible. But with Disraeli they often over-ran the customary hour. 'Twenty minutes over luncheon time!' he once boasted. 'Considered a miracle by the Court.' At times, these intimate audiences were 'all milk and honey' with no business being discussed at all, merely 'the most animated, interesting and confidential gossip'. Those who saw the Queen purely in terms of the heartbroken and humourless Widow of Windsor would have been astonished at Dizzy's behaviour with her. He teased her, he flattered her, he paid her the most extravagant compliments. He knew how to amuse her, how to interest her, how to win her round. Where Gladstone's bullying behaviour had achieved nothing, Dizzy's more adroit handling worked wonders. 'He had a way when we differed . . .' she later told Lord Rosebery, 'of saying "Dear Madam" so persuasively, and putting his head on one side.'

Within a few months of taking office he had even managed, wonder of wonders, to get her to alter her date of departure for Balmoral by two days, so as not to offend Tsar Alexander II.

It was often wondered how Queen Victoria—so astute, so honest and so sensible—could tolerate Dizzy's outrageous flattery. Surely she must suspect him of insincerity. She was no fool, she had a sharp eye for character, she was quick to recognize a charlatan. But it was precisely because of these qualities that she was able to appreciate Disraeli's flowery style. She realized that it was simply the expression of 'something poetic in his temperament', that behind the baroque façade was an essentially honest structure. If it suited him to behave more like a silver-tongued courtier than a serious-minded Prime Minister, then well and good. She knew that he was both these things.

Often one of the Queen's daughters, Princess Louise or Princess Beatrice, would have to knock on the door of the audience room and remind their mother that she had another appointment and so halt the 'charming flow' of their talk. Mr Disraeli 'had never been so delightful,' the Queen would sigh. 'You can easily conceive who the delightful person really was,' commented Disraeli. 'We are never so pleased as when we please others, and, in our gratified generosity, attribute to them the very results we have ourselves accomplished.'

On one occasion, when Disraeli was due to board his special train at five minutes past five exactly, the conversation proved so absorbing that Dizzy quite forgot to keep an eye on the time. Suddenly the clock struck five. Unceremoniously, he leapt to his feet and explained the situation. 'Run away, run away directly,' laughed Victoria. So he went scampering out of the room, hardly aware, he afterwards reported, that 'instead of being dismissed, I dismissed my Sovereign.'

Mr Disraeli, on paper, was hardly less entertaining than Mr Disraeli in the flesh. Where Gladstone's memoranda had been so ponderous that the Queen had to have précis made of them before she could understand them, Dizzy's were pithy, airy, scintillating. 'Mr Disraeli has a wonderful talent for writing in an amusing tone while seizing the points of an argument,' noted Ponsonby. Victoria's self-confidence, so badly shaken by Gladstone's erudition, was restored by Dizzy's blandishments; he never made her feel foolish. 'When I left the dining room after sitting next to Mr Gladstone I thought he was the cleverest man in England,' runs a story told by one of the Queen's grand-daughters. 'But after sitting next to Mr Disraeli I thought I was the cleverest woman in England.' This was the effect Dizzy had on many women, the Queen not least of all.

No wonder Gladstone always referred to him as 'the artful dodger'.

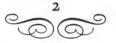

2

From time to time Disraeli was obliged to spend a few days at Windsor. This he never really enjoyed. He called the great battle-mented pile 'the temple of the Winds'. The Queen's passion for fresh air was something he could not share. While Victoria complained 'terribly of the sweltering clime of the realm she rules', Dizzy was never warm enough. He seemed, he grumbled, to spend half his time pacing the wind-swept Corridor. Icy blasts seemed to buffet him from every one of the many openings along what he maintained was its thousand-foot length.

He quickly tired of all the formalities of the Court. 'All is well as long as I can keep to my room, or a morning walk,' he told Lady Bradford, 'but *toilette* and evening mannerisms destroy me.' There were even times when he found the Queen exhausting. 'What nerve! What muscle! What energy!' he groaned. 'Her Minister is very deficient in all three.'

But there were compensations. Complain as he might, Dizzy undoubtedly enjoyed, not only the Queens' company, but the idea of all this royal hob-nobbing. To be on such intimate terms with the Court never quite ceased to delight and amuse him. Henry Ponsonby, who could never quite bring himself to trust Disraeli, admitted himself bemused by Dizzy's blend of reverence and cynicism. 'I so fully believe that Disraeli really has an admiration for splendour, for Duchesses with ropes of pearls, for richness and gorgeousness, mixed I also think with a cynical sneer and a burlesque thought about them. ... His speech here on the Palatial Grandeur, the Royal Physician who attended on him, the Royal Footman who answered his beck and nod, the rich plate etc—all was worked up half really, half comically into an expression of admiration for Royalty and the Queen. Yet there might also have been a sarcasm under it all.'

With Disraeli at the dinner table, Victoria could be extremely animated. Time and again, he reports on her high spirits, her good humour and her gaiety. 'What is he saying!' she smilingly demanded in German whenever she saw one of her children—Princess Christian or Prince Leopold—laughing at Disraeli's drily expressed witticisms. Yet one had to be careful. No less-favoured guest dare become too relaxed in the Queen's company. When Lady Derby asked the Queen if she had read Dizzy's latest book, *Lothair*, and Victoria answered that she had been the 'first person' to read it, her ladyship vivaciously went on to inquire if her Majesty had not found Theodora to be a '*divine* character'. At this, says Dizzy, the Queen looked both 'perplexed and grave'.

If Windsor was chilly, Osborne, in bad weather, was worse. Here, a great deal of time was spent out of doors. Although there were still times when Dizzy might delight in what he once called this 'Sicillian palazzo', with its columns, its urns and its balustraded, magnolia-scented terraces, there were other times when the rigours of the life there proved too much for him. Not only was there the crossing of the invariably choppy Solent but there was an endless to-ing and fro-ing between the royal yachts. One was forever balancing on some tilting, wind-lashed deck.

Unless it were actually raining—and sometimes even then—the Queen would have her large ecru parasol tent, fringed and lined with green, pitched on the lawns below the house. Here, surrounded by assorted dogs, liveried footmen, Highland attendants and black-clad ladies-in-waiting, the Queen would eat her breakfast and then deal with her despatch boxes. Here, too, she would receive Disraeli. 'The visit to Osborne was on the whole agreeable,' he once wrote. 'Our Sovereign hostess tried to make it so, but though I was much with her, I was very ill and could scarcely get through it.'

The Queen, in fact, was always very concerned about Disraeli's health. It was not only to spite the Prince of Wales that she once forbade Dizzy to risk going in an open boat to the Prince's yacht for dinner. She would scold him if he visited her when he had a cold and once, when they both had colds, he claimed that the 'kingdom was never governed with such an amount of catarrh and sneezing'. 'For fear of catching cold,' she once scribbled hurriedly to him, 'the Queen will excuse your wearing pantaloons this evening.' Victoria was forever urging him to see her doctor, Sir William Gull ('I was strong enough in mind and body to reject that,' he claimed) and if he were ill, she would bombard him with telegrams.

On one occasion he wrote to Ponsonby to tell him that he had recovered his youth 'by doing exactly what my medical friends have, for years, warned me not to follow: drinking very good wine.' Ponsonby promptly passed the letter on to the Queen. She was delighted. 'The Queen quite agrees,' she wrote. Mr Disraeli's letter was 'most amusing'.

It did not take Dizzy long to convert the relaxed and cheerful atmosphere between the two of them into something more intimate. During his first premiership, the Queen had sent him flowers. So now, to symbolize their increasingly close relationship, he chose flowers. Not, as one might expect, orchids or lilies, but simple spring flowers: snowdrops and primroses. He assured her that 'of all flowers, the one that retains its beauty longest, sweet primrose . . .' and that he liked primroses 'so much better for being wild'.

Victoria, charmed by such simplicity (as he knew she would be) was quick to enter into the spirit of the thing. Each time she sent him another offering of these artless flowers, she was rewarded with one of his lyrical letters. He would have imagined himself like Proserpine in Hades, he wrote, 'had the gift of primroses from Osborne not reminded him that there might yet be spring and tho' Proserpine be absent there is happily for him a Queen to whom he is devoted at Windsor.'

And he was ready to wax more lyrical still. Before long, his perfervid imagination had converted the dumpy, dowdy and sensible Victoria into something altogether more exotic. He pretended to believe that, like Edmund Spenser's Elizabeth I, she was a Faery Queen. Her flowers now became like 'an offering from the fauns and dryads of the woods of Osborne; and camellias, blooming in the natural air, become your Majesty's Faery Isle.' Primroses meant that 'your Majesty's sceptre has touched the enchanted isle'.

When she sent him snowdrops ('in a delicate-looking case, with a royal superscription') he pinned them on his breast to prove to his beribboned and bemedalled fellow guests at a banquet that he, too, had been decorated by a gracious Sovereign.

'Then, in the middle of the night,' he continued, 'it occurred to him that it might all be enchantment, and that, perhaps, it was a Faery gift and came from another monarch: Queen Titania, gathering flowers, with her Court, in a soft and sea-girt isle, and sending magic blossoms, which, they say, turn the heads of those who receive them.'

Can one wonder that the Queen was captivated?

Disraeli's vow to do whatever the Queen 'wished SHOULD be done' was put to an immediate test. Early in 1874 Archibald Tait, Archbishop of Canterbury, introduced the Public Worship Regulation Act, whereby he hoped to rid the Anglican Church of its Popish practices. The Bill had the Queen's fervent approval. Disraeli was less enthusiastic. Never very interested in Church affairs, he was all for leaving things as they were. In this he came up against the Queen. All a-tremble with indignation, she regaled him with stories about the extreme ritualistic practices of some of the High Church clergy. Did he know about those attending clergymen who, when the bishop accidentally spilt some of the altar wine, flung themselves face down on the floor and licked it up? How could such Romish behaviour be allowed to continue?

Disraeli had his own, somewhat less spectacular experiences of the pull between High and Low. Even at Hughenden Church there were dissensions. 'My friend the vicar will take what I call a collection and he calls an offertory, and it will be placed on what he calls an altar or what his parishoners call a table,' he once sighed.

Although not nearly as disturbed by the whole business as was his royal mistress, Disraeli applied himself to carrying out her wishes: he would shepherd the Bill through Parliament. His interest was aroused only when Gladstone, in a white-hot fury, denounced it. This was something Disraeli understood. In the House, he roundly attacked Gladstone's defence of this 'Mass in masquerade' and into the Queen's ears he whispered the sort of anti-Gladstone propaganda that she was only too ready to believe. 'As a statesman,' reported Dizzy, '[Gladstone] threw off the mask, and the only logical conclusion of his address was the disestablishment of that Church of which Your Majesty is the head.'

The Queen was suitably appalled. Without Mr Disraeli to protect her position as Defender of the Faith, Mr Gladstone would have them all sliding down the slippery slope to Rome. He had already disestablished the Anglican Church in Ireland. Was he indeed planning to do the same thing in England? Could Gladstone, in fact, be a secret Papist? John Brown was certainly ready enough to claim that Gladstone was 'a Roman'.

However, the Bill was passed and the headlong rush to Rome apparently prevented. The Queen was left with a gratifying feeling— fostered by the astute Disraeli—that her personal wishes had been carried out. Had her Prime Minister not assured her that 'the only object of Lord Cairns [the Lord Chancellor] and Mr Disraeli had been to further Your Majesty's wishes in this matter, which will always be with them a paramount object'? In other words, had the Bill not been an expression of her royal will? Had not the Opposition been disloyal— if not exactly treasonable—in challenging it?

The Bill passed, Dizzy hurried down to the Isle of Wight to report to the Queen on her great victory.

'Osborne was lovely, its green shades refreshing after the fervent glare of the voyage, and its blue bay full of white sails,' wrote Dizzy to Lady Bradford. 'The Faery sent for me the instant I arrived. I can only describe my reception by telling you that I really thought that she was going to embrace me.

'She was wreathed in smiles, and as she tattled, glided about the room like a bird. She told me it was "all owing to my courage and tact" and then she said, "To think of you having the gout all the time. How you must have suffered! And you ought not to stand now! You shall have a chair!"

'Only think of that! I remember that *feu* Lord Derby, after one of his severest illnesses, had an audience with Her Majesty, and he mentioned it to me as proof of the Queen's favour that Her Majesty had remarked to him "how sorry she was that she could not ask him to be seated." '

Dizzy did not, in fact, avail himself of the offer to sit (that would come at a later stage of their association) but what a triumph to have been asked.

The following month Disraeli visited Balmoral for the second and last time. Immediately he fell victim to its bracing climate. He caught a chill and had to keep to his bed. No more could he entertain the Queen with what Ponsonby calls his 'sparkling repartee' and the 'pungent and lively little arrows' of his conversation. But the solicitous Victoria visited him in his sickroom where he received her in dressing gown and slippers.

'What,' he asked Lady Bradford, 'do you think of that?'

4

With Disraeli's great programme of social reform—his manifestation of Tory Democracy—Queen Victoria was not deeply involved. She had never really interested herself in the conditions in which so many of her people lived; this was one of her greatest failings. Personally the Queen was kind-hearted, sympathetic, even sentimental, but her social conscience was never strong. She was still inclined to believe that all dissatisfaction was caused by agitators; that left alone, things would somehow work themselves out. When she praised the 'lower classes' so extravagantly, she was thinking of those cap-doffing Highland crofters or those ruddy-cheeked farm labourers rather than of the unhealthy, exploited and badly-housed urban masses.

Although Disraeli himself was hardly more interested in the details of social reform, he presided over the passing of a mass of progressive legislation. In fact, his administration passed more bills to ease the lives of the British working classes than did any other government during Queen Victoria's reign.

What concerned both the Queen and her Prime Minister far more actively was foreign policy. Here were the opportunities for the sort of *grande geste* they both appreciated; here was a field in which Britain could make her presence felt. For too long, reckoned the Queen, had Britain been prepared to 'swallow insults' and play a negative role; while Disraeli was itching for an opportunity to reassert British power in Europe. When it came to the question of enhancing their country's prestige, the hearts of Victoria and Disraeli beat as one.

Although Disraeli would have been happy enough to see British power affirmed in almost any quarter of the globe, it happened to be in what was loosely termed the East—the Balkans, the Levant, India— that he achieved his most spectacular successes. He had always, albeit inaccurately, been associated with the East. His youthful tour of the Middle East, his Jewish blood, his exotic appearance, his flowery speech, his oblique, almost oriental manner—all these tended to link him with those colourful, sun-steeped countries on, and beyond, the fringe of Europe. Whereas, in truth, his knowledge of these areas was of the scrappiest, Disraeli had the air of a man who knew them intimately.

It was by sheer coincidence, then, that one of the great set-pieces of the Victoria–Disraeli partnership should be concerned with the Near East: with that strategic waterway between the Mediterranean and the Red Seas—the Suez Canal.

At that time, in 1875, France had the greatest stake in the Suez Canal. The driving force behind the construction of the Canal had been a Frenchman, Ferdinand de Lesseps; the Canal had been ceremonially opened, in a final burst of Second Empire splendour, by the Empress Eugénie of the French in 1869; most of the shares of the Suez Canal Company were in French hands.

On the other hand, Britain had the greatest interest in the waterway. With this being the shortest route between Britain and India, over three-quarters of the ships using the Suez Canal were British.

Such shares as were not in French hands (some 177,000 out of the total of 400,000; that is, just under half the shares) were held by the debt-ridden Khedive of Egypt. Early in November 1875 the Khedive, finding himself more debt-ridden than ever, decided that he must sell his shares. He opened secret negotiations with two rival French syndicates. News of these negotiations reached the ears of Frederick Greenwood, editor of the *Pall Mall Gazette* and he, anxious to prevent the company from becoming entirely French-owned, urged the British government, in the person of the Foreign Secretary, Lord Derby (son of the late Lord Derby who had thrice been Prime Minister) to buy the shares. Always cautious, Derby hesitated.

But not Disraeli. On hearing the news, his imagination took wing. He was determined that the British government must buy the shares. What a *coup* that would be; what a fillip for British prestige. But there were difficulties. His cabinet was reluctant; one of the French syndicates already had an option; with Parliament not in session, the necessary £4,000,000 could not be voted immediately. Yet he refused to be discouraged. 'Scarcely breathing time!' he scribbled to the hardly less enthusiastic Queen Victoria. 'But the thing must be done.'

And done it was. Exercising, to the full, all his celebrated daring, panache and sense of timing, Dizzy applied himself to the problem. He talked his cabinet round, he informed the Khedive that Britain was willing to buy the shares, he let the French government know that his cabinet would be opposed to the shares falling into French hands. The

French syndicate, discouraged by its government, promptly renounced its option.

One problem remained. The £4,000,000 had to be found immediately. For this, too, Disraeli had a solution. During a cabinet meeting on the issue, he posted his secretary, Montagu Corry, outside the door. As soon as the cabinet had come to its decision, Dizzy put his head round the door and said one word: 'Yes'. Within ten minutes Corry was at New Court, being ushered into the presence of Baron Lionel de Rothschild. Rothschild was at table, eating muscatel grapes.

Corry told him that Disraeli needed four million pounds.

'When?' asked Rothschild.

'Tomorrow,' answered Corry.

Rothschild ate a grape and spat out the skin.

'What is your security?' he asked.

'The British Government,' said Corry.

'You shall have it.'

So Rothschild lent the money and Britain bought the Khedive's shares.

Disraeli was ecstatic. The thing accomplished, his first thought was of the Queen. 'It is just settled;' he wrote triumphantly on 24 November, 'you have it, Madam.' He promised to tell her, at the earliest opportunity, 'the whole wondrous tale' of the acquiring of the shares.

Like some exotic gift, the Suez Canal was being laid at the feet of the Faery Queen.

Whether the two of them actually believed this, one does not know. The truth was that not only was Disraeli in no position to present the Canal to Queen Victoria, he had not even acquired a controlling interest in it. The Khedive had held less than half the total shares. But what Dizzy had done was to prevent the Canal from becoming entirely French-owned and this was no mean achievement. Yet when the more prosaic Lord Derby made a speech to that effect—claiming that the government had merely acted to prevent the Canal from coming under the exclusive control of French shareholders—Victoria was incensed. Lord Derby was simply trying to pour cold water on Mr Disraeli's great triumph, she grumbled. The buying of the shares had been 'an immense thing'.

To Theodore Martin, then busy on the second volume of his monumental *Life of the Prince Consort*, the Queen declared that the Suez Canal *coup* was '*entirely* the doing of Mr Disraeli, who has *very large ideas* and *very lofty views* of the position the country should hold. His mind is so much greater, larger and his apprehension of things great and small so much quicker than that of Mr Gladstone.'

And when she saw Mr Disraeli in person she was, he reported, 'in ecstasies about "this great and important event".' She received him immediately; she was all smiles and coquetries; she swore that she had never seen him looking so well; she showed him all her telegrams of congratulation. Would he write in answer to the Prince of Wales's telegram? Bertie was so fond of him. At dinner that night, the Queen was in 'the tenth Heaven'—amusing, interesting, excited. 'Nothing could be more successful—I might say triumphant—than my visit,' he boasted.

Whatever others might say, Victoria and Disraeli were happy enough with the myth that a loyal Disraeli had presented his Sovereign with this great waterway linking Britain to India, the Mother Country to its Empire, West to East. And the majority of Her Majesty's subjects were no less happy to believe it. It was the sort of fanfare to set one's pulses pounding. It was spectacular proof of Britain's greatness.

Chapter Fifteen

I

For some years now the great sub-continent of India had been exerting an increasing fascination on the mind of Queen Victoria. Of all Britain's possessions across the seas, India was the most colourful, the most mysterious, the most exciting. Where the inhabitants of those other large British territories such as Canada, Australia and New Zealand were Englishmen enjoying a certain measure of self-government, the Indians were a subject people, belonging, as the Queen was apt to put it, 'to me'. More so than with any of the other colonies, the Queen felt personally associated with India; she regarded herself as being directly responsible for 'that enormous Empire which is so bright a jewel in her Crown'.

Disraeli shared her views. The thought of India, with its clamorous cities, its exotic peoples and its fabulously rich princes had always excited him. No less than the Queen did he regard this crowded sub-continent as the monarch's personal domain; the more British rule could be personified by the Sovereign, the better. The India Bill of 1858, whereby the British Crown had taken over the administration of India from the East India Company, had been described by Disraeli to the Queen as the mere 'ante-chamber to an imperial palace'. Surely the time had come for the entering of the imperial palace itself.

The first step was taken by the Prince of Wales. By the beginning of the year 1875 the thirty-three-year-old Bertie had decided that he wanted to tour India. The visit would kill several birds. The presence of the heir to the throne would more effectively symbolize the Crown than could any government official; the journey would afford a diversion for his notoriously restless nature; and, as he planned to travel without his wife, the lovely Princess Alexandra, Bertie would be given the opportunity for a few amatory escapades.

As the last two reasons were hardly likely to carry much weight with the Queen (and, in any case, Victoria's instincts were never to allow Bertie to do anything that he wanted to do) the Prince decided that he must first win Disraeli's support for the project. This the Prime Minister was only too ready to give. Unlike Gladstone, Dizzy was quick to appreciate that India was far more likely to appeal to the Prince's opulent tastes than was Ireland. A royal tour of India was exactly the sort of imperial gesture that Disraeli might have thought up himself. So, addressing Bertie as 'Sir, and dear Prince' on paper and, equally effectively, as 'young Hal' behind his back (and who could have looked more like a young Henry VIII?) Disraeli gave the plan his sanction. Using this, Bertie badgered his mother into agreeing to it.

But Victoria was far from happy about the project. It needed all Dizzy's celebrated tact to prevent her from changing her mind. Promising to undertake the entire management of the affair, he did his best to still the Queen's apprehensions. Where Gladstone would have presented her with a twenty-page memorandum of reasons for the desirability of the Prince's tour, Disraeli mentioned it as little as possible. Indeed, when he wrote to her on her fifty-sixth birthday that May, he mentioned the tour not at all; 'you live in the hearts and thoughts of many millions,' read the deft congratulatory phrases, 'though in none more deeply and more fervently than in the heart of him who, with humble duty, pens these spontaneous lines.'

How, in the face of such delectable language, could one fuss about Bertie's forthcoming journey?

But fuss she did. One aspect of the tour that particularly alarmed the Queen was that Princess Alexandra had announced her intention of accompanying her husband. 'The Wife,' as Dizzy reported to Lord Salisbury, 'insists upon going! When reminded of her children, she says "the husband has first claim".'

But whatever the Wife might say, the Mother was having none of it. Nothing, reported Disraeli, would induce the Queen to consent to the Princess's plan. Thwarted, Alexandra appealed to Disraeli. There was little he could do. He realized that the Prince of Wales was every bit as adamant about his wife not accompanying him as was the Queen. To the petulant Alexandra Bertie explained that it was difficult for ladies to travel about India; and indeed, the presence of the Princess of Wales would cause problems of protocol at the various Indian courts. But Lord Derby touched the heart of the matter when he claimed that 'Hal is sure to get into scrapes with women whether she goes or not, and they will be considered more excusable in her absence. . . .'

The Princess of Wales never ceased to regret that she had not been allowed to visit India. Forty years later she was still claiming that the one wish of her life had been to see 'that *wonderful*, beautiful country!'

Then, the question of finance worried the Queen. 'A Prince of Wales must not move in India in a *mesquin* manner,' she told Disraeli. 'Everything must be done on an imperial scale.' She, however, was not prepared to pay a penny towards it. So Disraeli was obliged to ask a far from sympathetic House of Commons for £112,000. This was granted, and to it was added £100,000 by the Indian government. Yet the Prince felt that he had been meanly treated. How, on this pittance, could he hope to match the gifts that would be given to him by the wealthy maharajahs? The long-suffering Dizzy was invited to Sandringham to listen to Young Hal's complaints about the parsimony of Parliament.

The Queen was perturbed too, about her son's proposed suite. To the indignation of the Prince (he 'manifested extraordinary excitement,' reported Dizzy) the Queen insisted that Disraeli submit all arrangements to her for approval before he discussed them with her son. There seemed, she said, to be a woeful lack of 'eminent men' and an alarming number of the 'fast set' among the Prince's travelling companions. On this occasion, however, Dizzy advised the Queen to give way. He undertook to warn those two arch practical jokers, Lord Carrington and Lord Charles Beresford, against any larking.

Finally, in October 1875, the Prince of Wales got away. Despite all Victoria's apprehensions (which took the form of advice, often by telegram *en clair*, for Bertie to be careful of what he ate and for him to be in bed by ten when possible) the tour was a great success. The Prince shot a prodigious amount of game, he delighted everyone with his particular blend of geniality and dignity, he carried out numberless public engagements with great gusto. To his mother, who passed on the information to Disraeli, he complained about the cavalier manner in which the British officials in India treated the princes and chiefs. Whatever his failings, the Prince of Wales was relatively free of religious, racial and social bigotry.

If the Prince was impressed by India—by the teeming game, the gorgeously uniformed troops, the berobed and bejewelled potentates, the unbelievably rich maharajahs—India was no less impressed by him. He was rightly regarded, not as a representative of the British government, but as a symbol of the Monarchy: his presence suggested that the Queen was as much the Sovereign of India—and not merely of India's conquerors—as she was of Great Britain.

Driving through the crowded streets of Bombay on his birthday, the Prince was greeted by a variety of illuminated signs, ranging from a cheerful 'Tell Mamma we're happy' to one that struck a particularly significant note. 'Welcome to our Future Emperor' it read.

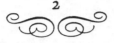

A point on which Queen Victoria was becoming increasingly touchy was whether a queen was equal to an empress. At one moment she would be dismissing as ridiculous the notion that a queen was somehow inferior to an empress; at another she would be wondering if it were not time that she herself became an empress. An undeniable fact was that all the leading monarchies of Europe—Russia, Germany and Austria—were empires and that, until the declaration of a republic, France had been an empire. And one had to admit that Empress *sounded* more impressive than Queen.

In recent years, Victoria had twice had occasion to feel indignation over this question of the relative importance of royal titles. The inauguration of the German Empire in 1871 had meant, not only that the Queen's daughter Vicky would one day be an empress, but that Vicky's father-in-law, the new German Emperor, Kaiser Wilhelm I, took it for granted that his heir was now superior to Queen Victoria's heir. This was something which the Queen was not prepared to stomach.

Then, in 1873, the Queen's second son, Prince Alfred, Duke of Edinburgh, became engaged to the Grand Duchess Marie Alexandrovna, daughter of Tsar Alexander II of Russia. This bizarre alliance caused endless ill feeling. More even, than Kaiser Wilhelm I, did Tsar Alexander II feel that an emperor was superior to a king; a grand duchess superior to a duchess. While the Tsar insisted that his daughter be called Imperial, 'as in all civilized countries', Victoria raged against these '*Asiatic ideas of their Rank*'.

Nor did the Tsar see any reason why his daughter should present herself at Balmoral for the Queen's customary inspection before the marriage. Why, suggested the Russian Empress, could Queen Victoria not cross to Cologne to meet the future bride? When the Queen's daughter, Princess Alice, wrote in support of this suggestion, Victoria exploded.

'I do *not* think, dear Child, that *you* should tell *me* who have been nearly 20 *years longer* on the throne than the Emperor of Russia and am the Doyenne of Sovereigns and who am a *Reigning* Sovereign which the Empress is *not—what I ought to do. I* think *I* know *that.* The proposal received on *Wednesday* for me to be *at Cologne . . .* tomorrow, was one of the *coolest* things *I* ever heard. . . . I *own everyone* was shocked.'

And once the marriage had taken place, the problems of protocol remained. Should the Duchess of Edinburgh be called Royal *and* Imperial and, if so, which took precedence? Did the title of Grand Duchess, or of Duchess of Edinburgh, come first? And was a Russian Grand Duchess more, or less, important than Queen Victoria's daughters?

Quite obviously, there was only one solution to these vexing questions. The Queen must become an Empress. 'The Empress-Queen,' said Disraeli to one of his cabinet colleagues at the beginning of 1876, 'demands her Imperial Crown.' She wanted to become Empress of India. And it fell, of course, to Disraeli to see that her royal wish was granted. The second great set-piece of the Victoria–Disraeli partnership was about to be assembled.

3

Although Disraeli was all in favour of the Queen assuming the title of Empress, he did not really consider the time opportune. He was not feeling particularly well and the parliamentary session was proving to be a difficult one. But, as had been the case with the Public Worship Regulation Bill, he allowed the Queen's wishes to override his.

There were, in fact, sound political reasons for the introduction of the Royal Titles Bill. It was not all a matter of personal, or even national, vanity. The title would give an air of stability and permanence to British rule in India. A British Empress of India would make the Russian Emperor think twice before advancing any more deeply into Asia. Not only in the drawing room, but across the North-West

Frontier, could Queen Victoria face Tsar Alexander II as an equal. The Prince of Wales's tour had struck the first blow for British prestige in India; the Queen's assumption of the title of Empress would strike the second.

But not everyone was so convinced of the sweet reasonableness of the argument. Much to the Queen's astonishment (and despite the fact that Disraeli had prevailed upon her to open Parliament in person) the Royal Titles Bill had an extremely choppy passage. Professing herself 'shocked and surprised', Victoria dismissed the opposition as 'a *mere* attempt to injure Mr Disraeli but which is most disrespectful and indecorous.' For his part, Mr Disraeli regarded the piloting of the Bill through the House as an exposure of weeks to a fiery furnace.

But the Bill was passed. On 1 May 1876 Victoria was declared Queen-Empress. She was highly delighted. Blithely ignoring the fact that she was Imperial only as far as India was concerned, the Queen signed herself 'V.R. & I.' on every possible occasion. Disraeli was rewarded with a vast portrait of herself: a copy of a painting by Joachim von Angeli. 'Now,' she said one day to Dizzy after their usual audience, 'I will show you your picture.' She led him into an adjoining room. 'There it stood,' he reported to Lady Bradford, 'not quite a full length, but a very large picture in a gorgeous frame with, I suppose, the Crown of an Empress at the top.'

Having admired the somewhat stony-faced but undeniably imperial likeness of his royal mistress, Dizzy fell to one knee.

'I think I may claim, Madam, the privilege of gratitude,' he breathed. 'She gave me her hand to kiss which I did three times very rapidly,' he said, 'and she actually gave me a squeeze.'

However gratifying these imperial triumphs, Disraeli's exposure to the fiery furnace had not left him unscathed. By the end of that parliamentary session, he felt that he could simply not face another. He was not well enough for the continued hurly-burly of the House of Commons. Either he must resign, or continue his premiership from the House of Lords. The Queen, quite naturally, would not hear of his resigning. Nor, one suspects, did he ever seriously think of doing so. There was only one course of action: Disraeli must be elevated to the peerage.

So elevated to the peerage he was. His obliging monarch created him Earl of Beaconsfield. (Dizzy always pronounced the name Beaconsfield as it was spelt: it was the field of the beacon, he would maintain, not a beckoning field.) On 11 August 1876 Disraeli made his last speech in the House of Commons. From then on he ran his government from the relative tranquillity of the House of Lords.

It was as the Earl of Beaconsfield then, that Dizzy gave his blessing to the events marking Victoria's proclamation as Empress of India.

At noon on 1 January 1877, at a Durbar on the great Plain of Delhi, Victoria was officially proclaimed Empress of India by the Viceroy, Lord Lytton. It was an occasion of considerable splendour. In a five-hundred-and-forty-word telegram, the Viceroy regaled the Queen with the day's multiple glories: the blazing sunshine, the gorgeousness of the potentates, the magnificence of the Indian army, the pomp of the ceremonial, the eloquence of the addresses, the apparently unfeigned joy and gratitude of the Queen's Indian subjects as they hailed the *Shah-in-Shah Padshah*—the Monarch of Monarchs.

'The Viceroy of India lays his humble congratulations at the feet of her Majesty,' ran Lord Lytton's orotund phrases, 'and earnestly prays that the Queen's loyal subjects, allies and feudatories of this country, may be to the Empress of India a New Year's Gift of inestimable value in return for the honour which she has conferred today upon this great dependency of the Crown.'

Only Disraeli could outdo such magniloquence and, of course, he did. That night, at a sumptuous banquet at Windsor, while the Queen sat—plump, imperious and all a-dazzle in her Indian jewellery—the newly ennobled Earl of Beaconsfield made a speech so florid that it could have come straight out of the pages of one of his novels. It brought even the Queen to her feet. After he had cried out 'Your Imperial Majesty' and the toast had been drunk, the new Empress of India astounded the company by rising to her feet and half-curtseying to her Prime Minister.

They both had reason to be pleased: he had made her an Empress and she had made him an Earl.

Chapter Sixteen

I

What was it exactly, that was making the partnership between Victoria and Disraeli so successful?

Those who saw the association purely in terms of a wily and accomplished old seducer buttering up a plain and susceptible widow were entirely misjudging the situation. It was true that Disraeli, on his own admission, believed that one could never flatter royalty too much and that Victoria's household claimed that he had 'got the length of her foot exactly', but there was much more to it than this. The situation was not all one-sided: Disraeli was no less drawn to the Queen than she was to him.

For them both, the paths of their past lives had converged at exactly the correct moment: circumstances, both emotional and political, were just right for the flowering of their extraordinary relationship.

'I am fortunate in serving a female sovereign,' said Disraeli. 'I owe everything to women; and if in the sunset of life I have still a young heart, it is due to that influence.' And not only was Dizzy serving a female sovereign but, more important, he was serving a middle-aged female sovereign. His taste had always been for dowagers rather than debutantes; his women friends, as the Russian Ambassador remarked, were 'toutes grand'mères'. How much more rewarding then, to be dealing with the greatest grandmother of them all. Here, surely, was the culmination of a life-time's association with matrons. Here was the mother-figure to end all mother-figures.

With so much experience behind him, it is not surprising that Disraeli knew exactly how to handle the Queen. Employing a shade more courtesy and a shade more deference, he treated her as he had treated all his women, whether they be wife, mistress or friend: gently, gallantly and above all, romantically. He had long ago realized that the Queen would respond to a personal approach: that he must cut through the splendour of her position and the stiffness of her bearing.

In short, he must treat her as a human being. More even than most monarchs, Queen Victoria needed someone with whom she could let herself go, and Dizzy had been quick to sense this. He knew that that dour expression and that imperious manner marked a shy, warm, indeed ardent temperament; that if treated with tact and affection, her reserve would melt.

And so, skilfully and consciously, Dizzy had set out to woo her—just as surely as he had wooed any of that long procession of wives and widows and dowagers. It might have been the most discreet, respectful and innocent of courtships but it was a courtship none the less.

Conscious as all this might have been on Dizzy's part, it was not entirely calculated and certainly not unscrupulous. This was the way he had always behaved. A born romantic, a natural gallant, he had quite easily embarked on his decorous flirtation with the Queen; it would not have occurred to him to approach her in any other fashion. With him, dalliance was second nature. The death of Mary Anne, which had undoubtedly left a void in his life, had none the less allowed him to carry his flirtation rather further than he might otherwise have done. And although, during much of this period, he was besotted by Lady Bradford, there were times when he actually imagined himself in love with Queen Victoria.

He certainly never minded encouraging the impression that the Queen was a little in love with him. Any suggestion that she might be jealous of his attentions to other women, he would pass on with great delight. When the Empress Augusta, wife of Kaiser Wilhelm I, spent a few days at Windsor in the spring of 1876, Disraeli was in his element. The old German Empress, with her brightly enamelled face, her skittish clothes, her vivacious manner (she looked not unlike the late Mary Anne), and her intellectual pretensions, could hardly have been in greater contrast to the English Queen. 'The two Empresses sate next to each other at dinner . . .' he reported gleefully to Lady Bradford. 'Carnarvon sate next to the Empress of Germany, and I sate next to the Empress of India. The conversation of the *partie carrée* was good: animated and natural—but whenever Augoosta had got involved in some metaphysical speculations with Carnarvon, the Faery took refuge in confidential whispers in which she indulged in the freest remarks on men and things. . . . After dinner I was attached to Augoosta who threw out all her resources, philosophical, poetic, political—till the Faery was a little jeal, for she had originally told Lady Ely that some one "was not to make his pretty speeches to

Augoosta, who only wanted to *draw him to her*!!!!" However, all went off very well, and the Faery made a happy dart and had the last word.'

Yet however flirtatious or seemingly irreverent Disraeli's behaviour might be, he never forgot that Victoria was the Queen of England. In truth, that remained her chief attraction. Cynical in so much else, Disraeli, in his attitude towards the throne, remained positively sentimental. He revered the Monarchy. And the fact that his monarch was a queen rather than a king brought all this royalist reverence into full play. A queen on the throne fired his imagination as no king could ever have done. Parchment-skinned and stiff-kneed he might be but, in his incurably romantic way, Disney saw himself as a knight, a liege-man, a loyal servant of his royal mistress. He liked to inform the House that he stood there 'by favour of the Queen'; he liked to pretend that he might lose his head at her command. He made a dull debate, says Philip Guedalla, 'sound like a tournament reported to the Queen of Beauty by her Unknown Knight'.

It was, claims one of Dizzy's biographers, 'after the romantic fashion of Raleigh's service to Queen Elizabeth that Disraeli conceived of his own service to Queen Victoria'. Once, on thanking her for a gift of pink may from Windsor, Dizzy wrote, 'It was a gift worthy of Queen Elizabeth, and of an age when great affairs and romance were not incompatible.'

For in Dizzy's imagination, this plump, homely, middle-aged constitutional monarch was transformed into a second Queen Elizabeth, a second Catherine the Great. In his eyes, and hers, she became the embodiment of Great Britain. Not only was he reviving her interest in the business of monarchy but he was making her more conscious of the importance of her position. He saw her, and encouraged her to think of herself, in her historical perspective: not merely as the ceremonial head of a self-governing nation, but as the latest in a glorious line of British monarchs; as the heir to King Alfred, William the Conqueror, the Plantagenets, the Tudors and the Stuarts.

He saw himself, and encouraged her to think of him, as the servant of the Crown rather than as the servant of the people. It could almost be said that he regarded the government of the country as a partnership between the Sovereign and her Prime Minister; a partnership to which they could each bring their vast store of knowledge and experience. Not only did he keep her fully informed on what was going on but he was forever asking for her opinion and advice. Never before had she felt so involved in the day-to-day workings of the government; never before had she considered herself to be so indispensable, so important, so powerful.

Disraeli was re-creating, or had led her to believe that he was re-creating, what he called 'a real Throne'.

2

And what, on the other hand, was it that attracted the Queen, so irresistibly, to Disraeli? The truth was that just as she fitted the mould of his previous women friends, so did he seem to typify the sort of man to whom she was always attracted. Dizzy might no longer be handsome but he had remnants of the looks to which she always responded: he was *outré*, mysterious, poetic. Exotics, such as he, had always exercised a strong fascination on her. In both appearance and manner he was an amalgam of all those men with whom she had been closely involved. He had the sagacity of King Leopold, the urbanity of Lord Melbourne, the gentleness of Prince Albert, the flamboyance of Napoleon III. He was part-mentor, part-lover. Only the more stalwart qualities of John Brown were missing, but then John Brown was on hand.

Indeed, John Brown and Disraeli together gave the Queen all the support and attention she craved. What one lacked, the other supplied. Where Brown made her feel like a helpless 'wumman', relying on him for protection, Dizzy made her feel like some desirable and almost mythical creature—an undoubted queen. If Brown supplied the reassurance, Dizzy supplied the romance. In the presence of either of them, she felt cherished.

No wonder that Queen Victoria found this period so blissful. It was like a more extended version of that other supremely exciting time, when she could flirt with the fascinating Napoleon III while remaining Prince Albert's '*Fräuchen*'.

Between them, Dizzy and Brown coaxed Victoria out of her long period of mourning. Her renaissance dates from this time when both men, in their very different ways, were paying her court. If she did not actually forget Prince Albert, she certainly spent less time thinking about him. This state was arrived at, however, only after considerable heartsearching. At first, she had felt distinctly guilty about the lessening of her grief. Dean Wellesley had been obliged to assure her that a more cheerful—or, at least, less doleful—frame of mind was nothing to be ashamed of. If God, in His wisdom, saw fit to provide her with comforting friends, she should accept them without question. She herself claimed that if one's husband were dead and one's children grown up, one had need of a devoted and sympathetic friend.

And now she had two. Gradually, in their reassuring company, her health improved, her interest was reawakened, her vitality revived. No one, seeing the Queen dancing with Brown at a gillies' ball at Balmoral or bantering with Disraeli in her tent at Osborne, could reconcile her with the grief-stricken Queen of popular imagination. In any case, to some, her unremitting stream of complaints had long since become suspect. Henry Ponsonby, in describing Disraeli's handling of her, claimed that 'his sympathy is expressed while his tongue is in his cheek—but are not her woes told in the same manner?'

An additional attraction as far as Victoria was concerned was the fact that Disraeli had also lost his life's partner. Here was a bond indeed. 'The Queen,' she had written on the death of Mary Anne, 'knows also *what* Mr Disraeli has lost and what he must suffer.' And Dizzy confessed to Lady Bradford that 'It is strange that I always used to think that the Queen, persisting in these emblems of woe, indulged in morbid sentiment, and yet it has become my lot, and seemingly an irresistible one.' Neither of them, of course, were anything like as grief-stricken as they pretended, but their respective losses brought them even closer, and that was comforting.

Politically, Disraeli could not have come to her at a more opportune time. After Gladstone, almost anyone would have been welcome but by now Victoria's views were in full accord with Disraeli's. Prince Albert's lessons in liberalism had served their day; the conservative creed of her new, and infinitely more entertaining teacher, was what she now wanted to hear. During Disraeli's term of office, their ideas became ever more closely interwoven; he had brought to her what she was coming, more and more, to value: his high regard for the monarchy, his faith in the working together of the aristocracy, the squirearchy and the lower classes, his belief in a strong foreign policy, and his dreams of imperial grandeur.

And he had brought something more. He had brought to her that element of glamour, of colour and of fantasy which always struck a chord in her passionate nature. More than any man she had ever known, Disraeli had the ability to kindle her imagination. Never before had Queen Victoria's innate romanticism been brought to such full flower. The outrageous flattery, the decorous flirtation, the make-believe of the Faery Queen, the gifts of primroses and snowdrops and violets, the entire magical, serio-comic plane on which the two of them moved, aroused an undercurrent of excitement in the normally sensible Queen. If it was not exactly love, it was something very like it.

In February each year, Victoria and Disraeli exchanged valentines. Here was yet another opportunity for some deliciously titillating flirtation. 'He wishes he could repose on a sunny bank, like young Valentine in the pretty picture that fell from a rosy cloud this morn,' wrote Dizzy on receiving Victoria's latest card, 'but the reverie of the happy youth would be rather different from his. Valentine would dream of the future, and youthful loves, and all under the inspiration of a beautiful clime! Lord Beaconsfield, no longer in the sunset, but the twilight of existence, must encounter a life of anxiety and toil; but this too, has its romance, when he remembers that he labours for the most gracious of beings!'

Years later, when Queen Victoria was a very old lady, she told Lord Rosebery that Disraeli had once sent her, without any inscription, a little box: 'on one side was a heart transfixed by an arrow, and on the other the word *Fideliter*.' Had that not been, asked her Majesty, 'touching'?

3

To set a public seal, as it were, on this close friendship between them, Queen Victoria decided to visit Disraeli at Hughenden. For the Queen, who rarely paid visits, this was a significant gesture indeed. Not since she had visited the adored Lord Melbourne at Brocket, over thirty-five years before, had Victoria shown any Prime Minister so signal a mark of royal favour.

The thing was more easily decided than done. After protracted negotiations it was arranged that the Queen and Princess Beatrice, attended by only one lady and one gentleman, would lunch at Hughenden on 15 December 1877. Too late for change did Victoria realize that the date was the anniversary of Mary Anne's death. At first, the Queen had considered driving from Windsor to Hughenden (when Dizzy told her that the drive took two hours, she answered that she could do it in an hour and half with *her* horses) but in the end she went by train. The royal party arrived, at High Wycombe station, at a quarter past one that Saturday afternoon.

Despite ill-natured remarks by Dizzy's political opponents of the Queen 'going ostentatiously to eat with Disraeli in his ghetto', the visit was a great success. 'It was a fine day, and with some gleams of sunshine,' wrote Disraeli. 'The Faery seemed to admire, and to be interested in, everything.' A welcoming arch, spanning the High Street of High Wycombe, and composed entirely of chairs, she pronounced as being 'very curious'. She admired Dizzy's 'pretty Italian garden'; she and Beatrice each planted another tree in Hughenden's already heavily wooded park. To Princess Beatrice, Dizzy presented 'the most beautiful bonbonnière you ever saw or fancied—just fresh from Paris.' He showed the Queen his famous portrait gallery of his friends and a 'very fine head of Lord Byron' whom, he assured the Queen with something less than accuracy, he had once known. Victoria, with her daughter and lady-in-waiting, lunched with Disraeli in one room; her equerry and Montagu Corry in another. At half past three, carrying off her host's Trentanova statuette as a souvenir, the Queen took her leave.

'Your Majesty left a dream of dignified condescension and ever-graceful charm,' wrote Disraeli to her afterwards.

All this intimacy between Sovereign and Prime Minister might have been overlooked had there not been a strong suspicion that there was something unconstitutional about it all. Not only did they spend hours closeted together but they even wrote directly to each other, without using the customary third person and without the knowledge of the Queen's private secretary. 'She is always at him,' grumbled Ponsonby, 'about something that we know nothing of.'

Was the Queen bringing too much influence to bear on Disraeli; or was he bringing too much to bear on her? Were they working too closely together? Was he perhaps encouraging her to be something more than a constitutional monarch? Surely all his flowery talk of her being the 'Directress' and 'Arbitress' of Europe was not only foolish but dangerous? 'Is there not just a risk,' asked Derby of Disraeli, 'of encouraging her in too large ideas of her personal power, and too great indifference of what the public expects?'

There was certainly a risk, but Disraeli was prepared to take it. Provided, that is, that the Queen was in accord with his ideas. He neither hesitated to encourage her authoritarianism nor to use her name to further his schemes. In her mind, Disraeli's policy became 'our' policy; and our policy, in turn became the 'imperial policy of England'. Any criticism of Disraeli's actions was to her a criticism of the Crown. For a constitutional monarch, this was a perilous path to be treading.

But it worked both ways. The Queen was no more Disraeli's cat's paw than he was hers. On more than one occasion he gave in to her wishes. When his colleagues muttered darkly against the pressure of 'the Court' or 'Balmoral', they were muttering against the Queen. Ponsonby even went so far as to report that Disraeli was 'a perfect slave to the Queen'. And Dizzy was once forced to remind Victoria that he was not her 'Grand Vizier'.

At no time was this personal and political co-operation between the two of them closer than during the flare-up, in the second half of the 1870s, of the ever-festering Eastern Question.

Chapter Seventeen

I

'I really believe,' wrote Dizzy to Lady Bradford in November 1875, ' "the Eastern Question", that has haunted Europe for a century and which I thought the Crimean War had adjourned for half another, will fall to my lot to encounter—dare I say to settle.'

Boiled down to its simplest, the complicated Eastern Question was the rivalry between Britain and Russia over the body of the 'Sick Man of Europe'—Turkey. Russia was anxious to see the sprawling Turkish Sultanate dismantled; Britain was determined to keep it shored up. Both Great Powers were motivated by self-interest, pure and simple. That Turkish rule over its European subjects—many of whom were Christian—was barbaric, corrupt and incompetent did not particularly bother either of the Great Powers. Russia saw a disintegrating Turkey as a happy hunting ground for territorial expansion; Britain saw a Turkey intact as a safeguard against Russian designs on India. In somewhat myopic British eyes, Constantinople was the 'Key to India'. For year after year it was stoutly, if mistakenly, maintained that to surrender to the Russians one inch of Turkish territory would be to jeopardize both the land and sea routes to India. To see the Russians in Constantinople was almost to see them in Calcutta.

With this exaggerated view of the situation both Victoria and Disraeli were in agreement. The Queen had always distrusted Russia; Disraeli, with his decidedly shaky geographical knowledge, never really appreciated the vastness of the distance between the Black and Red Seas. Moreover, he had no sympathy with the nationalism of those Slavs trying to free themselves of the Turkish yoke. Nationalists were generally radicals, and radicals he distrusted.

So when in the summer of 1875 rebellion broke out and spread through Turkey's European provinces, neither the Queen nor Disraeli were inclined to view the uprisings with much sympathy. On Russia threatening to intervene on behalf of the Christian Slavs against the infidel Turks, they became less sympathetic still. Nor, when rumours of unspeakable Turkish atrocities against their rebellious Bulgarian subjects began to filter through to England, did Disraeli take much notice. Airily, he dismissed the rumours as 'coffee-house babble'. Even the Queen, who treated the atrocity stories more seriously, claimed that it was the Russians who were to blame: by *instigating* the insurrection, they had *caused* the cruel Turkish retaliation.

Both were reckoning without Gladstone. He was taking the atrocity stories very seriously indeed. In September 1876 he published his famous pamphlet: *The Bulgarian Horrors and the Question of the East.* Let the Turks, ran his impassioned phrases, 'one and all, bag and baggage . . . clear out from the province they have desolated and profaned.' The pamphlet caused an extraordinary sensation. Within a month, over 200,000 copies had been sold and crowds were streaming to mass rallies to hear an indignant Gladstone thundering out against the infamy of the Turks.

With the publication of this inflammatory pamphlet, it became war to the death between Disraeli and Gladstone. The more a somewhat uneasy Disraeli pooh-poohed the atrocities, the more a righteously outraged Gladstone deplored them. Nor was the battle confined to the two statesmen. Almost the entire British population split into two warring factions: the 'Turks' against the 'Russians'.

The Queen, during the opening stages of this Balkan flare-up, had not been actively pro-Turk; it was only after Gladstone's denunciation of them that she took so violently anti-Russian a stand. She was able to convince herself, not only that the Russians had incited their fellow Slavs to revolt but that Gladstone had encouraged the Russians. It was the dreadful Gladstone who was to blame for everything. With each passing day the Queen's tirades against Gladstone became more and more shrill. From being merely tiresome and obstinate, he became a 'mischief-maker', a 'fire-brand', a 'half-madman'. His conduct was mischievous, shameful, unjustifiable, disgraceful. Her hatred of him became almost pathological.

Her attitude suited Disraeli perfectly. Indeed, many believed that it was he who not only encouraged, but instigated the Queen's near-hysterical loathing of Gladstone. Knowing how his Sovereign always saw politics in terms of personalities, Disraeli had every reason to stimulate her antipathy towards his great rival. The more she hated Gladstone, the more readily she would support Disraeli's anti-Russian policies. And although it is true that Victoria needed very little prompting in her detestation of Gladstone's personality and politics, it is not improbable that Disraeli deepened her loathing by enlightening her on one aspect of Gladstone's life which she would not, in the ordinary way, have come to hear about. This was his bizarre sex life.

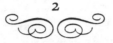

2

Even in his late sixties Gladstone remained a robust, energetic, full-blooded man. By nature impetuous and passionate, he had all his life exercised an iron self-control. In this he was helped by two things: his exceptional strength of character and his unquestioning belief in God. All instincts towards self-gratification had to be repressed, he maintained; humility and self-mortification must be the ideal.

To few aspects of his life did Gladstone apply this belief more rigorously than to his sex life. Faced with a sexual drive no less vigorous than his other drives, he did his utmost to sublimate it. In the main, this sublimation took the form of a lone campaign against prostitution: throughout his long life, Gladstone set himself the task of rescuing and reforming prostitutes.

There was no shortage of possible candidates. The field in which he so zealously carried out his self-imposed mission—an area bounded by Soho, Piccadilly and the Thames Embankment—was swarming with street-walkers. Late at night, armed with a stick for protection, Gladstone would roam the gas-lit pavements. Sometimes waiting to be accosted, sometimes making the first advance himself, sometimes even going into the brothels, he would endeavour to talk the women into giving up their way of life. He might offer to take them home for a meal, he might give them gifts of money, he might send them to some institution for 'fallen women'. Not only did he make generous contributions to rescue homes but he was instrumental in founding several of these institutions.

Inevitably, his strange behaviour led to gossip. From time to time he was seen in conversation with a prostitute, or entering a brothel, and on one occasion an attempt was made to blackmail him. Few men— the police among them—could believe that his interest was purely philanthropic. Occasionally his parliamentary colleagues would warn him of the dangers, both to his career and to his Party, but Gladstone refused to listen. So candid, so innocent, so honest seemed his reaction to these warnings, that his friends could not believe that his behaviour was inspired by anything other than the highest motives.

And so it may have been, but in not quite the way that they imagined. For Gladstone took his determination to be humbled and mortified very far indeed. To control his sexual torment, to master temptation, he is said to have read pornography and to have resorted to what he himself called 'strange and humbling acts' with the prostitutes whom he visited. And if he felt that his mortification at the hands of these women had not been severe enough, then, on reaching home, he would flagellate himself.

'Has it been sufficiently considered how far pain may become a ground of enjoyment?' confided Gladstone to his diary. 'How far satisfaction and even an action of delighting in pain may be a true experimental phenomenon of the human mind?'

Such admissions were for his eyes only and it is unlikely that anyone else would have guessed the lengths to which Gladstone was prepared to go in search of this pleasurable humiliation. But enough was known of his strange habits to cause not only misgivings, but deep distrust.

This would certainly have been Queen Victoria's reaction. Did Disraeli tell her about Gladstone and the prostitutes? A. C. Benson, the son of the Archbishop of Canterbury from 1882 to 1896, claimed that he did, while Gladstone himself was certain that the Queen's hostility was due to her having heard, and misconstrued, these stories. Viscount Gladstone, the Grand Old Man's son, always maintained—somewhat inaccurately—that it was only in the year 1876 that Queen Victoria turned against his father and that it was Disraeli's malicious gossip that had so turned her.

In fact, on Gladstone's own admission, the Queen had exercised her 'repellent power' on him long before Disraeli's present term of office, but it is not unlikely that these rumours put the seal on her distaste for Gladstone.

To Victoria, as to most Victorians, sexual morality was regarded as one of the most important moralities. One can well imagine with what moues of shocked disapproval she would have listened to Dizzy's tactfully worded revelations as the two of them sat, heads together, in her opulent drawing room. And not only would she have listened with disapproval, but with indignation. What right, she could have demanded, had this man who consorted with prostitutes—for whatever reason—to mount a fervent moral crusade against the Bulgarian atrocities? How dare he be so self-righteous? Both Victoria and Disraeli had always considered Gladstone to be a smug and sanctimonious old hypocrite; now, with him spending his days in denouncing the Turks and his nights in converse with prostitutes, they were sure of it.

3

In the spring of 1877 Russia declared war on Turkey. One would have imagined, from Queen Victoria's reaction, that Tsar Alexander II had declared war on her. She was incensed. It was like the Crimean War all over again but this time there was no Prince Albert to temper Victoria's bellicosity. On the contrary, there was Disraeli to encourage it. He 'has skilfully described the situation,' wrote a disapproving Ponsonby to his wife, 'as a struggle for mastery between England and Russia and that the point at issue is who shall be first, the Queen or the Czar. . . .'

This was the sort of political situation that Victoria appreciated.

That Disraeli himself took so elementary a view of the problem is unlikely. Although he was almost as much a Russophobe as his Sovereign, he was not really prepared to fight. He wanted to be in a position to threaten Russia with war if she showed any signs of occupying Constantinople, but he did not actually want war. Nor, he realized, did a sizeable section of the British population. Indeed, a great many people did not even approve of Disraeli's belligerent attitude towards Russia. Shocked by the Turkish atrocities, they were ready to believe that the Tsar, by taking up arms against Turkey, was merely fulfilling what he called 'a sacred mission'. Why, demanded one speaker of his wildly cheering audience, should Britain fight 'to uphold the integrity and independence of Sodom'?

This attitude was not confined to Disraeli's political enemies. Even in his cabinet there were dissenting voices. Neither the Foreign Secretary, Lord Derby, nor the Colonial Secretary, Lord Carnarvon, was prepared to make a stand; even Lord Salisbury, the Indian

Secretary, seemed to be undecided. Turkey, they reckoned, was simply not worth a war.

To Queen Victoria, all this was inexplicable. When Lord Carnarvon, known as 'Twitters', visited Windsor, he was treated to one of Victoria's most violently anti-Russian outpourings. 'She is ready for war,' wrote Carnarvon in alarm to Lord Salisbury, she 'says that rather than to submit to Russian insult she would lay down her crown.'

Within a few months it was the pacific 'Twitters' himself who was being castigated by the Queen. 'I pitched into him,' she assured Vicky, 'with a vehemence and indignation—[which] was at any rate inspired by the British Lion—and he remained shrinking but still craven-hearted!—wishing to say to the world we could not act!!! Oh! that Englishmen were now what they were!! but we could yet assert our rights—our position—and "Britons never will be slaves"—will yet be our Motto. I own I never spoke with such vehemence as I did last night.'

No wonder poor 'Twitters' slunk away like a 'naughty schoolboy'.

'Oh, if the Queen were a man,' cried Victoria, 'she would like to go and give those horrid Russians, whose word one cannot trust, such a beating.'

Even the Queen's adored Disraeli seemed, from her point of view, to be dragging his feet. As the Russians moved forward from victory to victory, so did the Queen's harangues to her Prime Minister become more impassioned. She was forever exhorting him to act more boldly, more quickly, more aggressively. 'The Faery writes every day and telegraphs every hour,' sighed the long-suffering Dizzy to Lady Bradford.

On one occasion, the almost hysterical Queen implied that Disraeli was not carrying out some promised course of action. Had he, or had he not, assured her that he would tell Russia that Britain was resolved to declare war if she reached, and refused to quit, Constantinople? Why then, had Lord Beaconsfield not told Russia so? At this, Dizzy was obliged to be a little sharp with her. Perhaps, he answered firmly, he had erred in confiding too much in her, particularly about plans which were still 'in embryo'.

The Queen repented immediately. 'She was *greatly grieved* that *he* thinks she meant *him* by what is said,' she protested. 'How could he think so? She meant his Colleagues. . . .'

Together, and without Dizzy telling his cabinet colleagues, the two of them hatched a plan whereby a secret emissary was sent to the Tsar to tell him that any renewed Russian campaign would lead to a British declaration of war. On this, Dizzy maintained blandly, his cabinet was absolutely united. The Tsar, who knew perfectly well that Disraeli's cabinet was anything but united on the issue, treated the emissary with great civility but pressed on with the war.

While the Queen bemoaned the fact that she was a constitutional monarch and was therefore unable to do what was 'right', the Tsar's ambassador in London described this partnership between Sovereign and Prime Minister as a conspiracy between 'a half-mad woman' and a 'political clown'.

But at no stage was there any conspiracy. Not, that is, as far as the Queen was concerned. Throughout these months of ferment, her attitude was always crystal clear: she wanted Russia put in its place. It was Disraeli's role that was more conspiratorial. As often before, he was making use of the Queen to further his own ends. Having worked her up into this warlike state, he used it to coax his divided cabinet into a more bellicose attitude, while depending upon their hesitancy to keep the Queen in check. This way he hoped to be able to threaten war, as he wished, without actually going to war, which was the Queen's wish. Yet all the while he was assuring Victoria that he lived only for Her, and worked only for Her and that without Her, all would be lost.

As the Russo–Turkish War dragged on, so did the Queen's belligerence begin to be echoed by a great many of her subjects. The further the Russians advanced, the more aggressive became British public reaction. Gladstone was jeered at in the streets and the windows of his house shattered. His second pamphlet on the Bulgarian atrocities had a poor reception. Crowds surged about the streets bellowing the music-hall song that gave birth to the word 'Jingoism'.

We don't want to fight but by Jingo if we do,
We've got the ships, we've got the men, we've got the money too.

The signing of an armistice between Russia and Turkey on the last day of January 1878 merely heightened this war fever. A rumour that Russia had ignored the terms of the armistice and was marching on Constantinople finally enabled Disraeli to jolt his irresolute cabinet into action. War credits were passed, a fleet of ironclads was despatched to Constantinople, arrangements were made to move troops from India to the Mediterranean and the reserves were called up. Much to the Queen's delight, first Lord 'Twitters' Carnarvon and then Lord 'Peace-at-all-price' Derby resigned. It looked as though Queen Victoria was about to get her war.

But Disraeli kept his head. This show of force was what he had all along been wanting. But he wanted nothing more. It alone would convince Russia of Britain's determination to stand firm; he was certainly not going to be stampeded into war.

But not everyone showed such restraint. One evening at the dinner table, the plump and ebullient Duchess of Teck—mother of the future Queen Mary—attacked him for his refusal to declare war.

'What are you waiting for, Lord Beaconsfield?' she demanded. 'The Queen is for you; the Army is for you—what *are* you waiting for?'

'The potatoes, Ma'am,' answered Dizzy.

4

Disraeli was proved right. The British show of strength halted the Russians. Hastily imposing the Treaty of San Stefano on the retreating Turks, Russia concluded the war.

But Dizzy, having got the whip hand, was not going to relinquish it immediately. He was not at all happy about the Treaty of San Stefano. So the ironclads remained off Constantinople and the troops were ordered from India. Climbing down yet again, Russia conceded that the Great Powers had a right to be consulted on the terms of the Treaty. A conference was decided upon. After a flurry of preliminary agreements between Britain and Russia, it was agreed to hold a congress at Berlin. Prince Bismarck, having followed up one memorable phrase (that the affairs of the Balkans were 'not worth the bones of a Pomeranian grenadier') with another (that he wished only to play the part of the 'honest broker' in the forthcoming conference) agreed to be President of the Congress.

The Congress of Berlin opened in mid-June, 1878. It was a month-long, magnificently staged affair. Dizzy, representing Great Britain, was in his element. In a series of amusing, incisive and colourful letters and in a diary which he called a 'rough journal for One Person only'

Dizzy detailed to the Queen the multiple glories of the Congress: the grandeur of the newly imperial German capital; the 'ceremonious and costumish' opening in the sumptuously decorated hall of the Radziwill Palace; the 'singularly various and splendid' costumes at a gala banquet in the Old Schloss; a 'splendid Rococo hall, which would have driven old Lord Malmesbury, with his frigid Ionic taste, quite crazy'; Bismarck's 'Rabelaisian monologues: endless revelations of things he ought not to mention'; the pretty Countess Karolyi's extraordinarily hearty appetite ('I never refuse a dish' was her far-from-idle boast); the huge *pilaff* at the banquet at the Turkish Embassy.

When the Iron Chancellor, afloat on a mixture of champagne and stout, advised the British Prime Minister not to put his trust in princes, Dizzy replied that 'he served one who was the soul of candour and justice, and whom all her Ministers loved'. That, at any rate, is what he told the Queen.

Nor was his Sovereign the only royal personage on whom Dizzy was ready to lavish praise. Old Kaiser Wilhelm I, convalescent after an assassin's attack, was spared his effusions but the Kaiserin was more than ready to hear them. In full evening dress, in daylight, Disraeli was received by the German Empress—that same brightly rouged, bewigged and beribboned old 'Augoosta' to whom the jealous Queen Victoria had once imagined that he was paying too much attention. 'She was very foolish,' reported Lord Salisbury, who had accompanied his Chief, 'and Beaconsfield's compliments were a thing to hear!'

The Empress Augusta's only son, Crown Prince Frederick, was married to Queen Victoria's eldest daughter Vicky—Crown Princess Victoria—and Disraeli was lavishly entertained by them in their palace at Potsdam: that 'Paradise of Rococo' as Dizzy called it. 'The Crown Prince and Princess have showered kindnesses on Lord Beaconsfield during his visit . . .' he reported to the Queen, 'and what makes them more delightful is, that he feels they must be, in no slight degree, owing to the inspiration of one to whom he owes everything.'

The Crown Prince he pronounced as being 'natural and cordial' and the Crown Princess who, although clever, had something of her mother's emotionalism, he called 'most animated and entertaining'. She seemed, he wrote with just a touch of exasperation to Lady Bradford, 'to know everything'.

Dizzy was touched to discover that Queen Victoria had given her daughter strict instructions about the care of his health. The Crown Princess was to see that he had fires in every room and that he was not to walk, much less stand, on any cold marble floors. Indeed, Queen Victoria had good reason to be worried about him. The never-ending round of meetings, banquets, balls and receptions, the clouds of cigar smoke and rivers of champagne were doing him no good at all. Before the Congress was over, Dizzy's doctor had to be sent for.

Absent royalties were not neglected either. Knowing how passionately Alexandra, Princess of Wales, was concerned with the problems of her brother, King George of the Hellenes, Dizzy did what he could to further the Greek cause at the conference table. 'I did yesterday something for Greece,' he reported to the Prince of Wales. 'It was very difficult but it was by no means to be despised. It was all done for Her Royal Highness's sake. I thought of Marlborough House all the time. . . .'

All in all, Disraeli achieved a great deal in Berlin. He emerged, in fact, as the hero, the 'Lion of the Congress'. He stood up to, and triumphed over, Russia in almost every essential; even threatening, it was rumoured, to order a train to take him home when Russia showed signs of resisting British demands. His masterstroke was the announcement, late in the Congress, that Britain had just gained control of Cyprus. In this way she was assured of an Eastern Mediterranean base to counteract any Russian advances in the area.

'This is progress,' exclaimed an admiring Bismarck. 'Evidently his idea of progress,' said Dizzy to the Queen, 'is seizing something.'

It was. But then so, no less evidently, was theirs.

No wonder that Bismarck who—in his astuteness, his cynicism, his national pride and his aristocratic viewpoint—resembled Disraeli, developed a great respect for him. '*Der alte Jude,*' he afterwards said, '*das ist der Mann.*'

The old Jew was the man indeed. If the Congress had not been quite, as Dizzy so graphically put it to the Queen, the surrender by the Emperor of Russia to the Empress of India, it was undoubtedly a triumph for British diplomacy. 'Peace with Honour' was what Disraeli claimed to have brought back. The cheering crowds that greeted him on his return to a triumphantly decorated London were ready to believe it.

And so was the Queen. She was ecstatic. She sent Ponsonby to Downing Street with a huge bouquet of 'Windsor flowers' to present to the returning hero. 'From the Queen!' bellowed Ponsonby above the roar of the crowd as the impassive-faced Dizzy alighted from his open carriage at the door of Number Ten.

'He has gained a wreath of laurels which she would willingly herself offer him . . .' wrote the Queen. Instead, his gratified Sovereign offered him a positive shower of honours: the Garter, a dukedom, a peerage for his brother or his nephew.

Rather than 'Peace with Honour', quipped one cynic, it was 'Peace with honours'.

Dizzy accepted only the Garter. 'He will not trust himself now in endeavouring to express what he feels to your Majesty's kindness. He thinks he is ennobled through your Majesty's goodness quite enough, though with infinite deference to your Majesty's gracious pleasure, he would presume to receive the Garter; but, as he always feels, your Majesty's kind thoughts are dearer to him than any personal distinction, however rich and rare. The belief that your Majesty trusts, and approves of, him is more precious than rubies!'

Three days after his return from Berlin, he was at Osborne. The Queen gave him a rapturous welcome. Never, since the days of Prince Albert, and perhaps not even then, had she been in such close personal and political rapport with anyone. It was one of the most exultant moments of her life. With the sentiments of the London *Times*, she would have been in complete agreement. Her beloved Disraeli was now 'at the pinnacle of Ministerial renown, the favourite of his Sovereign and the idol of Society.' And as she conferred the Garter, she must have felt, with the *Journal des Débats*, that 'the traditions of England' did indeed live on 'in the hearts of a woman and an aged statesman'.

Like the buying of the Suez Canal shares and the passing of the bill that made the Queen Empress of India, the British triumph at the Congress of Berlin was one of the great flourishes of the Victoria–Disraeli partnership.

Chapter Eighteen

While Disraeli's romantic association with Queen Victoria was flowering so spectacularly, his love affair with Selina, Countess of Bradford, was dying a death. At the start of their relationship, in 1873, he had imagined that she was returning his love. She might well have imagined so herself. It had no doubt been flattering for Selina to have the most famous man in England at her feet; to receive from him those hundreds of hundreds of letters, all assuring her of his slavish devotion, all keeping her *au fait* with events in his great world. How gratifying to know that cabinet meetings or ministers or ambassadors or special messengers were being kept waiting while a note was being scribbled to the effect that she was more important to him than all these, that the sun shone only when he had a hope of seeing her.

But before a year had passed, Selina's manner began to cool. Perhaps her husband objected, perhaps Dizzy was proving too pressing, perhaps she felt that she was making a fool of herself. Whatever the reason for her coolness, it had the effect, of course, of increasing Dizzy's ardour. His stream of letters continued unabated, his protestations of love multiplied.

'To see you, or at least to hear from you, every day, is absolutely necessary to my existence,' he would protest. 'To see you in society is a pleasure peculiar to itself; but different from that of seeing you alone; both are enchanting, like moonlight and sunshine.'

But not only had Selina no wish to see him every day ('Three times a week is so very little,' he complained) she had no wish to hear from him every day. At times she was quite firm with him. When he asked her to choose a sign by which he would recognize her at a masked ball, she advised him not to go. When his amorous outpourings became too embarrassing she would feel obliged to check him. 'Your view of correspondence, apparently, is that it should be confined to facts and not admit feelings,' he grumbled. 'Mine is the reverse.' Often, he wrote, he felt as if he were pouring forth these feelings, 'however precious, like water from a golden goblet on the sand.'

Worse, even, than Selina's unemotional responses or her rebukes were her silences. Often she did not bother to answer his letters; not even his telegrams. Never was he too immersed in his manifold duties and responsibilities, never did he feel too old or ill or tired to be aware of the fact that she had not written to him. 'While I was working at some Despatches last night in my room in the House of Commons, Monty knocked and came in triumphant with a telegram.... His countenance was radiant with my anticipated pleasure,' he told her. 'Alas! it was from the Mayor of Norwich. I fell in a clear heaven like a bird shot in full wing.'

Once, so violent was his longing for some word that he opened a letter from her addressed to Montagu Corry. 'It is heinous;' he confessed to his sympathetic secretary, 'I cannot defend or palliate my act.'

Yet nothing could stop the flow of his letters to Selina or to her more understanding sister, Lady Chesterfield. As much in love with love, perhaps, as he was with Lady Bradford, Dizzy felt compelled to go on pouring out his heart. That he was in his seventies—frail, pale and asthmatic—rendered him no less ardent, no less romantic. His nature, he had once said, demanded that his life be perpetual love, and surely an unrequited, or only half-returned love, was better than no love at all? 'I have lived to know that the twilight of love has its splendour and richness,' he rhapsodied; and if this twilight was not quite as splendid or as rich as he liked to pretend, what did it matter? With him sincerity and make-believe were always closely intertwined.

Yet, in the end, even he was obliged to admit that he was deluding himself. By 1878 he could sigh that 'I gave you feelings you could not return. It was not your fault; my fate and my misfortune.'

'I fear our Romance is over,' he wrote on another occasion, 'if indeed it ever existed except in my imagination—but still I sometimes dreamed that the dream might last until I slumbered for ever.'

Faced with Selina's indifference, Dizzy came to depend, more and more, on the one person of whose admiration, solicitude and devotion he could be quite certain. After all, Queen Victoria still most perfectly epitomized the indulgent and adoring mother-figure of his life-long search. *She* would never leave his letters unanswered.

'The Faery writes to me three or four times a day ... and her letters are worth reading,' he once told Selina's sister, Lady Chesterfield.

'It is impossible for them to be more kind than they are to me.'

But even with the Queen, Dizzy had to content himself with something less than her whole heart. For one thing, Victoria had a large family; for another, she had John Brown. But then Dizzy had never seen John Brown as a rival for the Queen's affection. More than any other man in Victoria's circle, Disraeli would have appreciated the nature of her relationship with her Highland gillie. He would have appreciated, too, the fact that she was able to divide her affections between Brown and himself; that each of them could appeal to different facets of her complex nature. He, after all, and in much the same way, was attracted to both the Queen and Lady Bradford. Dizzy understood Brown's role and was always grateful to him for coaxing the Queen out of her long period of mourning. Brown had eased Disraeli's task. For if Disraeli had heightened Victoria's interest in life, it was Brown who had first re-awakened it.

There were even times when Dizzy was able to reach Victoria through Brown. On once being asked why he did not propose a certain measure to the Queen, Disraeli answered that he must first make sure that it had the approval of 'the two J.B.s'—'John Bull and John Brown'.

For his part, John Brown approved of Disraeli. The astute Dizzy, unlike the others surrounding the Queen, had always taken care to treat Brown with the utmost friendliness and respect. And Brown, who was so touchy, so suspicious and so surly, was quick to respond to Dizzy's overtures. Those little messages to Brown with which Dizzy so often ended his letters to the Queen were greatly appreciated.

And, of course, the more Dizzy played up to Brown, the better he pleased the Queen. With Brown causing so much friction in the royal household, it was a joy for her to know that there was someone whom the rough-tongued gillie did not rub up the wrong way. Dizzy's tactful treatment of Brown could only increase Victoria's affection for her Prime Minister. It was yet another point in his favour.

But there were some subjects on which Victoria and Disraeli did not agree. Even with them, the course did not always run smooth. Indeed, during the year following his triumphant return from the Congress of Berlin, Disraeli all but fell out with the Queen.

First, though, there was a slight difference between them about the Queen's sailor son, Prince Alfred, Duke of Edinburgh. As Prince Alfred was married to the only daughter of the Tsar Alexander II, he tended to sympathize with Russia on the Eastern Question. This, the Queen considered bad enough but when Prince Alfred, in command of one of that fleet of ironclads off Constantinople, invited the aide-de-camp of the Commander-in-Chief of the Russian forces to dine aboard his ship, the Queen was furious. She insisted that her son be reprimanded. The Prince retaliated by threatening to demand a Court of Inquiry.

Disraeli, who considered that the Queen was making an unnecessary fuss, needed all his tact to smooth her ruffled feathers. 'The more Lord Beaconsfield attempts to deal with the business of the Duke of Edinburgh, the greater become the difficulties,' he wrote. 'Indeed, it costs Lord Beaconsfield more trouble than the Eastern Question itself.'

In the end, he managed to coax the Queen into adopting a more reasonable attitude.

Far more serious were their disagreements about the situation in South Africa. Sir Bartle Frere, the newly appointed Governor of the Cape Colony and High Commissioner for South Africa, was one of those 'prancing proconsuls' who firmly believed in an expansionist imperial policy. In this, he could count on the support of the Queen. Disraeli, on the other hand, was far more interested in maintaining Britain's newly established supremacy in Europe; he was anxious to avoid any costly and unsuccessful colonial ventures that might weaken Britain's prestige on the Continent. So when Frere, set on extending Britain's power in South Africa, let the cabinet know that he was contemplating a war against the Zulu in Natal, Disraeli was very put out. Frere was told that he must do his utmost to avoid any such war.

But the Governor refused to listen. In January 1879 he sent a British army, commanded by Lord Chelmsford, into Zululand. On 22 January, on the slopes of a dramatic-looking mountain named Isandhlwana, this British invading force was all but annihilated.

Disraeli was both appalled and angry. 'When a viceroy or a commander-in-chief disobeys orders,' he once said, 'he ought at least to be certain of success.' Not only had Frere disobeyed orders but Chelmsford had failed disastrously. Reinforcements had to be rushed out to Natal and Disraeli found himself with a full-scale war on his hands.

The Queen, although no less appalled at the disaster of Isandhlwana, was less inclined to blame Frere and Chelmsford. When the incensed Disraeli appointed Sir Garnet Wolseley to supersede, in effect, both Frere and Chelmsford, Victoria balked at the proposal. She had never liked Wolseley; she considered him too cocksure by half. Moreover, she thought it quite wrong for Lord Chelmsford to be superseded in the middle of what she felt sure was a very difficult campaign. In this she was right. Disraeli should either have dismissed both Frere and Chelmsford outright or else he should have given them his support.

But despite the Queen's protestations, Disraeli stuck by his decision to appoint Wolseley. The disgruntled Victoria was obliged to give way. She would sanction Wolseley's appointment, she declared, but she would not 'approve it'.

And, lest there be any lack of martial spirit on the part of the government, or any attempt to conclude a hasty peace, the Queen reminded Disraeli that 'if we are to maintain our position as a first-rate Power—and of that no one ... can doubt, we must with our Indian Empire and large Colonies, be Prepared for attacks and wars, somewhere or other, CONTINUALLY, and the true economy will be to be always ready. Lord Beaconsfield can do his country the greatest service by repeating that again and again, and by seeing it carried out.'

Among the troops despatched to South Africa was the young Prince Imperial of France, only child of the late Emperor Napoleon III and the Empress Eugénie. Since the fall of the Second Empire, the family had been living in exile in England and since his father's death in 1873, the Prince Imperial had been the Bonapartist Pretender to the French throne. Victoria was particularly fond of the still beautiful Empress, and for the twenty-three-year-old Prince she had developed a strong affection. The youngster had something of his late father's exotic air and charm of manner; to this was added a frankness and a vivacity inherited from his mother. All in all, he was the sort of high-spirited, swashbuckling, romantic young man to whom the Queen was always drawn.

Dizzy could not share Victoria's high opinion of the Prince

Imperial. Privately, in a letter to Lord Salisbury, he referred to him as 'that little abortion'. Pretenders to foreign thrones were always something of an embarrassment to a government: Disraeli had no quarrel with the French Republic and, as far as he was concerned, the less fuss made about the Prince Imperial the better.

So when the Prince, who had done his military training at Woolwich, expressed a wish to join the reinforcements going out to Natal, Disraeli would not hear of it. The venture would be fraught with risks. The government, already reeling under the blow of Isandhlwana, did not want the death of a French pretender on their hands.

But the Prince Imperial was determined to go. Both he and his mother, the Empress Eugénie, applied directly to the Commander-in-Chief of the British army—the Queen's cousin, the Duke of Cambridge. The Duke passed the Prince's application on to the Queen. She was charmed. What could be more natural than that the dear young Prince Imperial should be eager to repay her hospitality by fighting with her troops?

So between the two of them—the sympathetic Queen and the partisan Empress—the Prince got his way. The government agreed to let him go. 'Well,' Disraeli was afterwards to say, 'my conscience is clear. I did all I could to stop his going. But what can you do when you have to deal with two obstinate women?'

But on one thing Disraeli insisted. The Prince would be allowed to go to Natal in the capacity of a spectator only. He was not to be a combatant. In letters to Frere and Chelmsford, the cabinet's instructions were made abundantly clear.

They were ignored; ignored, moreover, by the Prince himself, who was itching to do some fighting. On 1 June 1879 he was killed in an ambush while on a reconnaissance mission. And if that were not bad enough, it was learned that he had been deserted by his companions and had been left, quite alone, to face the Zulu assegais.

The Queen was horrified. To make amends, both for the loss of his life and the cowardice of her soldiers, she was determined that the Prince be given a magnificent funeral. This, in turn, horrified Disraeli. Fearing the insult to republican France, he wanted the whole unhappy affair played down as much as possible. The Prince's death was certainly no fault of the British government; Disraeli's cabinet saw no reason why they should be associated with this manifestation of what Lord Salisbury called 'national self-reproach'.

When the Queen announced her intention of placing the Order of the Bath on the Prince's coffin with her own hands, Disraeli advised against it. To this advice she submitted. But when the cabinet decided against attending the funeral at all, she flew into one of her towering rages. So outspoken was her indignation that the cabinet was forced to relent. It was agreed that two ministers would go in full dress.

Disraeli, whom the Queen had been bombarding with telegrams for days, was finally obliged to journey down to Windsor in person. He went in considerable trepidation, expecting, as he put it, 'a distressing scene'. His apprehensions were justified. The Queen kept him for an hour and a half and talked, he confided to a friend, 'only on one subject'.

The funeral, on 12 July 1879, was every bit as impressive as the Queen had intended it to be. Arriving back at Windsor when it was over, Victoria at once sent a telegram to Disraeli, expressing her entire satisfaction at the day's proceedings. She was 'highly pleased' with all that had taken place.

'I hope,' wrote Dizzy to Lady Chesterfield, 'the French Government will be as joyful. In my mind, nothing could be more injudicious than the whole affair.'

3

Nor was the funeral of the Prince Imperial the last of the differences between Victoria and Disraeli to arise from the ill-fated Zulu War.

Lord Chelmsford, on learning that Sir Garnet Wolseley had been sent out to supersede him, advanced rapidly into Zululand and won a great victory at Ulundi, thus putting an end to the campaign. A delighted Queen Victoria, considering that the victory at Ulundi had made up for the disaster at Isandhlwana, was all for giving Lord Chelmsford a hero's welcome. Disraeli was not. When the Queen asked him to invite Chelmsford to Hughenden, Disraeli refused. In a very strong letter, he gave the Queen his reasons for this refusal. Victoria's answer was no less strong. But Dizzy remained firm. So while the Queen received Chelmsford at Balmoral, Disraeli made a point of not receiving him at Hughenden.

These little clouds of misunderstanding—and they were not more than that—upset both Victoria and Disraeli considerably. It was Dizzy who made the first move towards a reconciliation. He wrote to Lady Ely, the Queen's lady-in-waiting, knowing that she would show the letter to her royal mistress.

'My nature demands perfect solitude, or perfect sympathy . . .' he wrote. 'I am grieved, and greatly, that anything I should say, or do, should be displeasing to Her Majesty. I love the Queen—perhaps the only person in this world left to me that I do love; and therefore you can understand how much it worries and disquiets me, when there is a cloud between us.'

In the face of these mellifluous phrases, the clouds dispersed. When next they met, the sun was out and the Faery was all smiles.

Chapter Nineteen

Thanks largely to Disraeli, the Queen's relations with her eldest son, the Prince of Wales, were beginning to improve. Where the Prince Consort had always considered Bertie to be entirely feckless and foolish, Disraeli had a high opinion (or professed to have a high opinion) of the Prince's abilities. He made a show of consulting him, he kept him informed on certain issues, he tried to involve him in the business of the monarchy. Disraeli would have been quick to appreciate that the Prince's special qualities—his verve, his love of display, even his somewhat roisterous life style—could be of as much value to the monarchy as the Queen's very different virtues. Young Hal could certainly be relied upon to provide the monarchy with that show of splendour that the Queen, despite Dizzy's promptings, felt herself unable to provide. Not for a moment did Disraeli make the mistake of either ignoring or underestimating Victoria's heir.

This, in turn, made the Queen look at her son with new eyes. If dear, clever Lord Beaconsfield was prepared to take Bertie seriously, then perhaps there was more to him than she had hitherto imagined. And although Queen Victoria could never quite overcome her reservations about her heir's political talents, she did come to a gradual appreciation of his other good points.

However, Dizzy took good care to avoid any appearance of conniving with the Prince behind his mother's back. He realized that he had only to pay a few visits to Marlborough House—particularly if the Queen were on her, by now, annual Continental holiday—for there to be speculation on the exact nature of these meetings. 'It is enough to state that, while the Premier is of all ministers quite the most punctilious in his deference to the Crown, the Prince is wholly incapable of playing the part of Madcap Hal,' protested one High Tory journal. 'In fine, we are able to state on authority that neither political nor dynastic topics entered into the conversation of the Prince and the Premier.' The visits had been purely social.

Yet, despite their seeming rapport, the Prince and the Prime Minister were never entirely at ease in each other's company. Bertie was certainly in tune with Disraeli's politics—with his conservative and imperial creeds—but he could never quite shake himself free of the feeling that Dizzy might be making a fool of him. The Prime Minister's manner was altogether too flowery, too ironic, too enigmatic for the much less complicated Prince. For someone as thin-skinned and as huffy as Bertie, Dizzy's sardonic smile was distinctly unnerving.

And then Bertie, for all his panache, was not really Disraeli's sort of man. Bluff, restless and philistine, the Prince of Wales too closely resembled the sort of aristocratic oaf with whom Dizzy had never had anything in common.

But, needing each other, the two men put on a show of friendship. The Prince would invite the Prime Minister to Marlborough House or Sandringham and, on at least one occasion, Disraeli acted as peacemaker in one of those Society scandals through which the indiscreet Prince was forever picking his way.

On this social level, the Prime Minister had to tread no less cautiously than he did on the political. The Queen might be prepared to admit that Bertie was not entirely without good qualities but nothing would reconcile her to his frenetic social life. So it would not do for Disraeli to be seen too often at Marlborough House or Sandringham. 'This morning a telegram in cypher,' he once reported to Lady Bradford, 'disapproving of my going to Sandringham as I shall catch cold. A little jealous on that subject.' And on another occasion he announced that the Queen was 'delighted' that he was not going to Sandringham after all. There was always the chance, moreover, that Disraeli would find himself embroiled in one of those family political rows—between the Queen on the one hand and the Prince and Princess of Wales on the other.

One such source of trouble were the visits of Princess Alexandra to her native Denmark. Victoria strongly disapproved of Alix's prolonged absences from England and, on one occasion, insisted that she cut short her Danish holiday in order to be present at the State Opening of Parliament. (The Queen had conveniently forgotten with what wails of indignation she had previously refused to open Parliament.) Victoria's summons infuriated Alix. But the Queen remained firm and it fell to the unfortunate Disraeli, whose visit to Windsor had been made particularly unpleasant by the Queen's tirade against Alix's wilfulness, to insist that the Princess return. 'I fear very much that she will misunderstand my motives and conduct,' wrote Dizzy unhappily to the Prince of Wales.

He was less happy still about the Princess's ardent championship of her brother, King George I of the Hellenes. From the Congress of Berlin, a triumphant Dizzy had written to tell Princess Alexandra of his territorial achievements for Greece; as the years went by, however, these paper gains showed precious little sign of becoming a reality. This distressed Alix considerably. In heartfelt letters to the Queen, and to Disraeli's face, she attacked British apathy and British short-sightedness. One of the troubles, of course, was that whereas Alix's heart was with her brother's anti-Turkish and pro-Russian stand, both Victoria and Disraeli were in the opposite camp. 'The Greek question,' complained Disraeli to the Queen, 'is becoming a serious and painful question under that roof. . . .'

But there were more light-hearted moments. Late in 1879, the Prince of Wales suggested that he spend a night, *en garçon*, at Hughenden. At this Dizzy, who feared both the Prince's notorious restlessness and the Queen's possible disapproval of the visit, became distinctly apprehensive. But all went beautifully. The Prince was kept busy with drives, walks, whist, gargantuan meals and the antics of two famously witty fellow guests—Lord Rosslyn and Bernal Osborne. 'He praised the house, praised the dinner, praised the pictures, praised everything; was himself most agreeable in conversation, said some good things and told more,' reported a relieved Dizzy to Lady Bradford.

He was even more relieved at the Queen's reaction. 'I heard today from the Faery, who highly approves of the visit,' he wrote. 'I thought, on the contrary, we should have our ears boxed!'

What Bertie thought of his mother's close association with Disraeli is uncertain. One knows his opinion of her relationship with that other favourite, John Brown. No sooner had he become King than Edward VII had all his mother's pictures and busts and statuettes of the Highland gillie turfed out of the palaces and destroyed. With Disraeli, Edward VII confined himself to a destruction of letters. All Queen Victoria's letters to Disraeli, then in the possession of Lord Rothschild, the trustee of Hughenden, were sent for by the King. These letters have been described as being '*very* Private'. They are said to have dealt, among other things, with matters concerning various members of the Queen's family. King Edward VII had all these personal letters destroyed.

Only those dealing with political subjects were returned to Lord Rothschild.

What the '*very* Private' contents of these letters between Victoria and Disraeli were, one will never know.

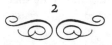

If the sun was again shining on the partnership between Victoria and Disraeli, the clouds were still heavily banked over Disraeli's administration. Hardly was the Zulu War over than the Prime Minister received news of another disaster. The entire British mission at Kabul in Afghanistan had been murdered. There was nothing for it but to embark on yet another war. That this Afghan War was more efficiently conducted than the Zulu War did not lessen a general feeling that it should not have been necessary to fight at all.

At home, too, there was trouble. An economic boom was coming to an end. Unemployment was increasing and four wet summers had resulted in four bad harvests. At Hughenden, Dizzy slithered about in the mud asking the farmers, in his dry fashion, whether the dove had left the Ark yet. But no little jokes could hide the fact that disenchantment with his administration was spreading.

By no one was this disenchantment being spread more vigorously than by Mr Gladstone. Although no election had been proclaimed, the Grand Old Man was conducting something very like an election campaign in his chosen constituency of Midlothian in Scotland. In that thunderous voice, to vast, enraptured audiences of simple, honest, God-fearing men, he castigated Disraeli's Satanic regime. He spoke up on behalf of the despoiled Zulu and the suffering Afghans; he attacked Disraeli's 'false phantoms of glory'—those immoral colonial wars and greedy annexations of foreign territory; he even lashed out against the 'theatrical bombast and folly' of Queen Victoria's new imperial title.

While the infuriated Queen noted that 'Mr Gladstone is going about Scotland, like an American stumping orator, making most violent speeches', Dizzy turned a deaf ear. He needed all his failing energies to get through a day's work, let alone pay heed to what one of his supporters calculated to be the eighty-five thousand, eight hundred and forty impassioned words declaimed by Mr Gladstone. Let his rival imagine that he represented the Divine Will, that the British people had been following a false prophet, that the Lord God of Hosts was now chastising an errant nation; the Lord of Darkness was not going to bother answering him. When Gladstone's triumphant tour was over, Dizzy could only write that 'It certainly is a relief that this drenching rhetoric has at length ceased: but I have never read a word of it.'

And on being asked how long he thought the Conservative Party would remain in power, Dizzy's answer was characteristically laconic. 'As long as Mr Gladstone is spared to us,' he said.

Yet despite his increasing ill-health, Dizzy could also strike sparks in the minds and hearts of men. His vision of Britain—of a proud, imperial, aristocratically-led Britain—was no less firmly held, or voiced, than was Gladstone's. At that year's Lord Mayor's Banquet, to an, admittedly tailor-made, audience of city merchants, Disraeli claimed that 'I know that they are men who are not ashamed of the Empire which their ancestors created; because I know that they are not ashamed of the noblest of human sentiments, now descried by philosophers—the sentiment of patriotism; because I know they will not be beguiled into believing that in maintaining their Empire they may forfeit their liberties.'

In society, too, Dizzy could still shine. He might be bent and frail and wheezy but he took no less pleasure in the social round. The opulence of the great London houses, the glitter of jewels and the shimmer of dresses, the richness of the food and the mellowness of the wine, the gossip and the laughter and the intrigue—all these still held their allure for him. And he, in turn, was no less sought after than he had ever been. He remained the centre of attraction; his presence could still enhance an evening. His behaviour was no less bland nor his tongue less sharp.

'Thank God,' he once said, as he turned from his inadequately heated food to his inadequately iced champagne, 'for something warm.'

3

On 5 February 1880, Queen Victoria opened Parliament in person. This was the fourth occasion during Disraeli's term of office that she had performed the ceremony. Although she still did not actually enjoy the duty, she no longer shirked it. Not only to secure adequate allowances for her children did she now expose herself to the public gaze; nor did she any longer describe the ceremony as '*great, trying* and *painful*' and one which 'the Queen *must* have *clearly understood* that she is *not* to be expected to do as a *matter of course, year after year*.' On the contrary, for this latest State Opening, the Queen consented to being on more prominent display than ever. Dizzy had asked that 'the procession should be as splendid as might be convenient to your Majesty.' There was nothing, he continued, 'which the great body of the people more appreciate than this spectacle . . . because the splendour of royalty delights the people'.

So the Queen, wearing a small diamond and sapphire coronet atop her diamond-edged cap with its floating tulle veil, drove to Parliament in a new State coach which sported so much glass that she could be seen more clearly than ever before.

The scene in the House of Lords that afternoon captured, in a way, the whole flavour of Disraeli's brilliant world. Here were gathered the peers and the judges and the bishops in their robes of scarlet and ermine, the ambassadors in their dark blue uniforms glittering with gold and flashing with orders, the representatives of the more exotic countries, such as Persia and China, resplendent in their robes, the bejewelled peeresses in their lavishly embroidered dresses of satin and velvet. Here were the princes and princesses of the royal family, the Archbishops of Canterbury and York, the Lord Chancellor, the great officers of the Court and the Royal Household, the pages of honour, Gold Stick, Silver Stick, gentlemen-at-arms, Yeomen of the Guard, pursuivants, heralds, equerries, gentlemen ushers, sergeants-at-arms.

And in the midst of this great 'sea of colour, beautifully variegated and harmonized' sat the Queen. This was Queen Victoria at her most impressive. On her golden throne were draped the crimson robes of state. Her black velvet dress, trimmed with miniver, was dramatically slashed by the blue Riband of the Order of the Garter; diamonds dazzled in her crown, in her ears and about her throat; the Koh-i-noor blazed on her breast. Plump, impassive, undeniably imperious she sat— Dizzy's Faery Queen—while the Lord Chancellor read out her speech to the hushed assembly. It was, as always, an unforgettable occasion.

One thing only spoiled the pageantry of this particular State Opening. Disraeli felt too weak to carry the heavy sword of State in the procession.

But if he could not carry it literally, he was confident of carrying it figuratively. The Tories won two by-elections early that year and the Queen was able to follow up her customary valentine to her beloved Prime Minister with a triumphant telegram: 'I am greatly rejoiced at the great victory . . .' she wired. 'It shows what the feeling in the country is.'

Disraeli agreed. So delighted was he, in fact, that he decided on an early election. Victoria, who had no doubt that the Tories would be returned 'stronger than ever', set off for Darmstadt to attend the confirmation of two of her grand-daughters.

While the Queen and her Prime Minister prepared themselves for the coming Tory victory, Gladstone took to the roads of Midlothian once more. With an energy that was astonishing in a man of over seventy, the Grand Old Man addressed meeting after meeting. Once more those burning, apparently God-inspired phrases rolled out across the intent, upturned faces of his listeners. With what the Queen must have regarded as unbelievable effrontery, he directed his call to 'the nation itself'. It was no use appealing, he cried out, to the aristocracy or the landed interest or the Established Church or the wealth and rank of the country; the People's William was appealing directly to the people.

The appeal was successful. The election was spread over two weeks and by the beginning of April 1880, it was clear that the Liberals would win.

Queen Victoria was at Baden-Baden when she received a telegram from Disraeli preparing her for his defeat. Its effect was overwhelming. 'This is a terrible telegram,' she exclaimed. So bitter, so indignant, so desolate was her reaction to the news that the long-suffering Ponsonby considered it as well that she was alone with her courtiers at Baden-Baden: 'some of the language used', he claimed, would hardly have been suitable for other ears.

For not only was the Queen about to lose her adored Disraeli but there was the prospect of Mr Gladstone to be faced. She would 'sooner *abdicate*,' she declared roundly, 'than send for or have any *communication* with that *half-mad firebrand* who would soon ruin everything and be a *Dictator*. Others but herself *may submit* to his democratic rule, *but not the Queen*.'

Disraeli's words to her were heartbreaking. 'His separation from your Majesty is almost overwhelming,' he wrote. 'His relations with your Majesty were his chief, he might almost say his only, happiness and interest in this world. They came to him when he was alone, and they have inspired and sustained him in his isolation.'

Victoria, answering him in the first person, expressed the hope that when they corresponded in the future 'which I hope we shall on many a *private* subject and without anyone being astonished or offended, and even more, without anyone knowing about it,' he too, would use the first person.

On her return to England, the Queen sent at once for Disraeli. Unpalatable as it might be, she had to face the question of his successor. As she would not hear of Gladstone, Dizzy suggested that she send for Lord Hartington, who was the leader of the Liberal Party in the House of Commons. But neither Lord Hartington, nor Lord Granville, the Liberal leader, was prepared to form a government without Gladstone. And Gladstone was certainly not prepared to serve under either 'Harty-Tarty' or 'Puss' Granville.

So the Queen braced herself to do what she had sworn she would rather abdicate than do: she sent for Gladstone. Without hesitation, he accepted the responsibility of forming a government.

On 27 April 1880, Disraeli travelled to Windsor to take formal leave of the Queen. For them both, it was a poignant occasion. The Queen's desolation was somewhat tempered by the fact that she was convinced that the new Liberal administration would never last. She felt sure that it would 'separate into many parts very soon, and that the Conservatives will come in stronger than ever in a short time.' In the meantime, Lord Beaconsfield was to promise 'for the country's, as well as my sake, to be very watchful and very severe, and to allow no lowering of Great Britain's proud position! It must not be lowered.'

She had been anxious to give Dizzy some tangible proof of her appreciation for all he had done for her. Would he not allow her to confer a barony on his nephew and heir, Coningsby Disraeli? He would not. But he asked that his true heir, the faithful Montagu

Corry, be made a peer. Victoria agreed, and Corry, now forty-one, became Lord Rowton. This elevation of the debonair Corry astonished some of Disraeli's critics. There had been nothing like it, snorted Gladstone, since Caligula had made his horse a consul.

'My audience was very long,' wrote Dizzy of this last official visit to Victoria, 'and everything was said that could be said. . . .' The Queen presented him with a bronze statuette of herself and made him promise that he would often come to see her.

'The downfall òf Beaconsfieldism,' wrote an elated Gladstone, 'is like the vanishing of some vast magnificent castle in an Italian romance.'

Neither Victoria, nor Disraeli himself, could have put it better.

Chapter Twenty

Disraeli's fall from power did not mean the end of his association with Queen Victoria. In the year of life that was left to him, the seventy-five-year-old Dizzy kept in close touch with the Queen. They wrote to each other ('Ever your affectionate and grateful friend V.R.I.' was how the Queen ended her letters) and on several occasions Dizzy was Victoria's guest at Windsor. In general, Disraeli kept off political topics. The Queen might assure him that 'I *never* write except on *official* matters' to Gladstone, and that 'I look always to *you* for ultimate help', but, in the main, Dizzy did not encourage her in this attitude. When Victoria appealed to him for political advice, he did his best to keep it as impartial as possible.

Yet even these exchanges had to be kept dark. Victoria would refer to some of her letters as '*very secret*' and knowing that Henry Ponsonby disapproved of the correspondence, she advised Dizzy not to write to her through her secretary. He could use her son Prince Leopold, or a groom-in-waiting, or a woman of the bedchamber: they were 'all QUITE SAFE' she assured him.

But it was, as always, as much for personal as political reasons that the Queen valued this continued contact. The old wizard could still weave his magic spells; he could still enchant Victoria with his romantic imagery. What a relief to turn from her glacial audiences with Gladstone to the warmth of Dizzy's letters or conversation. 'I feel so happy,' she told him on the first occasion after his fall that he dined with her at Windsor, 'that I think what has happened is only a horrid dream.'

His sympathy, his affection, his flattery, his flamboyance, his still undimmed ability to create a heady, sensual atmosphere afforded her as much pleasure as always. From Hughenden, at which he spent that summer of 1880, he wrote to her of the splendours of the countryside: of 'the mysterious and sultry' call of the cuckoo, of the cooing of the wood-pigeons, of the sweetness of the may-blossom. From Windsor she replied to say that 'I often think of you—indeed constantly—and rejoice to see you looking down from the *wall* after dinner.'

And if Dizzy looked down from the wall on the Queen at Windsor, she—in her Angeli portrait—looked down on him in the drawing room at Hughenden. He ate his Christmas dinner alone that year (Corry was looking after an invalid sister) but the Queen had not forgotten him. 'Oh Madam and most beloved Sovereign,' he wrote on Christmas Day. 'What language can express my feelings when I beheld this morning the graceful and gracious gifts upon my table. Such incidents make life delightful and inspire even age with the glow and energy of youth.'

Indeed, some of the glow and energy of youth seemed to have been restored to him during that summer of 1880. Warm weather always suited him ('I only live for climate,' he once claimed) and as he was feeling so much better, he decided to finish a novel which he had started before becoming Prime Minister. The result was his last published book, *Endymion*. Significantly, its theme was the influence of women on the career of a politician. Although its hero hardly resembled Disraeli, Endymion, like Dizzy, moved upwards, towards premiership, through a cloud of admiring, accomplished and ambitious women. It was almost as though, in this sunset blaze of his last novel (for, with all its faults, the book was scintillating), Dizzy was paying tribute to those female friends who had encouraged him in his own dazzling career: Sara Austen, his sister Sarah, his wife Mary Anne, Mrs Brydges Willyams and, not least of all, Queen Victoria. 'I owe everything to women;' he had once written, 'and if, in the sunset of life, I have still a young heart, it is due to that influence.'

Even without setting eyes on the manuscript, the publishing firm of Longman offered £10,000 for it. For its time, this was an exceptionally large advance. *Endymion* was published in November 1880 and the gratified Dizzy felt able to relax and enjoy the fine, almost burning, late autumn weather. 'I can sit on the southern terrace for a couple of hours,' he reported to the Queen, 'and feel like Egypt.'

But after Christmas the weather changed. It turned windy, icy, snowy. Disraeli left Hughenden on the last day of the year to move into his new London home, 19 Curzon Street. He was never to see his beloved Hughenden again. From his new home and in the teeth of biting east winds, Dizzy launched forth on his usual London round: to the House of Lords 'to make a speech on a falling Empire', or to those great London houses whose glitter he still could not resist. On one occasion, fortified by drugs, he gave a dinner party himself. On other nights he would sit alone in his sumptuous red and gold drawing room, his emaciated body wrapped in a long red dressing gown, one varnished black ringlet projecting from the red fez on his head. All around would be the sweet-scented flowers he had always loved and, as the winter turned gradually to spring, his Sovereign sent him the first of the primroses and the first of the violets. On 1 March 1881, the two of them—Victoria and Disraeli—dined together at Windsor Castle. It was their last meeting.

Less than a month later, Dizzy wrote the Queen his last letter. He had been ill for a week with bronchitis and, in pencil, he scrawled an answer to her anxious inquiry. 'I am prostrate though devoted,' he told her. His message did nothing to reassure Victoria. Knowing that he was in the care of the celebrated homoeopath, Dr Joseph Kidd, she was anxious that there be a second, more orthodox, medical opinion. Her wish, treated as a command, overcame the reluctance of a specialist in chest diseases to associate himself with a homoeopath, and he agreed to examine him. By now, however, Dizzy was past medical help, be it conventional or not.

Every day the Queen wired from Windsor for news. She sent him letters, she sent him primroses, she sent him violets. 'I sent some Osborne primroses and I meant to pay you a little visit this week, but I thought it better you should be quite quiet and not speak,' she wrote on one occasion. 'And I beg you will be very good and obey the doctors and commit no imprudence.'

When he became too weak to read her letters himself, he insisted, with that mixture of reverence and irony that was never to desert him, that his Sovereign's letter be read to him by a Privy Councillor. It was, and the voice of the Privy Councillor was heard intoning the royal, if first-person phrases: 'I send you some of your favourite spring flowers. . . .'

And in the end, not even his beloved Sovereign herself could escape his mordant wit. When it was suggested that she come and visit him, he decided against it. 'No, it is better not,' he said. 'She would only ask me to take a message to Albert.'

Disraeli died, on 19 April 1881 at half past four in the morning. He was seventy-six years of age.

John Brown broke the news of Disraeli's death to the Queen. One look at his doleful, tear-stained face was all Victoria needed to realize what had happened. She was desolate. In her own hand Victoria composed the announcement for Disraeli's death for the Court Circular and with tears blurring her eyes, wrote a letter of condolence to Montagu Corry. She had never lost a friend, she told Corry, 'whose loss will be more keenly felt'. Her dearest wish was to see Corry in order to hear about his master's last days. Corry duly hurried down to Osborne where, he told Lady Bradford, 'I found my every moment taken up by the Queen, with whom I passed hours telling her all she wished to know of her loved Friend. And she did love him.'

In her grief the Queen did not forget Lady Bradford. Knowing something of Disraeli's affection for Selina, she sent her an elaborately framed miniature of him on which were inscribed the words: 'In memory of the dear Earl of Beaconsfield. Born December 21, 1804; died April 19, 1881.'

To Lord Salisbury, the Queen admitted that she was '*quite* overwhelmed with this dreadful loss, irreparable to the country and Europe, to his many friends, and above all to herself! His devotion, unselfishness, and kindness she can *never, never* forget; her gratitude is everlasting as well as her regret to have lost *one* whose dear memory will ever live in her heart. . . .'

The Queen, with her penchant for funerals, was quite prepared for Disraeli to go to his grave in the most grandiose manner possible. Even Gladstone, assuming that Dizzy would have liked to have gone out with a flourish, decided that a State funeral at Westminster Abbey was called for. But on reading Disraeli's will, it was discovered that he had left instructions to be buried, quietly, beside Mary Anne at Hughenden. Gladstone was astonished. He could not bring himself to believe that Dizzy's wish for a simple funeral was anything other than a final piece of charlatanism; his crowning affectation. 'As he lived so he died,' grumbled Gladstone, 'all display without reality or genuineness.'

But Victoria was touched. She considered the choice of Hughenden Church entirely typical of him. Just as he had always preferred primroses to orchids, so would he have preferred a humble village church to Westminster Abbey. He had always 'hated display', she announced emphatically.

With protocol preventing a Sovereign from attending the funeral of a subject, Victoria was obliged to miss the great day—26 April 1881. But heading the galaxy of mourners were three of her sons: the Prince of Wales, the Duke of Connaught and Prince Leopold. The Queen sent two wreaths of primroses. On her card she wrote: 'His favourite flowers from Osborne, a tribute of affection from Queen Victoria.'

The royal revelation that primroses were Disraeli's 'favourite flowers' started a cult. Immediately, the primrose was adopted by his friends and disciples. Each year, on the anniversary of Disraeli's death, his supporters would be seen sporting little bunches of primroses and later, when his statue rose in Parliament Square, great wreaths of his 'favourite flowers' would be heaped about the plinth. In time, when a great Conservative body was founded, it chose the title of The Primrose League.

Yet there was considerable scepticism about the Queen's claim that primroses had been her Prime Minister's favourites. Was the choice of this unassuming spring flower—like his choice of Hughenden Church above Westminster Abbey—not merely another example of his insincerity? 'Tell me . . .', asked Gladstone of Lady Dorothy Nevill, 'on your honour now, did you ever hear Lord Beaconsfield express particular admiration for primroses? The glorious lily, I think, was much more to his taste.'

But Victoria knew better. Primroses were a part of the make-believe, magical, midsummer night's dream of a world in which the two of them had moved; the world in which she had been transformed into the Faery Queen and he into her devoted liegeman. To others the choice might seem paradoxical but then, what couple other than the Queen and her Prime Minister could afford to choose so artless and unostentatious a flower to symbolize their romantic association?

Victoria's tribute did not end with those wreaths of primroses. Above Disraeli's seat in the chancel in Hughenden Church, she had a huge marble tablet erected in his memory. 'This memorial is placed by his grateful Sovereign and Friend, Victoria R.I.' ran the frank inscription beneath his marble profile, and to these words were added, even more significantly, a quotation from Proverbs: 'Kings love him that speaketh right'.

At one stroke, the Queen was professing her love for Disraeli and taking a swipe at Gladstone.

Four days after Disraeli's funeral, with Princess Beatrice and Lady Ely in tow, Victoria travelled to Hughenden to visit his grave. As the Queen dearly loved a pilgrimage, she took the route which Dizzy had happened to take—through the estate of Sir Philip Rose—on the last occasion that he visited Windsor from Hughenden. It was a showery, blustery day. The little church was filled with flowers and more flowers were heaped on the coffin which lay in the specially opened vault. Dizzy's remains lay beside those of the two women who had given him so much devotion: Mary Anne and Mrs Brydges Willyams. And now the third, the Queen herself, added a wreath of china flowers to the other tributes.

From the church, Victoria went on to the house. Here memories of her previous visit came flooding back. Sadly she trailed through the rooms—the library, the drawing room with her portrait on the wall, his little sitting room. Every piece of furniture, every ornament, every picture, was a heartbreaking reminder of him. 'I seemed to hear his voice, and the impassioned eager way he described everything,' wrote Victoria. Corry, no less heartbroken than the Queen, gave her the dagger that Dizzy had brought back from Constantinople over fifty years before.

Through the wind and the rain the Queen drove back to Windsor. If one thing could have comforted her in her grief, it would have been Corry's assurance that in Disraeli's coffin 'there lies, and will ever lie, close to that faithful heart, the photograph of the Queen *he* loved. . . .'

3

What were the fruits, for Queen Victoria, of this idyll with Disraeli? They were many, and they were magnificent. The Queen emerged as a very different woman from the one whose hands Disraeli had kissed six years before. Then she had been a withdrawn, doleful, insecure, self-obsessed, self-pitying and hypochondriacal creature, clinging to the late Prince Consort's set of precepts and constantly bewailing the fact that she was being pushed beyond her limits. But now, with Disraeli having—by his tact and his blandishments and his thinly-veiled flirtation—revived her spirits and built up her self-confidence, Queen Victoria was an altogether more remarkable figure.

For one thing, her health had improved. Or perhaps it was merely that she did not dwell at such length on her often imagined ills—her 'nerves', her 'poor head', her lack of energy. She was as energetic now as she had been in the Prince Consort's time. 'I danced a Quadrille and a valse (which I had not done for eighteen years) with dear Arthur, who valses extremely well,' she admitted, 'and I found I could do it, as well as ever!'

And from valsing with Arthur, she went on to executing exhilarating reels with her grandsons, Prince Eddy and Prince George. In short, the Queen had learnt how to enjoy herself again. Instead of always looking back she began to look forward.

No longer did she follow so slavishly the patterns of life laid down by the Prince Consort. Instead of going always to his beloved Germany, she went to those sun-steeped southern countries more generally associated with Disraeli—to the South of France, to Italy, even on one occasion, to Spain. In other ways too, Victoria had thrown off the influence of dearest Albert. She no longer felt that she must always be improving herself, that she must strive to be cultured or intellectual or serious-minded. Dizzy had appreciated her for what she was; he had made her realize that there was no need for her to be self-conscious about her intellectual shortcomings.

And he had been right. Queen Victoria was no fool. Encouraged to think for herself and not always to wonder how Albert would have reacted to a particular situation, the Queen began to follow her own intuition and to put her trust in her own considerable judgement. Her opinions—once freed of Albert's inhibiting insistence on impartiality—became more firmly held and emphatically voiced. Her particular traits—her sagacity, her shrewdness, her common sense, her toughness—came into full play. Egged on by Disraeli, she became more and more convinced that what she felt was always right.

And not only had Dizzy given her self-confidence, he had given her a sense of vocation. Instead of complaining that she was overworked and of having to be urged on to make an effort, she busied herself as never before. Her zest became little short of miraculous. She was forever hectoring her ministers; her stream of letters, always formidable, became a flood. During one international crisis, the War Office was bombarded with no less than seventeen notes and telegrams, all in the course of a single day, urging more resolute action. It was up to her, she decided, to keep her ministers on the right path. Without her constant vigilance, without those snowstorms of telegrams or those drifts of letters—with their underlinings and their capital letters and their exclamation marks—things might so easily be allowed to slip.

The Queen emerged from her association with Disraeli as an unquestioning Conservative. Her views might not always have been those of an orthodox Tory but from now on she found that she had very little sympathy with the Liberals. The Prince Consort's lessons in political impartiality—that sure rock on which constitutional monarchy must stand—were forgotten; or, if not exactly forgotten, they were re-interpreted. The Liberals, argued the Queen blandly, had moved so far to the left that the Conservatives were now the exponents of that pure and shining liberalism of the Prince Consort's day.

In fact, even the Queen's concept of her role as a constitutional monarch had undergone a change. Lord Derby's fear lest Disraeli give Victoria too inflated an opinion of her position had to some extent been justified. All that talk of her being the 'Arbitress' and 'Dictatress' of Europe had gone to her head. She was by now determined not to be a mere cypher, a mere puppet-like signer of Bills and opener of Parliaments. And Dizzy, not only in, but out of, office had encouraged her in this attitude.

'I *do* think Dizzy has worked the idea of personal government to its logical conclusion . . .' complained Mary Ponsonby to her husband, the Queen's private secretary. 'If there comes a real collision between the Queen and the House of Commons, it is quite possible that she would turn restive, *dorlotée* as she has been by Dizzy's high-sounding platitudes, and then her reign will end in a fiasco. . . .'

One of Dizzy's most misleading pieces of constitutional advice had been given to her just a few months before his death. In her Speech from the Throne for the parliamentary session of 1881 (written, of course, by her ministers) was an announcement to the effect that British troops would be withdrawn from Kandahar in Afghanistan. This the Queen refused to sanction. With such cowardly, retrogressive, 'little England' policies she wanted no truck. At the end of an extremely stormy cabinet meeting at Osborne, with the Queen's exasperated ministers threatening resignation, Sir William Harcourt, the Home Secretary, assured her that 'the Speech of the Sovereign' was merely 'the Speech of the Ministers'. What he was saying, in effect, was that she was obliged to make it whether she approved of its contents or not.

Harcourt's claim astonished the Queen. She appealed to Disraeli. His answer was devastating in its sophistry. At one stroke, he brushed aside the entire concept of ministerial responsibility. Sir William Harcourt's principle, he answered unblinkingly, 'is a principle not known to the British Constitution. It is only a piece of Parliamentary gossip.'

It was no wonder that Queen Victoria had a somewhat exaggerated idea of her prerogatives; or rather, that she dug in her heels at any sign of their being whittled away. A minister's first allegiance, she would argue, should be to his sovereign. She would rather abdicate than yield up any of her rightful powers.

Then too, Dizzy had made Queen Victoria aware of the glories of imperialism. At the time of the Prince Consort's death, the imperial idea had been in its infancy; imperialism had still been a vague and suspect doctrine. The British Empire had been a haphazard affair, a collection of widely scattered, widely varying and only loosely connected possessions, which a great many politicians had been only too ready to scrap. But Disraeli, by his expansionist policies and his bold gestures, had made Victoria conscious of her position as the Sovereign of this jumble of people and territories, the Queen–Empress of the greatest Empire that the world had ever known. For the following two decades, Queen Victoria would symbolize the strident, swaggering and, in so many ways, glorious ideal that was the British Empire.

Was Victoria in love with Disraeli? Not, one imagines, in the generally accepted sense of the term. Nor is the particular form taken by her love important. What is important is its effect on her character and future development. Disraeli made the Queen feel, for the first time in many years, like a desirable woman; a woman who was worth flirting with, and joking with, and buttering up. Once again she felt herself to be the most important person in someone's life. Her ego, as she basked in the apparently whole-hearted attention of this fascinating man, was given a tremendous fillip. She felt appreciated, not so much for her position, as for herself.

This had been Disraeli's supreme achievement for Queen Victoria:

this building up of her confidence both as a monarch and a woman. By opening her eyes to the possibilities of her position, by bringing into flower her innate sense of majesty, by boosting her self-assurance, Disraeli transformed Victoria. Without him, she could so easily have remained a recluse, becoming less popular, more neurotic and more lethargic by the year. Whether the British monarchy could have survived twenty-five more years of Victoria's seclusion is doubtful. But by setting fire to her imagination, by treating her as a great queen and an attractive woman, Disraeli re-fashioned Victoria.

'For today,' he had written to her on her fifty-sixth birthday, 'which has given to my country a Sovereign whose reign, it is my hope and ambition, may rank with that of Elizabeth, has also given to me, her humble, but chosen servant, a Mistress, whom to serve is to love. . . .'

How could Queen Victoria possibly have resisted such a call?

By this transforming of the Widow of Windsor into the Faery Queen, Disraeli enabled Victoria to develop into the revered, magnificent and almost mythical figure of her old age: the Doyenne of Sovereigns, the Great White Queen, the *Shah-in-Shah Padshah*, the Grandmama of Europe, Victoria *Regina et Imperatrix*.

Notes on Sources and Bibliography

Notes on Sources

Unless otherwise indicated, all quotations from Queen Victoria are taken from the Queen's letters and journals, both published and unpublished. These quotations are from three sources: *The Letters of Queen Victoria* 9 vols., John Murray, London 1907–1930; *Victoria R.I.* by Elizabeth Longford, Weidenfeld and Nicolson, London, 1964; and *Queen Victoria, Her Life and Times* by Cecil Woodham-Smith, Hamish Hamilton, London 1972.

Similarly, unless otherwise indicated, all quotations from Benjamin Disraeli, Earl of Beaconsfield, are from the Hughenden Papers, *The Life of Benjamin Disraeli* 6 vols., by W. F. Monypenny and G. E. Buckle, John Murray, London 1910–1920; and *Disraeli* by Robert Blake, Eyre and Spottiswoode, London, 1966.

PART ONE

Chapter One

Greville, *The Greville Memoirs*. Victoria on Albert ('full of goodness . . .') Victoria, *Girlhood*. Disraeli on Victoria's first Council ('A hum of . . .') Disraeli, *Sybil*.

Chapter Two

Disraeli ('A female friend . . .') Disraeli, *Henrietta Temple*. Maria Disraeli on Disraeli ('clever boy . . .') Blake, *Disraeli*. Disraeli ('There is no fascination . . .') Disraeli, *Vivian Grey*. Sara Austen to Disraeli ('I have now gone through it . . .') Blake, *Disraeli*, and to Sarah Disraeli ('Really he is an excellent . . .') Jerman, *The Young Disraeli*. Disraeli's feelings for Sarah ('a passion . . .') Blake, *Disraeli*, and his letter to her ('I have no wife . . .') Disraeli, *Correspondence*. Disraeli ('In society nothing must be discussed . . .') Disraeli, *Vivian Grey*. Disraeli in Malta ('that damned bumptious . . .') Gregory, *Autobiography*. Sexual adventures ('Mercury . . .') Blake, *Disraeli*. Disraeli on destiny, Disraeli, *Contarini Fleming*. Disraeli to Sarah ('By the bye . . .') Disraeli, *Correspondence*. Henrietta ('such an affectionate . . .' and 'I am not very eloquent . . .') Blake, *Disraeli*. Count d'Orsay, Fraser, *Disraeli and his Day*.

Chapter Three

Lord Holland on Victoria's looks, Cecil Woodham-Smith, *Queen Victoria*. Greville, *The Greville Memoirs*. Lady Grey ('I hope you are amused . . .') Cecil, *Lord M*. Greville, *The Greville Memoirs*. Lord David Cecil on relationship, Melbourne on Duchess of Kent, Victoria on Melbourne ('a most truly honest . . .') and Victoria to Cabinet ('they wished to treat me . . .') Cecil, *Lord M*. Albert and women ('great dislike . . .') Grey, *Early Years*.

Chapter Four

Philip Guedalla, *Bonnet and Shawl*. Disraeli to Sarah ('a pretty little thing . . .') Disraeli, *Correspondence*, and on taking Mary Anne in to dinner, Blake, *Disraeli*. Disraeli's dress ('What is the meaning . . .') Fraser, *Disraeli and his Day*. Mary Anne to her brother, Hardwick, *Mrs Dizzy*. Disraeli's letter to Mary Anne, quoted in full in Appendix I, Blake, *Disraeli*. Mary Anne's account book entry, Monypenny, *Disraeli*, and her letter to Peel, Blake, *Disraeli*. Disraeli to Mary Anne ('Health, my clear brain . . .') Hardwick, *Mrs Dizzy*. Disraeli to Sarah on Victoria ('great grace . . .') Disraeli, *Correspondence*. Mary Anne on royal meeting, Monypenny, *Disraeli*.

Chapter Five

Lord M on Albert ('The Prince understands . . .') Longford, *Victoria R.I.* Greville, *The Greville Memoirs*. Lord M on Albert ('Three months ago . . .') Woodham-Smith, *Queen Victoria*. Greville, *The Greville Memoirs*. Victoria on sexual side of marriage ('a complete violence . . .') Victoria, *Dearest Child*. Mary Anne on Disraeli's looks, Maurois, *Disraeli*, her relationship with Disraeli ('One evening . . .') Gregory, *Autobiography*, with Baroness de Rothschild, Cohen, *Lady de Rothschild*, and her scatty conversation ('Oh yes! I love Oxford . . .') James, *Rosebery*. Hughenden ('a terribly gaudy . . .') Gower, *Reminiscences*, Ralph and James Disraeli's comments ('clever arrangements . . .') and Disraeli's dyed ringlets ('My hair will be white . . .') Hardwick, *Mrs Dizzy*. Lord Stanley to the Queen, Victoria, *Letters*.

Chapter Six
The Queen and Stanley on Disraeli, and Victoria on Disraeli's letters, Victoria, *Letters*. First clash between Disraeli and Gladstone, Blake, *Disraeli*. Disraeli's letter to Albert, Victoria, *Letters*.

Chapter Seven
Napoleon III on visiting Windsor ('delighted to avail . . .') Victoria, *Letters*. Clarendon and Greville, *The Greville Memoirs*. Disraeli and Mary Anne in Paris, Monypenny, *Disraeli*. Napoleon III on Disraeli, Malmesbury, *Memoirs*.

Chapter Eight
Disraeli's letters to Mrs Brydges Willyams, Blake, *Disraeli*. Disraeli's letters to the Queen, Victoria, *Letters*. Disraeli on Osborne, Blake, *Disraeli*. Disraeli as Viceroy ('It is quite on the cards . . .') Monypenny, *Disraeli*. Sarah to Mary Anne ('Remember . . .') Hardwick, *Mrs Dizzy*.

Chapter Nine
Greenwood on Disraeli, Londonderry, *Letters*. Albert's letter to Bertie, ('upon a subject . . .') Magnus, *King Edward*. Phipps to Palmerston, Woodham-Smith, *Queen Victoria*. Disraeli to Lady Londonderry, Londonderry *Letters*. Victoria on Disraeli's tributes to Albert, Monypenny, *Disraeli*.

Chapter Ten
Disraeli's letter to Mrs Brydges Willyams, Blake, *Disraeli*. Exchanges between Victoria and Disraeli, Monypenny, *Disraeli*. Description of Disraeli ('this miserable . . .') Pearson, *Dizzy*. Henry Ponsonby, *Life*. Buckingham Palace ('These commanding . . .') Longford, *Victoria R.I.* Victoria to Vicky, Victoria, *Dearest Mamma*. Balmoral ('Stagnation . . .') Ponsonby, *Life*.

Chapter Eleven
Gladstone on Reform Bill ('a smash . . .) Blake, *Disraeli*. Mary Anne ('I had got him . . .') Kebbel, *Lord Beaconsfield*. Brown and Victoria, Longford, *Victoria R.I.* Lady Palmerston ('We are all dreadfully . . .') Palmerston, *Letters*. Clarendon ('Mrs Dizzy . . .') Kennedy, *My Dear Duchess*. Victoria ('It must be a proud . . .') Monypenny, *Disraeli*. Disraeli ('Yes, I have climbed . . .') Fraser, *Disraeli and his Day*.

Chapter Twelve

Lady Augusta Stanley, Monypenny, *Disraeli*. Disraeli on Ward Hunt and Ireland ('yearned for the occasional . . .') Victoria, *Letters*. Victoria's biographer ('There for the first time . . .') Benson, *Queen Victoria*. Spring flowers, Monypenny, *Disraeli*. Ponsonby on Brown, Ponsonby, *Life*. Disraeli on Corry, ('Male society . . .') Zetland (Editor), *Letters of Disraeli*. Victoria on Mary Anne's elevation ('The Queen can truly . . .') Monypenny, *Disraeli*.

Chapter Thirteen

Victoria, Disraeli and Gladstone ('used to engage . . .') Russell, *Diary*. Gladstone ('I think it has been . . .' and 'The repellent . . .') Magnus, *Gladstone*. Fraser, *Disraeli and his Day*. Mary Anne to Corry ('He told me to turn . . .') Blake, *Disraeli*, and letter to Disraeli ('If I should depart . . .') Monypenny, *Disraeli*. Ponsonby on Disraeli, Monypenny, *Disraeli*. Lady Cardigan, Blake, *Disraeli*. Lady Bradford, Zetland, *Letters*. Disraeli ('the whole gamut . . .') Monypenny, *Disraeli*. Disraeli ('than to have a heart . . .') Zetland, *Letters*. Victoria's exchanges with Gladstone, Magnus, *Gladstone*.

PART TWO

Chapter Fourteen

Unless otherwise indicated, all quotations are from Zetland, *Letters*. Disraeli and Corry ('Darling . . .') Field, *Uncensored Recollections*. Disraeli on portrait ('Oh, is it not hideous . . .') Torrens, *Twenty Years*. Victoria on Millais portrait, Millais, *Life*. Windsor uniform ('as a mark . . .') Monypenny, *Disraeli*. Victoria to Rosebery, James, *Rosebery*. Ponsonby on Disraeli's memoranda, Blake, *Disraeli*. Queen's grand-daughter ('When I left the dining room . . .') Marie-Louise, *Memories*. Ponsonby on Disraeli's snobbishness ('I so fully believe . . .') and medical advice ('by doing exactly what . . .') Ponsonby, *Life*. Rothschild and Corry exchange, Monypenny, *Disraeli*. Disraeli to Victoria ('the whole wondrous tale . . .') Victoria, *Letters*.

Chapter Fifteen

Lord Salisbury ('The wife . . .') Magnus, *King Edward*. Lord Derby ('Hal is sure . . .') Blake, *Disraeli*. Victoria and Prince and Princess of Wales, Magnus, *King Edward*. Victoria and portrait ('Now I will show you . . .') Zetland, *Letters*. Lord Lytton's telegram, Victoria, *Letters*.

Chapter Sixteen

Disraeli ('I am fortunate . . .') and Empress Augusta, Zetland, *Letters*. Guedalla, *Idylls of the Queen*. Victoria's biographer ('after the romantic . . .') Monypenny, *Disraeli*. Ponsonby ('his sympathy is expressed . . .') Longford, *Victoria R.I.* Disraeli to Lady Bradford. Zetland, *Letters*. Valentine, *Victoria, Letters*. Lord Rosebery, James, *Rosebery*. Queen ('going ostentatiously . . .') Blake, *Disraeli*. Disraeli ('The Faery seemed to admire . . .') Zetland, *Letters*. Ponsonby, *Life*. Derby ('Is there not just a risk . . .') Monypenny, *Disraeli*. Ponsonby ('Perfect slave . . .') Ponsonby, *Life*.

Chapter Seventeen

Gladstone's sex life, Gladstone, *Diaries*. Ponsonby ('He has skilfully . . .') Longford, *Victoria R.I.* Carnarvon to Salisbury, Blake, *Disraeli*. Duchess of Teck and potatoes, Marie Louise, *Memories*. Salisbury and Empress Augusta, Gladstone, *After Thirty Years*. Disraeli and Crown Princess, Zetland, *Letters*. Disraeli and Greece ('I did yesterday . . .') Magnus, *King Edward*. Comments on Berlin success, *Times* and *Journal des Débats*, July, 1878.

Chapter Eighteen

Unless otherwise indicated, all quotations in Section I are from Zetland, *Letters*. Disraeli and Corry ('It is heinous . . .') Blake, *Disraeli*. Disraeli ('the two J.B.s . . .') Anon, *Notebooks*. Disraeli and Prince Alfred, Blake, *Disraeli*. Disraeli ('a distressing scene . . .' and 'I hope the French . . .') Zetland, *Letters*.

Chapter Nineteen

High Tory Journal ('It is enough . . .') *Whitehall Review*. To Lady Bradford ('This morning . . .') Zetland, *Letters*. Disraeli to Prince of Wales ('I fear very much . . .') Battiscombe, *Queen Alexandra*. Bertie's visit ('He praised . . .') Zetland, *Letters*. Letters ('*very* Private . . .') Esher, *Journals*. Scene in House of Lords, *Times*, February 1880. Queen on by-election victory, Blake, *Disraeli*. Queen on Disraeli's defeat Ponsonby, *Life*, and to Disraeli ('for the Country's . . .' and 'Which I hope we shall . . .') Monypenny, *Disraeli*. Last audience, Zetland, *Letters*. Gladstone ('The downfall of . . .') Blake, *Disraeli*.

Chapter Twenty

Queen ('I feel so happy . . .') Monypenny, *Disraeli*. To Lady Bradford ('I owe everything . . .') Zetland, *Letters*. Queen ('I sent some Osborne primroses . . .') Monypenny, *Disraeli*. Disraeli and message to Albert, and Victoria's letter to Corry, Blake, *Disraeli*. Corry to Lady Bradford, Zetland, *Letters*. Gladstone ('as he lived . . .') Magnus, *Gladstone*. Gladstone to Lady Dorothy Nevill, Nevill, *Reminiscences*. Mary Ponsonby, *A Memoir*. Disraeli to Victoria ('for today . . .') Victoria, *Letters*.

Bibliography

Acton, Lord: *Letters of Lord Acton to Mary Gladstone*. Macmillan, London, 1913.

Anon: *The Notebooks of a Spinster Lady*. Cassell, London, 1919.

Anon ('X'): *Myself Not Least*. Thornton Butterworth, London, 1925.

Baily, F. E.: *Lady Beaconsfield and her Times*. Hutchinson, London, 1935.

Battiscombe, Georgina: *Queen Alexandra*. Constable, London, 1969.

Benson, E. F.: *Queen Victoria*. Longmans, London, 1935.

Blake, Robert: *Disraeli*. Eyre and Spottiswoode, London, 1966.

Bolitho, Hector: *The Reign of Queen Victoria*. Collins, London, 1949.

Brett, Reginald B.: *The Yoke of Empire*. Macmillan, London, 1896.

Burghclere, Lady (Editor): *A Great Lady's Friendships*. Macmillan, London, 1933.

Cardigan, Countess of: *My Recollections*. Eveleigh Nash, London, 1909.

Cartwright, Julia (Editor): *The Journals of Lady Knightly of Fawsley*. John Murray, London, 1915.

Cecil, Algernon: *Queen Victoria and her Prime Ministers*. Eyre and Spottiswoode, London, 1952.

Cecil, Lord David: *The Young Melbourne*. Constable, London, 1939.

Cecil, Lord David: *Lord M*. Constable, London, 1954.

Cohen, Lucy: *Lady de Rothschild and Her Daughters*. John Murray, London, 1935.

Disraeli, Benjamin: *Novels and Tales by the Earl of Beaconsfield*. Longmans, Green and Co., London, 1881.

Disraeli, Benjamin: *Home Letters 1830–1831*. John Murray, London, 1885.

Disraeli, Benjamin: Lord Beaconsfield's Correspondence with his Sister, 1832–1852. (Editor Ralph Disraeli), John Murray, London, 1886.

Disraeli, Benjamin: *The Letters of Disraeli to Lady Bradford and Lady*

Chesterfield (Editor, the Marquis of Zetland) 2 vols. Ernest Benn, London, 1929.

Disraeli, Benjamin: *Letters from Benjamin Disraeli to Frances Anne, Marchioness of Londonderry.* (Editor, Marchioness of Londonderry) Macmillan, London, 1938.

Ellis, S. M. (Editor): *Unpublished Letters of Lady Bulwer Lytton to A. E. Chalon R.A.* Eveleigh Nash, London, 1914.

Esher, Reginald Viscount: *Journals and Letters.* (Editor, Maurice V. Brett) 2 vols. Ivor Nicholson and Watson, London, 1935.

Field, W. O.: *Uncensored Recollections.* Eveleigh Nash and Grayson, London, 1924.

Fraser, Sir William: *Disraeli and His Day.* Kegan Paul, London, 1891.

Froude, J. A.: *Lord Beaconsfield.* Sampson Low, London, 1890.

Furniss, Harry: *Some Victorian Men.* John Lane, London, 1924.

Gladstone, Viscount: *After Thirty Years.* Macmillan, London, 1928.

Gladstone, W. E.: *The Gladstone Diaries.* Clarendon Press, Oxford, 1968–75.

Gorst, Harold E.: *The Earl of Beaconsfield.* L. Blackie, London, 1900.

Gower, Lord Ronald: *My Reminiscences.* 2 vols., Kegan Paul, London, 1883.

Gregory, Sir William. *Autobiography.* John Murray, London, 1894.

Greville, Charles: *The Greville Memoirs.* (Editors, Lytton Strachey and Roger Fulford) 8 vols. Macmillan, London, 1938.

Grey, Charles: *The Early Years of H.R.H. The Prince Consort.* Smith, Elder and Co., London, 1867.

Guedalla, Philip: *Idylls of the Queen.* Hodder and Stoughton, London, 1937.

Hardie, Frank: *The Political Influence of Queen Victoria 1861–1901.* Oxford University Press, Oxford, 1935.

Hardie, Frank: *The Political Influence of the British Monarchy 1868–1952.* Batsford, London, 1970.

Hardwick, Mollie: *Mrs Dizzy.* Cassell, London, 1972.

James, Robert Rhodes: *Rosebery.* Weidenfeld and Nicolson, London, 1963.

Jerman, B. R. *The Young Disraeli.* Princeton University Press, Oxford University Press, 1960.

Kebbel, T. E.: *Life of Lord Beaconsfield.* W. H. Allen, London, 1895.

Kennedy, A. L. (Editor) '*My dear Duchess*'. John Murray, London, 1956.

Lee, Sir Sydney: *King Edward VII.* 2 vols., Macmillan, London, 1927.

Longford, Elizabeth: *Victoria R.I.* Weidenfeld and Nicolson, London, 1964.

Magnus, Sir Philip: *Gladstone.* John Murray, London, 1954.

Magnus, Sir Philip: *King Edward the Seventh.* John Murray, London, 1964.

Mallet, Marie: *Life with Queen Victoria.* John Murray, London, 1968.

Malmesbury, J. H. H., Earl of: *Memoirs of an ex-Minister.* Longmans, London, 1884.

Marie Louise, Princess: *My Memories of Six Reigns.* Evans, London, 1956.

Martin, Sir Theodore: *Life of His Royal Highness the Prince Consort.* 5 vols., Smith, Elder and Co., London, 1877–1880.

Martin, Sir Theodore: *Queen Victoria as I knew Her.* Blackwood, London, 1908.

Maurois, André: *Disraeli.* John Lane, London, 1951.

Meynell, Wilfred: *Benjamin Disraeli: An unconventional biography.* 2 vols., Hutchinson, London, 1903.

Millais, John Guille: *Life and Letters of Sir John Everett Millais.* Methuen, London, 1905.

Monypenny, W. F. and Buckle, G. E.: *The Life of Benjamin Disraeli.* 6 vols., John Murray, London, 1910–1920.

Nevill, Lady Dorothy: *Reminiscences.* Edward Arnold, London, 1900.

Palmerston, Lady: *Letters.* (Editor, Tresham Lever). John Murray, London, 1957.

Pearson, Hesketh: *Dizzy.* Methuen, London, 1951.

Ponsonby, Arthur: *Henry Ponsonby: His life from his Letters.* Macmillan, London, 1930.

Ponsonby, Sir Frederick: *Sidelights on Queen Victoria.* Macmillan, London, 1930.

Ponsonby, Mary: *A Memoir, Some Letters and a Journal.* John Murray, London, 1927.

Raymond, E. T.: *Disraeli: the Alien Patriot.* Hodder and Stoughton, London, 1925.

Reid, T. Wemyss: *Life, Letters and Friendships of Richard Monckton Milnes.* Cassell, London, 1890.

Russell, G. W. E. (One Who Has Kept a Diary): *Collections and Recollections.* Smith, Elder and Co., London, 1899.

Seton-Watson, R. W.: *Disraeli, Gladstone and the Eastern Question.* Macmillan, London, 1935.

Somervell, D. C.: *Disraeli and Gladstone*. Faber and Faber, London, 1932.

Sykes, James: *Mary Anne Disraeli*. Benn, London, 1928.

Torrens, W. M.: *Twenty Years in Parliament*. Richard Bently, London, 1893.

Victoria, Queen: *Leaves from the Journal of Our Life in the Highlands, 1848–1861*. Smith, Elder and Co., London, 1868.

Victoria, Queen: *The Letters of Queen Victoria: A Selection of Her Majesty's Correspondence*. First Series 1837–1861 (Editors, A. C. Benson and Viscount Esher), 3 vols.; Second Series 1862–1885 (Editor G. E. Buckle), 3 vols.; Third Series 1886–1901 (Editor G. E. Buckle), 3 vols., John Murray, London 1907–1932.

Victoria, Queen: *The Girlhood of Queen Victoria; A Selection from Her Majesty's Diaries between the years 1832 and 1840*. 2 vols. (Editor Viscount Esher) John Murray, London, 1912.

Victoria, Queen: *Further Letters*. Thornton Butterworth, London, 1938.

Victoria, Queen: *Dearest Child: Letters between Queen Victoria and the Princess Royal*. (Editor Roger Fulford) Evans Bros., London, 1964.

Victoria, Queen: *Dearest Mamma: Letters between Queen Victoria and the Crown Princess of Russia*. (Editor Roger Fulford) Evans Bros., London, 1968.

Victoria, Queen: *Your Dear Letter: Private Correspondence of Queen Victoria and the Crown Princess of Prussia*. (Editor Roger Fulford) Evans, London, 1971.

Woodham-Smith, Cecil: *Queen Victoria: Her Life and Times*. Hamish Hamilton, London, 1972.

Newspapers, Periodicals and Works of Reference

The Times, Morning Post, Journal des Débats, Whitehall Review, Pall Mall Gazette, Illustrated London News, Graphic, Punch, Annual Register, Dictionary of National Biography, Encyclopaedia Brittanica.

Index